LIBRARY

Learning
Resource Centre

THE MAUDSLEY
The Maudsley Series

The Maudsley Series

HENRY MAUDSLEY, from whom the series of monographs takes its name, was the founder of The Maudsley Hospital and the most prominent English psychiatrist of his generation. The Maudsley Hospital was united with the Bethlem Royal Hospital in 1948 and its medical school, renamed the Institute of Psychiatry at the same time, became a constituent part of the British Postgraduate Medical Federation. It is now a school of King's College, London, and entrusted with the duty of advancing psychiatry by teaching and research. The South London & Maudsley NHS Trust, together with the Institute of Psychiatry, are jointly known as The Maudsley.

The monograph series reports high quality empirical work on a single topic of relevance to mental health, carried out at The Maudsley. This can be by single or multiple authors. Some of the monographs are directly concerned with clinical problems; others are in scientific fields of direct or indirect relevance to mental health and that are cultivated for the furtherance of psychiatry.

Editor
Professor A. S. David MPhil MSc FRCP MRCPsych MD

Assistant Editor
Professor T. Wykes BSc PhD MPhil

Previous Editors

1955–1962	Professor Sir Aubrey Lewis LLD DSc MD FRCP and Professor G. W. Harris MA MD DSc FRS
1962–1966	Professor Sir Aubrey Lewis LLD DSc MD FRCP
1966–1970	Professor Sir Denis Hill MB FRCP FRCPsych DPM and Professor J. T. Eayrs PhD DSc
1970–1979	Professor Sir Denis Hill MB FRCP FRCPsych DPM and Professor G. S. Brindley MD FRCP FRS
1979–1981	Professor G. S. Brindley MD FRCP FRS and Professor G. F. M. Russell MD FRCP FRC(ED) FRCPsych
1981–1983	Professor G. F. M. Russell MD FRCP FRCP(ED) FRCPsych
1983–1989	Professor G. F. M. Russell MD FRCP FRCP(ED) FRCPsych and Professor E. Marley MA MD DSc FRCP FRCPsych DPM
1989–1993	Professor G. F. M. Russell MD FRCP FRCP(ED) FRCPsych and Professor B. H. Anderton BSc PhD
1993–1999	Professor Sir David Goldberg MA DM MSc FRCP FRCPsych DPM

The Maudsley Series

Vulnerability to Psychosis

From Neurosciences to Psychopathology

Edited by Paolo Fusar-Poli, Stefan J. Borgwardt and Philip McGuire

Psychology Press
Taylor & Francis Group
HOVE AND NEW YORK

First published 2012
by Psychology Press
27 Church Road, Hove, East Sussex BN3 2FA

Simultaneously published in the USA and Canada
by Psychology Press
711 Third Avenue, New York NY 10017

*Psychology Press is an imprint of the Taylor & Francis Group,
an Informa business*

British Library Cataloguing in Publication Data
A catalogue record for this book is available from the British Library

Library of Congress Cataloging in Publication Data
Vulnerability to psychosis: from neurosciences to psychopathology/edited
by Paolo Fusar-Poli, Stefan Borgwardt, and Philip McGuire.
     p.; cm. — (Maudsley series)
  Includes bibliographical references and index.
     ISBN 978-1-84872-087-9 (hardback: alk. paper) 1. Psychoses—Physiological
aspects. 2. Nervous system—Diseases—Complications. 3. Mental illness.
I. Fusar-Poli, Paolo. II. Borgwardt, Stefan. III. McGuire, Philip.
IV. Series: Maudsley series.
  [DNLM: 1. Psychotic Disorders—physiopathology. 2. Brain—physiopathology.
  3. Early Diagnosis. 4. Genetic Predisposition to Disease. 5. Psychotic Disorders—
  diagnosis. 6. Risk Factors. WM 200]
  RC512.V85 2011
  616.89—dc23   2011015183

ISBN: 978–1–84872–087–9 (hbk)
ISBN: 978–0–203–33268–9 (ebk)
ISSN: 0076–5465

Typeset in Times New Roman by RefineCatch Limited, Bungay, Suffolk
Printed and bound in Great Britain by TJ International Limited, Padstow, Cornwall
Cover design by Lisa Dynan

Contents

Plates

Figures

Tables

Contributors

Dr Marta Agosti, King's College London, Institute of Psychiatry, De Crespigny Park, London SE5 8AF, UK

Dr Stefan Borgwardt, Department of Psychiatry, University of Basel, c/o University Hospital Basel, Petersgraben 4, CH-4031 Basel, Switzerland, and King's College London, Institute of Psychiatry, De Crespigny Park, London SE5 8AF, UK

Dr Lisa Bortolotti, School of Philosophy, Theology and Religion, University of Birmingham, Birmingham B15 2TT, UK

Dr Elvira Bramon, King's College London, Institute of Psychiatry, De Crespigny Park, London SE5 8AF, UK

Prof. Matthew Broome, Warwick Medical School, University of Warwick, Coventry CV4 7AL, UK, and King's College London, Institute of Psychiatry, De Crespigny Park, London SE5 8AF, UK

Dr Michael T. Compton, New York State Psychiatric Institute, Columbia University, New York, NY 10032-1098, USA

Prof. Cheryl M. Corcoran, New York State Psychiatric Institute, Columbia University, New York, NY 10032-1098, USA

Dr Nicolas Crossley, King's College London, Institute of Psychiatry, De Crespigny Park, London SE5 8AF, UK

Dr Jennifer Dale, Department of Psychiatry, University of Birmingham, Birmingham B15 2FG, UK

Dr Fern Day, King's College London, Institute of Psychiatry, De Crespigny Park, London SE5 8AF, UK

Dr Paolo Fusar-Poli, King's College London, King's Health Partners, Institute of Psychiatry, De Crespigny Park, London SE5 8AF, UK

Dr Oliver Howes, King's College London, Institute of Psychiatry, De Crespigny Park, London SE5 8AF, UK

Dr Meredith Kelly, New York State Psychiatric Institute, Columbia University, New York, NY 10032-1098, USA

Dr Charlotte Marriott, Coventry and Warwickshire Partnership Trust, Wayside House, Wilsons Lane, Coventry CV6 6NY, UK

Prof. Philip McGuire, Prof. of Psychiatry & Cognitive Neuroscience, Head Department of Psychosis Studies, Academic Director, Psychosis Clinical Academic Group, King's College London, King's Health Partners, Institute of Psychiatry, De Crespigny Park, London SE5 8AF, UK

Dr Cristina Merino, Birmingham and Solihull Mental Health Foundation Trust, 50 Summer Hill Road, Ladywood, Birmingham B1 3RB, UK

Dr Barnaby Nelson, Centre for Youth Mental Health, The University of Melbourne, 35 Poplar Road, Parkville VIC 3052, Australia

Dr Mark Opler, New York State Psychiatric Institute, Columbia University, New York, NY 10032-1098, USA

Dr Carmine Pariante, King's College London, Institute of Psychiatry, De Crespigny Park, London SE5 8AF, UK

Dr Marco Picchioni, King's College London, Institute of Psychiatry, De Crespigny Park, London SE5 8AF, UK

Prof. Ralf Pukrop, Department of Psychiatry and Psychotherapy, University of Cologne, Kerpener Str. 62, D-50937 Cologne, Germany

Dr Valerie Purdie-Vaughns, New York State Psychiatric Institute, Columbia University, New York, NY 10032-1098, USA

Prof. Anita Riecher-Rössler, Department of Psychiatry, University of Basel, c/o University Hospital Basel, Petersgraben 4, CH-4031 Basel, Switzerland

Prof. Stephan Ruhrmann, Department of Psychiatry and Psychotherapy, University of Cologne, Kerpener Str. 62, D-50937 Cologne, Germany

Dr James M. Stone, King's College London, Institute of Psychiatry, De Crespigny Park, London SE5 8AF, UK

Dr Timothea Toulopoulou, King's College London, Institute of Psychiatry, De Crespigny Park, London SE5 8AF, UK

Dr Ahtoy J. Wonpat-Borja, New York State Psychiatric Institute, Columbia University, New York, NY 10032-1098, USA

Prof. Stephen J. Wood, Melbourne Neuropsychiatry Centre, Sunshine Hospital, PO Box 294, St Albans, VIC, 3021, Australia

Dr Lawrence H. Yang, New York State Psychiatric Institute, Columbia University, New York, NY 10032-1098, USA

Prof. Alison R. Yung, Orygen Youth Health Research Centre and the Centre for Youth Mental Health, The University of Melbourne, 35 Poplar Road, Parkville VIC 3052, Australia

Acknowledgements

Our aim for this book was to gather in one volume the perspectives of leading international researchers and clinicians on the interaction of environmental with genetic and neurodevelopmental factors before the onset of psychosis. We also wanted the book to stimulate ourselves and other readers and hope that we have succeeded in passing on our combined findings and arguments regarding vulnerability to psychosis. May our readers be inspired by this book to pursue their essential work on this important topic!

This ambitious task, however, could not have been accomplished without the help, inspiration, and support of many people: We are deeply grateful to all patients and contributors from centers worldwide. A special thank you goes to Renate Smieskova, Kerstin Bendfeldt, Jacqueline Aston, Rolf-Dieter Stieglitz, Andor Simon and Doris Blaser for advice and recommendations during preparing and editing this book.

Last but not least, we gratefully acknowledge the untiring support of our families, constant sources of encouragement and inspiration! Their willingness to bear with our sometimes extensive absorption into our work cannot be appreciated enough.

Paolo Fusar-Poli
Stefan Borgwardt
Philip McGuire

1 Introduction

*Stefan Borgwardt, Paolo Fusar-Poli and
Philip McGuire*

Early clinical intervention in psychosis has recently become a major objective of
mental health services, and the development of specialist early intervention
services has greatly facilitated research on the early phases of the disorder.
Research at this stage is potentially a way of investigating the mechanisms
underlying psychosis, as the same individuals can be studied before and after the
onset of illness, often with minimal confounding effects of previous treatment.
The identification of a clinical syndrome (an "at risk mental state") that reflects an
"ultra high risk" predisposition to psychosis is fundamental to both clinical and
research work in this area.

Endorsing the genetic high-risk approach, putative endophenotypes can be
evaluated for association with genetic risk for schizophrenia by comparing the
unaffected co-twins or the unaffected relatives of patients with normal controls.
Alternatively, "close in", i.e., clinical high-risk, approaches are able to identify a
group at high risk of psychosis with higher transition rates than those observed in
studies purely based on genetic inclusion criteria. The latter approach, focusing
on individuals who are considered to be at increased risk for psychotic disorders,
is based primarily on the presence of clinical symptoms. This clinical strategy
aims at identifying neural changes occurring prior to the onset of psychosis and
may improve our ability to predict schizophrenia outcomes based on the combined
perspectives of both neural and clinical characteristics observed at the baseline
assessment.

The presence of individuals who are at high risk but not psychotic is consistent
with evidence that schizophrenia results from the interaction of environmental
with genetic and neurodevelopmental factors, with the latter associated with
clinical, neurobiological and neuropsychological features before the onset of
psychosis. Over the past years, neuroscience techniques such as: structural brain
imaging—magnetic resonance imaging (MRI) and diffusion tensor imaging
(DTI); functional brain imaging—positron emission tomography (PET), single-
photon emission computed tomography (SPECT), functional magnetic resonance
imaging (fMRI); neurochemical imaging—magnetic resonance spectroscopy
(MRS); and computerized models (Virtual Reality), have rapidly developed as
powerful tools to explore the neurophysiological basis of vulnerability to
psychosis.

This monograph is indented to provide a state-of-the-art review of
neurobiological research in people at high risk of psychosis, with a particular

focus on the processes that may underlie the transition from a high-risk state to a first episode of frank psychosis. These neurobiological findings will be presented in the context of what is now known about the psychopathology and cognitive impairments that are evident in people at high risk of psychosis, and environmental factors that may influence the risk of the onset of illness. The monograph thus aims to bring together a diversity of new information from a range of different research modalities, which are sometimes studied separately.

2 Neuroscience, continua and the prodromal phase of psychosis

Matthew Broome, Jennifer Dale, Charlotte Marriott, Cristina Merino and Lisa Bortolotti

Introduction

Our focus in this chapter is to address some of the challenges that arise when a purely neuroscientific conception of the prodromal phase of psychosis is considered. Two clear challenges arise, both of which have been discussed in the wider literature on schizophrenia and psychopathology. The first is how models of a continuum of psychosis can be reconciled with a scientific understanding of the prodrome as a discrete constellation of signs and symptoms. The second issue is wider: psychopathology may not be able to be defined solely by reference to the brain (Broome & Bortolotti, 2009). Given the importance of psychopathology in the delineation of "prodromal" or "ultra-high-risk" states this difficulty may also limit our optimism in being able to characterize the prodrome by wholly biological variables. These challenges are by no means isolated to psychiatry and psychosis research but touch on mainstream and wide-ranging debates in cognitive neuroscience around the naturalization of meaning in the brain.

Schizophrenia, development and the prodrome

It has been apparent for almost two decades that there is a developmental component to schizophrenia. In its simple form, this model postulates that genes involved in neurodevelopment and/or environmental insults in early life lead to aberrant brain development, which in turn predisposes to the later onset of psychosis (Bullmore et al., 1998; McDonald, Fearon, & Murray, 1999; Murray & Lewis, 1987). However, more recent formulations incorporate the role of social factors such as urban upbringing, social isolation, and migration (Boydell, van Os, McKenzie, & Murray, 2004; Morgan et al., 2007), and point to an interaction between the biological and psychological in a cascade of increasingly deviant development (Howes et al., 2004).

Prospective studies show that children who later develop schizophrenia are more likely than peers to show subtle developmental delays and cognitive impairments, they also tend to be solitary and socially anxious (Cannon et al., 2002; Jones, Rodgers, Murray, & Marmot, 1994). Some evidence suggests that individuals destined to develop schizophrenia fail to learn new cognitive skills as they enter adolescence, thus appearing to show a relative decline compared with their peer group (Fuller et al., 2002; Jones et al., 1994). The combination of neurocognitive and emotional deviance increases the likelihood of developing minor quasi-psychotic symptoms: indeed a prospective study in Dunedin showed pre-schizophreniform individuals to be more likely to manifest such symptoms as early as age 11 years (Cannon et al., 2002; Poulton et al., 2000). It is postulated that in those destined to develop psychosis the strength, frequency, and associated distress of the odd ideas and experiences increases, and, at some ill-defined point, the individual crosses a threshold into the pre-psychotic or prodromal phase (Broome, Woolley, Tabraham et al., 2005).

The continuum and prodromal phase of psychosis

It is now clear that not only many children but also a proportion of the general adult population experience brief or isolated psychotic phenomena without coming into contact with psychiatric services (Johns & van Os, 2001). For example, in the Dunedin cohort, 25% of the entire population reported having experienced isolated or transient delusions or hallucinations at the age of 26 years though only 3.7% met criteria for a schizophreniform illness. Initially, there was considerable scepticism that such minor symptoms bore any relation to the frank and persistent hallucinations and delusions experienced by schizophrenic patients. However, van Os, Linscott, Myin-Germeys, Delespaul, and Krabbendam (2009) reported that the very same risk factors that are associated with clinical schizophrenia (single state, unemployment, urban living, etc.) are also associated with the occurrence of minor psychotic symptoms in the Dutch general population. Johns et al. (2004) confirmed these findings in a large sample ($n = 8,580$) of the British general population. Factors independently associated with psychotic symptoms were lower IQ, poorer educational qualifications, cannabis dependence, alcohol dependence, victimization, stressful life events, and neurotic symptoms. Such findings have suggested that psychosis is best considered as a dimension extending well into the general population (Verdoux & van Os, 2002).

To investigate this dimensional idea further, van Os and colleagues conducted a systematic review of the available evidence on the prevalence and incidence of psychotic symptoms and experiences in the general population (van Os et al., 2009). They found a median prevalence rate of around 5% and a median incidence rate of around 3%, demonstrating rates much higher than those recognized for clinically significant non-affective psychotic disorder. They also found, in their meta-analysis of demographic characteristics, that the prevalence of subclinical psychotic experiences or symptoms is associated with the same variables that are well recognized for schizophrenia, namely male gender, single marital status, unemployment and being from an ethnic minority or migrant group. They suggest that these findings support the notion of a continuum between subclinical and clinical psychosis, as does their finding that the risk factors for schizophrenia are also significant for subclinical psychosis, including urbanicity, traumatic life events and cannabis use.

Several research groups have identified characteristics of young people thought to be at "ultra high risk" of developing frank psychosis (Broome, Woolley, Johns et al., 2005; Klosterkötter, Hellmich, Steinmeyer, & Schultze-Lutter, 2001; McGlashan, Miller, & Woods, 2001; Morrison et al., 2004; Riecher-Rössler et al., 2006; Yung & McGorry, 1996; Yung et al., 1998, 2003). These individuals are described as experiencing cognitive dysfunction as the earliest detectable anomaly, followed by attenuated "negative" symptoms such as decreased motivation and socialization (Cornblatt, Lencz, & Obuchowski, 2002). Later, positive psychotic symptoms develop but are not sufficient in intensity or duration to meet formal criteria for frank psychotic illness. This constellation of symptoms has been combined with having: (i) a first-degree relative with psychosis; or (ii) a diagnosis of schizotypal personality disorder plus a decline in function, to create what is termed an "at risk mental state" or ARMS. Yung and colleagues reported that the presence of the "at risk" mental state in their clients predicted a 40% transition rate to frank psychosis within 12 months. If one accepts psychosis as a dimension, then the "at risk mental state" is likely to cover a segment of it, and the point of transition to frank psychosis is somewhat arbitrary. This relates to the first concern we outlined above: the ARMS could be viewed as being a segment of the continuum coupled with help seeking, decline of function and/or distress. A "Psychosis Proneness-Persistence-Impairment Model" has been suggested by van Os and colleagues, whereby transitory subclinical psychotic experiences can become persistent, and eventually of clinical significance, if "at-risk" individuals are exposed to additional environmental risk factors (van Os, 2009), such as those discussed above.

It has been pointed out by van Os and Delespaul (2005) that the highest transition rates occur in those "at-risk" populations that have been most highly selected, and that the process of screening and referral into these populations makes a major contribution to the success of researchers in identifying individuals at such high risk of transition. Thus, the application of ARMS criteria to the general population may have much less predictive power than in a clinic to which individuals suspected of being in a pre-psychotic phase have been specially referred. One reason for this loss of power is the evidence discussed above that psychosis exists as a continuous phenotype in the general population. A second reason is that the commonest outcome of subclinical psychotic symptoms in a general population is remission (Hanssen, Bak, Bijl, Vollebergh, & van Os, 2005). On this account, the clinical population is different from the general population not in the level of psychotic psychopathology, but rather in the prevalence of additional factors that lead to those symptoms being persistent and distressing.

The strategy of "sample enrichment" is utilized by most prodromal services to increase their ability to predict transition in an at-risk population. However, such enhanced predictive power may be falsely attributed to the psychopathological measure employed (van Os & Delespaul, 2005). Thus, the high predictive value may be consequent upon how the patients that make up a prodromal service are selected, rather than their psychopathology. Pathways may carry greater predictive power than mental-state abnormalities. This is not necessarily because those so detected are any less at risk, but rather that the greater proportion of those in the general population who would meet "at-risk" criteria for developing psychosis will never make it through the various selection procedures that account for the sample enrichment. However, such epidemiological criticisms may be more valid for some services than others, which have fewer "filters" between the person experiencing early psychotic symptoms and the clinician (Broome, Woolley, Johns et al., 2005). This is an obvious example of the more general problem that findings from cohort, epidemiological, and at-risk studies have not yet been fully integrated. Thus, neurodevelopmental theorists have struggled to explain what converts a developmentally impaired or socially isolated adolescent with odd ideas and experiences into a psychotic individual. Similarly, it is not yet clear what differentiates an individual in the community who experiences hallucinations and holds delusional beliefs but never sees a psychiatrist, from the individual who reaches a specialized clinic for those at risk of psychosis where he/she is considered as prodromal. The work of Hanssen et al. (2005) suggests that the intensity of the experiences is important but so too, they suggest, is depression. Escher et al. (Escher, Romme, Buiks, Delespaul, & van Os, 2002) also believe that the co-existence of affective disturbance is a major factor in determining whether young people who experience minor psychotic symptoms will progress to psychotic disorder that requires care. This shift away from a brain and symptom-based conception of clinical high risk, to one based around epidemiology and pathways through services has important theoretical ramifications in how we think of mental illness. Contrary to prevailing ideology in the DSM-IV (American Psychiatric Association, 1994), disorders are determined, at least in part, by a series of epidemiological factors and selection filters, by health behaviour of the individual and society, and by the beliefs and attitudes of health and legal professionals.

Normativity and delusions

Another argument for conceiving of psychosis as a continuum as opposed to a gradation of discrete stages comes from reflecting about the nature of psychopathology itself. Not only may the criteria of disorders themselves be not wholly dependent on neuroscientific or other biological variables, but the psychopathological symptoms used in the definitions of the disorders, or the items in the assessment tools we use to characterize the prodrome, are also contingent upon wider, normative, issues that are unlikely to be able to be reduced or correlated with brain function. A clear example, and one crucial in the prodrome, is that of delusions and disorders of thought content. In the case of delusions a merely neurobiological investigation becomes problematic early on. Unlike some other symptoms of psychosis, delusions are not discrete either temporally or in terms of their demarcation from other mental states—it would seem inconceivable to instruct a subject to button-press when deluded and when non-deluded, for example, in a neuroimaging experiment (Broome & McGuire, 2008). Delusions are usually thought of as false beliefs that are maintained in the face of strong counterevidence but as any clinician can attest, there is a lot more to a delusion than merely being wrong. Most contemporary accounts of delusion view them as non-discrete mental states, a symptom observed when a number of differing dimensional attitudes to a belief are adopted. Characteristics of delusions include having an implausible content, being reported with conviction, being unfounded, being distressing, causing preoccupation, and not being shared by others (Freeman, 2007). Delusions may lead to the subject's whole experience of themselves and of the world being altered. What was once banal, and beneath conscious attention, becomes salient and self-referential (Broome, Woolley, Johns et al., 2005; Broome, Woolley, Tabraham et al., 2005; Kapur, 2003; Kapur, Mizrahi, & Li, 2005). The normative, socially conditioned, rules for linking reasons, causes and explanations can be disrupted, and we are left with the hallmark of delusion: namely, that the reasons the person gives for holding his or her delusional beliefs either do not look like reasons or are not regarded as intersubjectively good reasons (Bortolotti & Broome, 2008, 2009a, 2009b). The effect of an inappropriate dopamine-driven generation of salience to otherwise neutral representation may lead to the private creation of affect-laden meaning and new reason-relations that cannot be shared or recognized by others as valid. Delusions held without doubt are extremely resistant to counterevidence or counterargument, contributing to the isolation of the person reporting and believing them. This shows how delusions manifest behaviourally and interpersonally: it is by observing how the person behaves with respect to his or her beliefs, and by witnessing such behaviour in the process of the giving and asking of reasons that one suspects delusions, not in viewing a brain scan or a genetic sequence. In other words, the diagnosis of delusions is based on the observation of behaviour that violates accepted norms (e.g., of rationality for belief reports). Listing these features of delusions helps us realize that the idea of what is pathological in delusion cannot be fully captured without referring to psychological notions and an interpersonal dimension. This does not mean that it is *a priori* impossible to reduce the concept of delusion to its biological underpinnings or to arrive at its physical aetiology, but that focusing on local brain dysfunctions won't begin to give us a sense of why the delusion is a disorder, and why both the clinically trained and lay interlocutor can spot that something is awry when conversing with a person with delusions—delusions stretch our folk-psychological categories and practices.

Odd beliefs and delusions are a remarkably heterogeneous phenomena and it has been notoriously difficult to offer an all-inclusive definition or to operationalize criteria to enable their reliable detection. This is not so much due to conceptual woolliness or confusion but rather to the fact that the term "delusion" does not pick out or index a discrete psychological state or natural kind: such difficulty carries over into the "disorders of thought content" delineated by tools such as the Comprehensive Assessment of At-Risk Mental State (CAARMS), where attenuated symptoms of abnormal thought content are distinguished from full-blown delusions using problematic criteria such as intensity, frequency and distress. Over the years there have been numerous ways to subclassify delusions: primary or autochthonous ("delusions") or secondary ("delusion-like ideas";

Jaspers, 1959/1997), based upon whether the interviewer's empathic skills (*Verstehen*) can be used to understand the narrative genesis of the belief or not, by theme or content, by congruity with mood, or by degree of fixity and conviction. Even if one focuses on a subtype of delusion defined by theme, for example persecutory delusions, these difficulties do not go away. Despite an explicit definition being offered (Freeman & Garety, 2000), persecutory delusions are still a psychologically complex phenomenon. Nevertheless, clinicians can usually agree on whether delusions are present or not, and, despite being difficult to define, they serve as important criteria in the diagnosis of mental illness in the psychiatric classifications. This may be because delusions show themselves when a belief tends to have characteristics that lie at the extreme end of several related, but not necessarily dependent, dimensions. These dimensions include such things as plausibility, foundation of the belief, conviction, level of distress incurred, preoccupation evoked, and degree of being shared by others (Freeman, 2007). The problem in defining delusions becomes clear: how are the dimensions weighted? Are they normally distributed? Do they correlate with one another? How "low" can one score on one dimension if scoring "highly" on the others and still be deluded? What are the cut-offs for each dimension for "delusionality" and are they altered by the scores on other dimensions? Which elements are necessary to be deluded? Part of the answers to these questions, particularly those of cut-off, threshold, and interaction will lie outside of natural science: what does society view as being deluded? This cannot be determined by biological or psychological research in itself as the dimensions integral to delusions are themselves defined using epistemic criteria, some of which may be more socially constructed (for example, plausibility) whereas others link into more basic and profound issues in rationality and judgement (foundedness). Further, certain beliefs have special rules of justification which apply to them (such as religious belief).

Cognitive neuropsychology will have a crucial role in understanding the various processes, including perceptual and affective, as well as information processing, that may underpin shifts up and down the dimensions linked to "delusionality". These issues of cut-off, threshold, and interaction not only demarcate delusion threshold but also challenge our ideas around the attenuated symptoms used to characterize clinical high-risk states for psychosis. Given this framework, one can appreciate the role of functional neuroimaging and cognitive neuroscience. Although on this analysis delusions are not amenable to a smooth reduction from symptom to circuits, as hoped for by the movement of biological realism in psychiatry, they can be deconstructed into several discrete phenomena. Imaging, and cognitive neuroscience more broadly, will have a crucial role in determining the neural correlates of the processes that may impact upon shifts in these dimensions, and with positron emission tomography (PET), may also allow progress into the biological physiology of such dimensions (for example, dopaminergic salience in relation to preoccupation, foundedness, and distress). A further methodological advance is linking longitudinal research with imaging: functional magnetic resonance imaging (fMRI) when used in high-risk studies (whether clinical or genetic studies) is a powerful method of linking biological variables (neural activations) with cognitive variables (such as reasoning biases) and the evolution of psychopathology, such as delusions, and the transition to psychosis.

Neuroscience and social psychiatry

We have seen that delusions are defined and diagnosed on the basis of behaviour that defies norms (e.g., epistemic norms of rationality for beliefs). These considerations challenge a narrowly biological conception of the prodrome of psychosis. Extending some of these arguments slightly, we shall suggest that there are good reasons to think that mental states are not only dependent upon the world, but in part constituted by it. Here, we try and draw some parallels between the philosophical doctrine of externalism and the current rebirth of social psychiatry, particularly evident in schizophrenia research.

> Psychiatry has recently rediscovered its roots. It seemed as if its long history of interest in the impact of society on the rates and course of serious mental illness had been forgotten, overtaken by the inexorable advance of neuroscience and genetics.
>
> (Morgan, McKenzie, & Fearon, 2008, p. 1)

This quote echoes the peculiar phenomenon that at the turn of the millennium, the close of the "decade of the brain", there was a return to social psychiatry. Despite the impact neuroimaging and genetics had made on understanding mental illness, and on psychiatry's understanding of itself, the impact of society on the epidemiology and prognosis of mental illness was again a serious academic concern. It had become clear that contrary to the old World Health Organization (WHO) study there was marked heterogeneity in the rates of schizophrenia, and, further, that some of this heterogeneity could be explained by urban birth and upbringing, migration, ethnicity, and what Cantor-Graae and Selten termed "social defeat" (Cantor-Graae & Selten, 2005; Selten & Cantor-Graae, 2005; Selten, Cantor-Graae, & Kahn, 2007). A particularly important body of research is the Medical Research Council (MRC) Aetiology and Ethnicity in Schizophrenia and Other Psychoses (AESOP) study that demonstrated a twenty-fold rate increase in the incidence of psychosis in London, compared with Nottingham and Bristol, and the very highest rates being within the black and ethnic minority groups (Fearon et al., 2006; Fearon & Morgan, 2006; Kirkbride et al., 2006, 2007; Morgan, Abdul-Al et al., 2006; Morgan, Fearon et al., 2006; Morgan et al., 2005a, 2005b, 2007). These epidemiological findings were compounded both by continuum models of psychosis suggesting that rates of psychotic experience in a non-help-seeking population were dependent upon many of the same variables as explained cases of the disorder, and by a seeming failure in the neurodevelopmental model of schizophrenia to explain how someone with odd ideas and developmental delay became a person with a frank psychotic disorder. Hence, as Morgan alludes to in the quote above, for the problems that the study of schizophrenia brings to researchers and clinicians the answers provided by neuroscience and genetics may not be enough. Trying to connect psychological, biological, and social models of psychosis became important, and trying to empirically test the relationships between these varieties of variables became a focus of psychosis research. Such an approach needs to be built into the burgeoning research programme into prodromal schizophrenia and clinical high-risk states.

Increasingly, accounts of psychosis relating to neuropsychological function, dopamine, symptoms, stress, and social isolation have been published with ingenious experiments testing various hypotheses. A very influential account is the salience theory of Kapur (2003; Kapur et al., 2005). Here, Kapur links dopamine dysregulation to the aberrant salience of both internal and external representations and to the symptomatology of psychosis. According to the "dopamine hypothesis of schizophrenia: version III" proposed by Howes and Kapur (2009) presynaptic dopamine dysregulation is the final common pathway to psychosis, as a result of what they term multiple "hits" (i.e., risk factors), including fronto-temporal dysfunction, genes, stress and drugs. These "hits" interact and lead to increased striatal dopamine release, which leads to aberrant salience or the altered appraisal of stimuli, resulting in psychosis. Taking the salience theory further, van Os proposed the term "salience dysregulation syndrome" as an alternative for the construct of schizophrenia, which would allow categorical and dimensional representations of psychosis to be combined, with the central tenet being a fundamental alteration in salience attribution (van Os, 2009).

In a series of remarkable experiments, Myin-Germeys, van Os, and other colleagues from Maastricht (Myin-Germeys, Delespaul, & van Os, 2005; Myin-Germeys, Krabbendam, Delespaul, & van Os, 2003a, 2003b; Myin-Germeys, Peeters et al., 2003; Myin-Germeys, van Os, Schwartz, Stone, & Delespaul, 2001) demonstrated a relationship between psychotic experiences and stress and "daily hassles", and, further, that this sensitivity was in part consequent upon the reactivity of the participants' dopaminergic system and their history of life events, and that neuropsychological impairment ameliorated this sensitivity. Ellett and colleagues (Ellett, Freeman, & Garety, 2008) demonstrated how the experience of walking through a busy urban street increased anxiety levels, negative beliefs about others, and exaggerated reasoning biases linked to the formation and maintenance of delusions. Hence, for schizophrenia and other psychotic disorders, we are left with the heterogeneity of incidence rates, with the role the urban environment, being part of an ethnic minority group and/or being a migrant plays, plus data suggesting that being in the urban environment has an immediate and measurable impact upon levels of paranoia in both healthy controls and patients.

This rebirth of social psychiatry has led to a renewed interest in external factors to the brain in the genesis of psychosis. The idea of an environment, or lived experience, that was somehow "psychotogenic" became a consequence of some of the data outlined above, which stressed how much variance in psychopathology could be attributable to context and exposure. Given these findings, and that with Morgan many commentators view them as a challenge to wholly neuroscientific or genetic accounts of mental illness, can it be suggested that psychopathology may be consequent upon factors external to the brain? Given the effect the world, and specifically urban experience, may have on both the rates and symptoms of psychosis, can external factors to the brain have a role, in terms of information processing and cognition, on the aetiology of psychosis? The idea here is that much as a list on a piece of paper may supplement the neurally encoded memory we have of what we want to shop for in the supermarket, certain cognitive acts may be subserved or supplemented by physical entities or relationships in the external world (Rowlands, 2003). Certainly, empirical data suggest that working memory and other neuropsychological, internal deficits may be linked to the onset of psychosis and perhaps an increasing reliance on external vehicles of cognition.

Do certain environments yield particular information if the individual is in a given "internal" (neurochemical, affective, neuropsychological) state? It is the case that what I experience when walking down Electric Avenue in Brixton, London, bears the informational content that I am Haile Selassie, and hence God Incarnate for the Rastafarians. The deluded are not simply mistaken: the world and internal events become meaningful in a non-public manner.

Clinical and ethical implications

We have seen that the prodromal phase of psychosis may represent a segment of a continuum of psychotic experiences within the general population, with some cases progressing to frank psychosis. However, a significant proportion resolve spontaneously, and many do not experience distress or seek help. In addition, we have discussed that psychotic symptoms cannot be defined by purely neurobiological factors. So, how do we as clinicians judge when and to whom we should target intervention? Furthermore, what kind of intervention would be appropriate, acceptable and effective?

The principle of early intervention in psychosis is now widely accepted. However, early detection and intervention in individuals with ARMS is a more controversial area, but one that has generated an enormous amount of research interest and investment. While targeting interventions with the purpose of preventing or delaying the onset of psychosis is hugely appealing, a number of authors have highlighted ethical and clinical concerns (Cornblatt et al., 2002; McGlashan et al., 2001; McGorry, Yung, & Phillips, 2001; McGuire, 2002; Warner, 2005). These concerns focus on the validity of the ARMS criteria and the related problem of "false positives" and we will discuss these briefly in turn.

Even in research trials there is huge variability in transition rates from ARMS to psychosis. For example, in the original Personal Assessment and Crises Evaluation (PACE) trial using the ultra high risk (UHR) criteria there was a transition rate of 35–40% over 12 months. However, other research groups using the same or similar criteria have reported 12-month transition rates of as much as 54% in the Prevention through Risk Identification, Management & Education (PRIME) clinic at Yale University and as little as 15% in the Cognitive Assessment and Risk Evaluation (CARE) clinic in San Diego. In the original PACE clinic, a significant reduction in transition rates over time has also been observed, with a 6-month transition rate of only 9.2% being reported in 2007 (Haroun, Dunn, Haroun, & Cadenhead, 2006; Miller & McGlashan, 2000; Miller et al., 2002; Yung et al., 1998, 2003, 2007). This may be a positive effect due to treatments being more effective at the very early stages of illness or a negative "dilution effect" due to finding more "false positives" (see below). As we have already discussed, it is also likely that when criteria used to detect at-risk individuals are applied to less highly selected populations false-positive rates will be much higher. It could be argued that the tools used are not yet well enough refined, relying on arbitrary cut-off points to select those at risk of developing psychosis. Yet, this does not fit with the conceptualization of psychosis being a dimensional variable, with varying degrees of risk of developing a psychotic illness in the "at-risk" population, and such risk possibly being attributable to environmental factors. Currently the instruments used rely on the presence of subclinical features of psychosis, or "state and trait" markers, to the exclusion of important environmental variables.

There is concern about the potential harmful consequences of over treatment and stigmatization of individuals identified as being at risk, who will never develop a psychotic illness (Warner, 2005). These are the so-called "false positive" at-risk individuals—i.e., those who are not prodromal for psychosis ultimately. Also, where antipsychotics are used as an intervention, there is a risk of iatrogenic dopamine sensitization and symptom rebound on drug withdrawal (Warner, 2005). Despite these concerns, in the proposed revisions for DSM-5 (http://www.dsm5.org/ProposedRevisions) there is a new category referred to as "attenuated psychotic symptoms syndrome" (Carpenter, 2009; Heckers, 2009) that is suggested for inclusion or as part of the appendix. This construct is largely based upon attenuated positive symptoms, as discussed above, and like the measures used to assess the "at-risk mental state" may pick out a group that may merge with those members of the normal population who have unusual experiences, and hence also relies on the possibly false assumption that the risk of psychotic disorder is best indexed by the presence of certain symptoms. The DSM-5 proposal seems to conflate a "risk syndrome" with the earliest signs of the disorder, a *forme fruste*, in linking their category with the retrospective abnormalities seen in cohorts with the disorder. Although detection of those at risk of psychosis is an important ethical, scientific and clinical duty reifying this research programme into a DSM-5 category may have the problematic consequence of over identification of people as at risk, missing those who are genuinely likely to develop psychosis, and offering needless or, indeed, harmful interventions to those whose outcome may be benign. An ethical concern many clinicians working in this area routinely come into contact with is the tension between reassurance and normalization of the unusual experiences with the follow-up and monitoring present in high-risk services, and genuine appreciation of risk. The monitoring and care offered, may themselves, by their impact on anxiety, appraisals, etc., thus have the paradoxical effect of increasing, rather than decreasing, the rate of transition in an at-risk group if not delivered in services of certain levels of skill and expertise. Expanding clinical awareness and service delivery may lead to this and other unwanted, and unforeseen, outcomes.

Possible solutions and future directions

Supporters of early detection and intervention argue that in spite of the high false-positive rate, those identified are by definition help seeking and in need of some form of care, whether or not they go on to develop psychosis or another non-psychotic disorder (McGorry, 2008). They also argue that the risk of lack of or delayed care, in terms of clinical and functional outcomes, far overshadows the theoretical one of premature labelling and over treatment (McGorry, 2008). Further, it seems clear that those clients, even if they do develop a psychotic illness, may have a better outcome after having been through early detection services (Valmaggia et al., 2009).

Contemporary classifications (such as DSM-IV or ICD-10) offer criteria for rather stable conditions (e.g., schizophrenia), but do not consider early phases of psychosis. However, the diagnosis of a psychotic disorder is based on the presence or absence of characteristic symptoms, and it is well known that the presence of such symptoms varies during the course and treatment of these illnesses (McGorry et al., 2009; Salvatore et al., 2009; Whitty et al., 2005). The clinical staging model, which has been widely used in clinical medicine but virtually ignored in psychiatry, will provide a coherent clinicopathological framework, which will restore the utility of diagnosis and promote early intervention. Such staging will define the progression of the disease in time and where a person lies along this continuum of the course of the illness. The staging will indicate a continuum of increasing risk, with unspecific conditions at the initial stages and more defined clinical-diagnostic profiles at the later stages (Raballo & Laroi, 2009).

At least four stages along a continuum can be now identified: first, a premorbid phase with endophenotypic vulnerability traits and risk factors but no significant psychosocial impairment; second, an early prodromal phase with anomalous subjective experience, initial psychosocial impairment, deterioration of quality of life and inter-peer performance; third, a late prodromal phase of subthreshold attenuated psychotic symptoms and/or brief, limited, intermittent psychosis (this phase would map onto that captured by most measures to determine the prodrome); and, fourth, a phase with full-blown prolonged psychotic symptoms, susceptible to develop into schizophrenia (Raballo & Laroi, 2009).

The advantages of considering a clinical staging model are substantial. A stratification of interventions could be developed for conditions not considered in the available diagnostic classifications. We will have a view of psychosis as a progression through at-risk mental states, which could lead to a spectrum of phase-specific treatments, providing earlier, safer, and more effective clinical interventions with potential to clarify the biological basis of psychiatric disorders, minimize stigma and reorganize mental health care (McGorry, Hickie, Yung, Pantelis, & Jackson, 2006; McGorry et al., 2009; Raballo & Laroi, 2009). Yung and McGorry advocate the use of clinical staging so that treatment can be tailored according to the stage of illness, preventing over treatment and reducing stigma (McGorry, 2008; Yung et al., 2007). This would allow for a period of observation, monitoring and treatment of non-psychotic psychiatric disorders (such as depression, anxiety and substance-misuse disorders). Specific treatments such as cognitive therapy and low-dose antipsychotics would be employed only in the presence of worsening or non-responsive subclinical psychotic symptoms, or where these symptoms were coupled with suicidality or dangerousness.

The scope and limits of biological psychiatry

These concerns regarding the naturalization of the prodromal phase of psychosis, and of the psychopathology that determines the presence of the ARMS, challenge our current conceptualization of mental disorders generally. To what extent should psychiatric disorders be thought of as strictly analogous to other medical disorders? While it is natural to suppose that psychiatric conditions share some features of physical disorders (e.g., they present obstacles to the satisfaction of an individual's interests and negatively affect the well-being of that individual), they also have distinctive features. We want to argue that some of these features can be adequately characterized only by using the vocabulary of the mental. We do not deny that psychiatric disorders can be described as disturbances of neurobiological mechanisms, but we insist that they are pathological because of the way in which they manifest, and they manifest as disturbances of the mind. Mental illness is mental precisely because in order to establish whether certain behaviour is disturbed we need to apply psychological concepts. This is of course orthogonal to the question about how these disturbances are caused, and it is likely to be correct that brain dysfunction and brain deficits will most likely be at the basis of these behavioural manifestations.

Equating the natural with neurobiology can constrain our understanding of mental illness. Neurobiological psychiatry had become the paradigm in the field and thus it has led to a rejection of the potential contributions of alternative approaches in clinical practice and psychiatric research. Neurobiology can explain why a certain disorder occurred, and how best we should treat it, and can enlighten the connections between that disorder and other aspects of normal or abnormal functioning. But it cannot be an exhaustive and exclusive explanation of the reason why the observed deviation from normal functioning is *pathological*.

Currently, psychopathological states and mental disorders use criteria that rely on psychological terms and refer to deviations from norms (ethical, epistemic, social, etc.). Mental illness itself can be thought of as the kind of disorder one identifies when normal reason giving, all other things being equal, breaks down. Thus, concretely speaking, a brain scan, genetic abnormality, blood test, etc., can never *a priori* serve as the sole criteria for the diagnosis of mental illness. Such tests can serve to diagnose disorders that use those criteria in their definition, or further elucidate physiology. However, to diagnose mental illness, one talks to one's patients. To bring biological investigations into diagnostic use, we can "eliminate" mental illness and choose to redefine psychiatric disturbances using other criteria than those we now employ. This approach would lead to a radical shift in both the profession (and possible existence) of psychiatry, as well as to a change in the wider societal perception and understanding of mental illness. It also leads to a conceptual difficulty: it doesn't take an expert to recognize that someone is mentally disordered, but how would one decide whether dopamine quantal size, functional MRI activations, or repeats of genetic polymorphisms were abnormal in the absence of a disordered person? And this is the crux of the issue: for biological psychiatry to have any validity, and to be anything more than neuroscience, the main object of study needs to remain the person. The normal and the abnormal themselves are not properties of the brain.

We need a psychological and mental vocabulary to explain what makes them pathological. Why would anyone think that the use of a mental vocabulary already implies a tendency to anti-scientific feelings? The philosopher John McDowell (McDowell, 1996, 1998) reminds us that one shouldn't believe that the domain of scientific investigation encompasses all that is natural and real, and talks about there being a second nature:

> The therapy I offer is a reminder of the idea of second nature, which tends, I suggest, to be forgotten under the influence of a fascination with modern science. The idea of actualizations of conceptual capacities does indeed belong in a logical space that contrasts with the one in which modern science delivers its distinctive kind of understanding. But we should not allow the logical space of scientific understanding to hijack the very idea of the natural. The idea of actualizations of conceptual capacities belongs in the logical space of reasons, but conceptual capacities are part of the second nature of their possessors.
>
> (McDowell, 1998, p. 367)

It is the structure of this second nature that helps us provide an account of what mental illnesses are, *really*. Mental illness is apparent in the realm of reasons, as abnormal, skewed, or constrained behaviour. Changes in interpersonal behaviour and reason giving map on the broad categories of mental illnesses we are familiar with. Mental illnesses *as illnesses* manifest at the level of observable behaviour and deviations from epistemic, moral or social norms. What one sees in biological terms may be changes in receptor function, abnormal neurotransmitter metabolism, or underdeveloped orbitofrontal cortex. But such changes are not "disordered" in and of themselves.

Conclusions

There is an increasing move away from studying solely discrete, categorical psychotic illnesses and more into a continuum model of psychosis. As well as casting the nosological status of established diagnostic categories such as schizophrenia in doubt, it also impacts upon the status of the prodromal phase or at-risk mental state. There is a tension in it being viewed both as a syndrome and collection of mental-state abnormalities, if a somewhat fuzzy category, and it being a region of the psychosis continuum with somewhat arbitrary borders. The danger lies, perhaps, in the false assumption that categories are more likely to have discrete pathophysiology (Broome, 2006) whereas it may be that there is a rich diversity of variables to be examined that may serve as risk factors for a given individual progressing along the continuum to frank psychosis, particularly in the latter stages from at risk to first episode. As such, they are proximal markers or causes that may be useful as predictors or as targets for therapeutic intervention. It is important for the authors of the DSM-5 and the proposed revisions to include these and other difficulties. Further, it is incumbent on researchers and clinicians to be reflective and critical of their own assumptions and ideology and follow the data: all potential variables need to be viewed as equal candidates, at least at first, and examined rigorously and dispassionately.

Related to these issues is a narrower research question as to whether focusing on the at-risk phase is worthwhile in understanding psychosis. The epidemiological data (An der Heiden & Häfner, 2000) suggests that the vast majority of those who develop a psychotic disorder go through a prodromal phase. However, this phase is currently characterized in a variety of different ways, with some groups studying the prodromal phase of psychosis, others the prodrome of schizophrenia, and with others distinguishing between an early and late prodromal phase or attenuated negative and attenuated positive syndrome. Further, there are still the groups who may enter frank illness with an acute, rapid and intense onset of illness and thus focusing on those with a more gradual and insidious prodromal illness may lead to us examining the risk factors for a psychotic illness with a poor prognosis, rather than one that may have a more benign outcome.

In this chapter we have argued that some psychological notions that are epistemic in character, such as those of rationality and self-knowledge, and some features of the external environment that affect the compliance with social and moral norms in the individual, play an important role in the detection and diagnosis of mental illness, of the ascription of certain mental-state abnormalities and in the demarcation of the clinical high-risk mental state for psychosis. As such, studying the brain solely will not enable us to understand the onset of psychosis and the preceding prodromal phase: a close attention to continua and normativity is also required.

References

American Psychiatric Association. (1994). *Diagnostic and statistical manual of mental disorders* (4th ed.). Washington, DC: Author.

An der Heiden, W., & Häfner, H. (2000). The epidemiology of onset and course of schizophrenia. *European Archives of Psychiatry and Clinical Neuroscience, 250,* 292–303.

Bortolotti, L., & Broome, M. (2008). Delusional beliefs and reasoning giving. *Philosophical Psychology, 21,* 821–841.

Bortolotti, L., & Broome, M. (2009a). The future of scientific psychiatry. In M. Broome & L. Bortolotti (Eds.), *Psychiatry as cognitive neuroscience: Philosophical perspectives* (pp. 365–375). Oxford, UK: Oxford University Press.

Bortolotti, L., & Broome, M. R. (2009b). A role for ownership and authorship in the analysis of thought insertion. *Phenomenology and Cognitive Sciences, 8*, 205–224.

Boydell, J., van Os, J., McKenzie, K., & Murray, R. M. (2004). The association of inequality with the incidence of schizophrenia—an ecological study. *Social Psychiatry and Psychiatric Epidemiology, 39*, 597–599.

Broome, M., & Bortolotti, L. (Eds.). (2009). *Psychiatry as cognitive neuroscience: Philosophical perspectives.* Oxford, UK: Oxford University Press.

Broome, M. R. (2006). Taxonomy and ontology in psychiatry: A survey of recent literature. *Philosophy, Psychiatry, and Psychology, 13*, 303–319.

Broome, M. R., & McGuire, P. K. (2008). Imaging and delusions. In D. Freeman, R. Bentall, & P. A. Garety (Eds.), *Persecutory delusions: assessment, theory and treatment* (pp. 281–301). Oxford, UK: Oxford University Press.

Broome, M. R., Woolley, J. B., Johns, L. C., Valmaggia, L. R., Tabraham, P., Gafoor, R., et al. (2005). Outreach and support in South London (OASIS): Implementation of a clinical service for prodromal psychosis and the at risk mental state. *European Psychiatry, 20*, 372–378.

Broome, M. R., Woolley, J. B., Tabraham, P., Johns, L. C., Bramon, E., Murray, G. K., et al. (2005). What causes the onset of psychosis? *Schizophrenia Research, 79*, 23–34.

Bullmore, E. T., Woodruff, P. W., Wright, I. C., Rabe-Hesketh, S., Howard, R. J., Shuriquie, N., et al. (1998). Does dysplasia cause anatomical dysconnectivity in schizophrenia? *Schizophrenia Research, 30*, 127–135.

Cannon, M., Caspi, A., Moffitt, T. E., Harrington, H., Taylor, A., Murray, R. M., et al. (2002). Evidence for early childhood, pan-developmental impairment specific to schizophreniform disorder: Results from a longitudinal birth cohort. *Archives of General Psychiatry, 59*, 449–456.

Cantor-Graae, E., & Selten, J. (2005). Schizophrenia and migration: A meta-analysis and review. *American Journal of Psychiatry, 162*(1), 12–24.

Carpenter, W. (2009). Anticipating DSM-5: Should psychosis risk become a diagnostic class? *Schizophrenia Bulletin, 35*(5), 841–843.

Cornblatt, B., Lencz, T., & Obuchowski, M. (2002). The schizophrenia prodrome: Treatment and high-risk perspectives. *Schizophrenia Research, 54*, 177–186.

Ellett, L., Freeman, D., & Garety, P. A. (2008). The psychological effect of an urban environment on individuals with persecutory delusions: The Camberwell walk study. *Schizophrenia Research, 99*(1–3), 77–84.

Escher, S., Romme, M., Buiks, A., Delespaul, P., & van Os, J. (2002). Independent course of childhood auditory hallucinations: A sequential 3-year follow-up study. *British Journal of Psychiatry, 43*(Suppl.), s10–18.

Fearon, P., Kirkbride, J. B., Morgan, C., Dazzan, P., Morgan, K., Lloyd, T., et al. (2006). Incidence of schizophrenia and other psychoses in ethnic minority groups: Results from the MRC AESOP Study. *Psychological Medicine, 36*, 1541–1550.

Fearon, P., & Morgan, C. (2006). Environmental factors in schizophrenia: The role of migrant studies. *Schizophrenia Bulletin, 32*, 405–408.

Freeman, D. (2007). Suspicious minds: The psychology of persecutory delusions. *Clinical Psychology Review, 27*, 425–457.

Freeman, D., & Garety, P. A. (2000). Comments on the content of persecutory delusions: Does the definition need clarifying? *British Journal of Clinical Psychology, 39*, 407–414.

Fuller, R., Nopoulos, P., Arndt, S., O'leary, D., Ho, B.-C., & Andreasen, N. C. (2002). Longitudinal assessment of premorbid cognitive functioning in patients with schizophrenia through examination of standardized scholastic test performance. *American Journal of Psychiatry, 159*, 1183–1189.

Hanssen, M., Bak, M., Bijl, R., Vollebergh, W., & van Os, J. (2005). The incidence and outcome of subclinical psychotic experiences in the general population. *British Journal of Clinical Psychology, 44*, 181–191.

Haroun, N., Dunn, L., Haroun, A., & Cadenhead, K. (2006). Risk and protection in prodromal schizophrenia: Ethical implications for clinical practice and future research. *Schizophrenia Bulletin, 32*, 166–178.

Heckers, S. (2009). Who is at risk for a psychotic disorder? *Schizophrenia Bulletin, 35*(5), 847–850.

Howes, O. D., & Kapur, S. (2009). The dopamine hypothesis of schizophrenia: Version III–The final common pathway. *Schizophrenia Bulletin, 35*(3), 549–562.

Howes, O. D., McDonald, C., Cannon, M., Arseneault, L., Boydell, J., & Murray, R. M. (2004). Pathways to schizophrenia: The impact of environmental factors. *International Journal of Neuropsychopharmacology, 7*(Suppl. 1), S7–S13.

Jaspers, K. (1997). *General psychopathology* (new ed.). Baltimore, MD: Johns Hopkins University Press. (Originally published 1959)

Johns, L. C., Cannon, M., Singleton, N., Murray, R. M., Farrell, M., Brugha, T., et al. (2004). Prevalence and correlates of self-reported psychotic symptoms in the British population. *British Journal of Psychiatry, 185*, 298–305.

Johns, L. C., & van Os, J. (2001). The continuity of psychotic experiences in the general population. *Clinical Psychology Review, 21*, 1125–1141.

Jones, P., Rodgers, B., Murray, R., & Marmot, M. (1994). Child development risk factors for adult schizophrenia in the British 1946 birth cohort. *Lancet, 344*, 1398–1402.

Kapur, S. (2003). Psychosis as a state of aberrant salience: A framework linking biology, phenomenology, and pharmacology in schizophrenia. *American Journal of Psychiatry, 160*, 13–23.

Kapur, S., Mizrahi, R., & Li, M. (2005). From dopamine to salience to psychosis—Linking biology, pharmacology and phenomenology of psychosis. *Schizophrenia Research, 79*, 59–68.

Kirkbride, J. B., Fearon, P., Morgan, C., Dazzan, P., Morgan, K., Tarrant, J., et al. (2006). Heterogeneity in incidence rates of schizophrenia and other psychotic syndromes: Findings from the 3-center AESOP study. *Archives of General Psychiatry, 63*, 250–258.

Kirkbride, J. B., Morgan, C., Fearon, P., Dazzan, P., Murray, R. M., & Jones, P. B. (2007). Neighbourhood-level effects on psychoses: Re-examining the role of context. *Psychological Medicine, 37*, 1413–1425.

Klosterkötter, J., Hellmich, M., Steinmeyer, E. M., & Schultze-Lutter, F. (2001). Diagnosing schizophrenia in the initial prodromal phase. *Archives of General Psychiatry, 58*, 158–164.

McDonald, C., Fearon, P., & Murray, R. (1999). Neurodevelopmental hypothesis of schizophrenia 12 years on: Data and doubts. In J. Rapoport (Ed.), *Childhood onset of "adult" psychopathology* (pp. 193–220). Washington, DC: American Psychiatric Press.

McDowell, J. (1996). *Mind and world.* Cambridge, MA: Harvard University Press.

McDowell, J. (1998). Precis of mind and world. *Philosophy and Phenomenological Research, 58*, 365–368.

McGlashan, T. H., Miller, T. J., & Woods, S. W. (2001). Pre-onset detection and intervention research in schizophrenia psychoses: Current estimates of benefit and risk. *Schizophrenia Bulletin, 27*, 563–570.

McGorry, P. (2008). Head to head. Is early intervention in the major psychiatric disorders justified? Yes. *British Medical Journal, 337*, a695.

McGorry, P. D., Hickie, I. B., Yung, A. R., Pantelis, C., & Jackson, H. J. (2006). Clinical staging of psychiatric disorders: A heuristic framework for choosing earlier, safer and more effective interventions. *Australian & New Zealand Journal of Psychiatry, 40*, 616–622.

McGorry, P. D., Nelson, B., Amminger, G. P., Bechdolf, A., Francey, S. M., Berger, G., et al. (2009). Intervention in individuals at ultra high risk for psychosis: A review and future directions. *Journal of Clinical Psychiatry, 70*, 1206–1212.

McGorry, P. D., Yung, A., & Phillips, L. (2001). Ethics and early intervention in psychosis: Keeping up the pace and staying in step. *Schizophrenia Research, 51*, 17–29.

McGuire, P. (2002). Prodromal intervention: The need for evaluation. *The Journal of Mental Health, 11*, 469–470.

Miller, T. J., & McGlashan, T. H. (2000). Early identification and intervention in psychotic illness. *Connecticut Medicine, 64*, 339–341.

Miller, T. J., McGlashan, T. H., Rosen, J. L., Somjee, L., Markovich, P. J., Stein, K., et al. (2002). Prospective diagnosis of the initial prodrome for schizophrenia based on the Structured Interview for Prodromal Syndromes: Preliminary evidence of inter-rater reliability and predictive validity. *American Journal of Psychiatry, 159*, 863–865.

Morgan, C., Abdul-Al, R., Lappin, J. M., Jones, P., Fearon, P., Leese, M., et al. (2006). Clinical and social determinants of duration of untreated psychosis in the AESOP first-episode psychosis study. *British Journal of Psychiatry, 189*, 446–452.

Morgan, C., Fearon, P., Hutchinson, G., McKenzie, K., Lappin, J. M., Abdul-Al, R., et al. (2006). Duration of untreated psychosis and ethnicity in the AESOP first-onset psychosis study. *Psychological Medicine, 36*, 239–247.

Morgan, C., Kirkbride, J., Leff, J., Craig, T., Hutchinson, G., McKenzie, K., et al. (2007). Parental separation, loss and psychosis in different ethnic groups: A case-control study. *Psychological Medicine, 37*, 495–503.

Morgan, C., Mallett, R., Hutchinson, G., Bagalkote, H., Morgan, K., Fearon, P., et al. (2005a). Pathways to care and ethnicity. 1: Sample characteristics and compulsory admission. Report from the AESOP study. *British Journal of Psychiatry, 186*, 281–289.

Morgan, C., Mallett, R., Hutchinson, G., Bagalkote, H., Morgan, K., Fearon, P., et al. (2005b). Pathways to care and ethnicity. 2: Source of referral and help-seeking. Report from the AESOP study. *British Journal of Psychiatry, 186*, 290–296.

Morgan, C., McKenzie, K., & Fearon, P. (2008). Introduction. In C. Morgan, K. McKenzie, & P. Fearon (Eds.), *Society and psychosis* (pp. 1–10). Cambridge, UK: Cambridge University Press.

Morrison, A. P., French, P., Walford, L., Lewis, S. W., Kilcommons, A., Green, J., et al. (2004). Cognitive therapy for the prevention of psychosis in people at ultra-high risk: Randomised controlled trial. *British Journal of Psychiatry, 185*, 291–297.

Murray, R. M., & Lewis, S. W. (1987). Is schizophrenia a neurodevelopmental disorder? *British Medical Journal (Clinical Research Edition), 295*, 681–682.

Myin-Germeys, I., Delespaul, P., & van Os, J. (2005). Behavioural sensitization to daily life stress in psychosis. *Psychological Medicine, 35*, 733–741.

Myin-Germeys, I., Krabbendam, L., Delespaul, P., & van Os, J. (2003a). Can cognitive deficits explain differential sensitivity to life events in psychosis? *Social Psychiatry & Psychiatric Epidemiology, 38*, 262–268.

Myin-Germeys, I., Krabbendam, L., Delespaul, P., & van Os, J. (2003b). Do life events have their effect on psychosis by influencing the emotional reactivity to daily life stress? *Psychological Medicine, 33*, 327–333.

Myin-Germeys, I., Peeters, F., Havermans, R., Nicolson, N. A., Devries, M. W., Delespaul, P., et al. (2003). Emotional reactivity to daily life stress in psychosis and affective disorder: An experience sampling study. *Acta Psychiatrica Scandinavica, 107*, 124–131.

Myin-Germeys, I., van Os, J., Schwartz, J. E., Stone, A. A., & Delespaul, P. A. (2001). Emotional reactivity to daily life stress in psychosis. *Archives of General Psychiatry, 58*, 1137–1144.

Poulton, R., Caspi, A., Moffitt, T. E., Cannon, M., Murray, R., & Harrington, H. (2000). Children's self-reported psychotic symptoms and adult schizophreniform disorder: A 15-year longitudinal study. *Archives of General Psychiatry, 57*, 1053–1058.

Raballo, A., & Laroi, F. (2009). Clinical staging: A new scenario for the treatment of psychosis. *Lancet, 374*, 365–367.

Riecher-Rössler, A., Gschwandtner, U., Borgwardt, S., Aston, J., Pflüger, M., & Rössler, W. (2006). Early detection and treatment of schizophrenia: How early? *Acta Psychiatrica Scandinavica Suppl., 429*, 73–80.

Rowlands, M. (2003). *Externalism: Putting mind and world back together again.* Chesham, UK: Acumen.

Salvatore, P., Baldessarini, R. J., Tohen, M., Khalsa, H. M., Sanchez-Toledo, J. P., Zarate, C. A., Jr., et al. (2009). McLean–Harvard International First-Episode Project: Two-year stability of DSM-IV diagnoses in 500 first-episode psychotic disorder patients. *Journal of Clinical Psychiatry, 70*, 458–466.

Selten, J.-P., & Cantor-Graae, E. (2005). Social defeat: Risk factor for schizophrenia? *British Journal of Psychiatry, 187*, 101–102.

Selten, J.-P., Cantor-Graae, E., & Kahn, R. S. (2007). Migration and schizophrenia. *Current Opinion in Psychiatry, 20*, 111–115.

Valmaggia, L. R., McCrone, P., Knapp, M., Woolley, J. B., Broome, M. R., Tabraham, P., et al. (2009). Economic impact of early intervention in people at high risk of psychosis. *Psychological Medicine, 39*, 1617–1626.

van Os, J. (2009). A salience dysregulation syndrome. *British Journal of Psychiatry, 194*, 101–103.

van Os, J., & Delespaul, P. (2005). Toward a world consensus on prevention of schizophrenia. *Dialogues in Clinical Neuroscience, 7*, 53–67.

van Os, J., Linscott, R. J., Myin-Germeys, I., Delespaul, P., & Krabbendam, L. (2009). A systematic review and meta-analysis of the psychosis continuum: Evidence for a psychosis proneness-persistence-impairment model of psychotic disorder. *Psychological Medicine, 39*(2), 179–195.

Verdoux, H., & van Os, J. (2002). Psychotic symptoms in non-clinical populations and the continuum of psychosis. *Schizophrenia Research, 54*, 59–65.

Warner, R. (2005). Problems with early and very early intervention in psychosis. *British Journal of Psychiatry, 48*(Suppl.), s104–s107.

Whitty, P., Clarke, M., McTigue, O., Browne, S., Kamali, M., Larkin, C., et al. (2005). Diagnostic stability four years after a first episode of psychosis. *Psychiatric Services, 56*, 1084–1088.

Yung, A. R., & McGorry, P. D. (1996). The prodromal phase of first-episode psychosis: Past and current conceptualizations. *Schizophrenia Bulletin, 22,* 353–370.

Yung, A. R., Phillips, L. J., McGorry, P. D., McFarlane, C. A., Francey, S., Harrigan, S., et al. (1998). Prediction of psychosis—A step towards indicated prevention of schizophrenia. *British Journal of Psychiatry, 172,* 14–20.

Yung, A. R., Phillips, L. J., Yuen, H. P., Francey, S. M., McFarlane, C. A., Hallgren, M., et al. (2003). Psychosis prediction: 12-month follow up of a high-risk ("prodromal") group. *Schizophrenia Research, 60,* 21–32.

Yung, A. R., Yuen, H. P., Berger, G. E., Francey, S., Hung, T.-C., & McGorry, P. (2007). Declining transition rate in ultra high risk (prodromal) services: Dilution or reduction of risk? *Schizophrenia Bulletin, 33,* 673–681.

3 Defining the risk for psychosis: Can neuroscience help psychopathology?

Alison R. Yung, Stephen J. Wood and Barnaby Nelson

Introduction

The identification of risk factors of particular disorders is a goal in both general medicine and psychiatry. One strategy in general medicine is genetic testing, enabling "at risk" status to be diagnosed before any symptoms of disorder are present. Thus, treatment can be applied with the aim of prevention of disorder. But what of identifying individuals "at risk" of psychotic disorders such as schizophrenia? There are no genetic tests for these disorders, nor even any aetiopathological diagnostic investigations. How can "at-risk" status for psychotic disorders be recognized? A number of attempts have been made to define certain groups as "at risk" either of schizophrenia or of psychotic disorders more generally. This chapter will explore the different strategies that have been used, and examine the role of neuroscience in understanding risk models and increasing our ability to refine risk factors.

Why study risk factors for psychotic disorder?

There are two reasons for studying risk factors for psychotic disorder.

1   Early intervention: that is, identification and treatment of individuals at risk of psychotic disorder allows the possibility of preventing, delaying or ameliorating the onset of full-blown psychosis and psychotic disorder.
2   The opportunity to study risk factors and processes before and around the time of the onset of schizophrenia and related disorders. This could aid our understanding of the aetiology of schizophrenia and assist us to distinguish if there are any core features of schizophrenia, in contrast to features that are epiphenomena or consequences of disease. This would in turn enable development of treatment approaches that target the core features.

Thus identifying risk factors for schizophrenia and other psychotic disorders is certainly a worthwhile aim. The next section describes different approaches to this problem.

Family-history approaches

One approach to identifying individuals' risk factors for schizophrenia is to study family members of patients with the disorder (Asarnow, 1988; Cornblatt & Obuchowski, 1997). Thus, a group with presumably an increased genetic risk is identified, and additional risk factors, which make the transition to a frank psychotic disorder more likely, can be examined. This is known as the "high-risk" approach. Assessments usually begin when subjects are children, with follow-up continuing over many years with the aim of detecting the development of psychotic disorder at some stage in the person's life span. Researchers using the high-risk family-history approach acknowledge that the transition rate to a psychotic disorder is likely to be small and results may well not be generalizable beyond the genetically defined high-risk group (Asarnow, 1988; Cornblatt & Obuchowski, 1997). Furthermore intervention in these "at-risk" individuals is not practical due to the low degree of risk. Indeed, these genetic high-risk studies never claimed early intervention as a goal, focusing instead on investigating causal pathways into schizophrenia and other psychotic illnesses.

Mednick and colleagues (Mednick, Parnas, Schulsinger, & Mednick, 1987) modified the genetic high-risk strategy by focusing on adolescent offspring who were entering the peak age of risk (i.e., they added in the risk factor of age). This approach made the high-risk paradigm more practical. However, the number developing a psychotic disorder from this cohort is still not expected to be large and the number of false positives too high to make any intervention practical.

Similarly, the Edinburgh High-Risk project (Hodges, Byrne, Grant, & Johnstone, 1999; Johnstone et al., 2000; P. Miller, Byrne, Hodges, Lawrie, & Johnstone, 2002) studied individuals with presumed high genetic liability for schizophrenia, including both first- and second-degree relatives of schizophrenia probands. Like the Mednick approach, this study also recruited young adults (aged 16 to 25) who would pass through the period of maximum risk of developing schizophrenia during the planned 10 years of the study.

The findings from genetic studies and the role of neuroscience within this strategy are certainly of interest. However, this is beyond the scope of this chapter, which will focus more on clinical and psychopathological approaches and neurological findings within these.

Longitudinal general population studies

Longitudinal general population cohort studies, such as the 1946 British birth cohort study (Jones, Rodgers, Murray, & Marmot, 1994), ALSPAC (Golding, Pembrey, & Jones, 2001), NEMESIS (Hanssen, Bak, Bijl, Vollebergh, & van Os, 2005) and the Dunedin study (McGee, Williams, Poulton, & Moffitt, 2000), collect data at multiple time points and examine a range of outcomes over time. Large numbers (several thousands) are required to detect risk factors for rare outcomes such as psychotic disorders. Several risk factors have been identified using this method. For example, delayed walking, speech problems, solitary play preference in childhood and low educational test scores at ages 8, 11, and 15 years were all risk factors for schizophrenia in the 1946 British birth cohort study. Neuroscience may provide the explanation for some of these risk factors. Delayed walking, other motor abnormalities, speech problems and learning difficulties are likely to be related to some form of neurodevelopmental abnormality. This may be a static lesion, with different manifestations over time: delayed milestones in early childhood, manifest learning difficulties in later childhood and psychotic symptoms in adolescence or young adulthood (Benes, 2003). This is consistent with different presentations according to age of neurological conditions such as Huntington's disease and frontotemporal dementia (Velakoulis, Walterfang, Mocellin, Pantelis, & McLean, 2009). Alternatively, or additionally, social factors may interact with these apparent neurodevelopmental abnormalities. For example, a child with learning and behavioural problems may be bullied at school, or not well parented, resulting in further stress. This could further affect brain development and result in worsening behaviours or additional symptoms and signs. Other findings from longitudinal studies may also have neurobiological explanations. Stress is a common factor in the possible mechanisms of many of the documented risk factors (Mortensen et al., 1999; Torrey, Miller, Rawlings, & Yolken, 1997). For example, growing up in an urban environment was found to be a risk factor for schizophrenia in the Dutch NEMESIS study (van Os, 2004; van Os, Hanssen, de Graaf, & Vollebergh, 2002). The reasons for this are unclear, but explanations include increased exposure to environmental stress such as high traffic density, noise and violence (Spauwen, Krabbendam, Lieb, Wittchen, & van Os, 2006). Low social capital including poor social cohesion, exclusion and discrimination, all possibly increased in an urban environment, may also increase stress (Boydell et al., 2003; van Os & McGuffin, 2003). Stressful life events in general (Frangou & Murray, 2000) and childhood trauma (Bendall, Jackson, Hulbert, & McGorry, 2008) may increase the risk for psychosis, as well as a number of other mental disorders.

How could stress cause psychosis? Stress and the brain

The hypothalamic-pituitary-adrenal (HPA) axis is considered a key biological factor mediating the link between childhood trauma and the development of psychiatric illness. There is a vast literature showing that early life adversity affects the development of the HPA axis and can lead to persistent alterations in neuroendocrine and behavioural responses to stress (Cirulli, Berry, & Alleva, 2003; Heim, Newport, Mletzko, Miller, & Nemeroff, 2008). Patients with psychosis display both an increased emotional reactivity to stress (Myin-Germeys, van Os, Schwartz, Stone, & Delespaul, 2001) and HPA dysregulation (Phillips et al., 2006). One aetiological pathway to psychosis might be that early life trauma results in an enhanced sensitivity to stress via alterations in HPA-axis regulation, thereby contributing to vulnerability to develop psychopathology under stressful circumstances.

Other common risk factors for schizophrenia identified include low socio-economic status, obstetric complications, illicit drug use and childhood trauma.

The direction of causality of low socioeconomic status and schizophrenia has also not been established. It may be that those who experience psychotic illness drift down through society via unemployment, unstable relationships, social isolation and withdrawal (Aro, Aro, & Keskimaki, 1995; McNaught et al., 1997). On the other hand, lower socioeconomic status is associated with greater stress.

Social defeat is another mechanism that has been proposed to explain the role of urban environment, low socioeconomic status and experience of discrimination in increasing risk for schizophrenia. The theory posits that social defeat leads to dopaminergic hyperactivity and sensitization (and/or increased baseline activity) of the mesolimbic dopamine system and thereby increases the risk for schizophrenia (Selten & Cantor-Graae, 2007).

This hypothesis is supported by animals models, which have found that monkeys (Morgan et al., 2002) and rats (Tidey & Miczek, 1996) show dopaminergic hyperactivity in the mesocorticolimbic system after social defeat. Evidence for a role of brain-derived neurotrophic factor (BDNF) in mediating the long-term effect of social defeat has also been found in mice (Berton et al., 2006).

Pregnancy and birth complications are also associated with increased risk of schizophrenia. This is thought to be due to hypoxic or ischaemic neuronal injury (Geddes & Lawrie, 1995; McNeil, 1995; Warner, 2001). Several of these risk factors are non-specific to psychosis but associated with many psychiatric sequelae. For example, in the case of childhood trauma, there is a demonstrated association between child sexual abuse and a subsequent increase in rates of childhood and adult mental disorders (Spataro, Mullen, Burgess, Wells, & Moss, 2004).

Finally, psychotic-like experiences were identified as risk factors for schizo-phreniform disorder in the Dunedin study (Poulton et al., 2000). This study found that children at age 11 with psychotic-like experiences had an increased risk of schizophreniform disorder at age 26 compared to children who did not have such experiences. However, most of the children with psychotic-like experiences did not develop a psychotic disorder. This study is consistent with findings from prodromal or ultra high risk research, discussed at more length below.

Longitudinal studies have added much to our knowledge of risk factors for psychotic disorders, and schizophrenia in particular. Neuroscience has developed explanatory models for many of these factors. However, one of the problems with longitudinal studies is the long length of follow-up required before associations can be investigated. They also need high numbers, and for possible risk factors to be identified and measured early on. One modification of whole population cohort studies is to narrow the study group to those more likely to develop the outcome of interest. As mentioned previously, studying people with a family history of psychotic illness is one such approach. The cohort is enriched as the expected incidence of schizophrenia and other psychoses is higher than in the general population.

Psychosis proneness

An alternative method of enriching the study group is to focus on those who are hypothetically "psychosis prone". Chapman and colleagues (Allen, Chapman,

Chapman, Vuchetich, & Frost, 1987; Chapman & Chapman, 1987; Chapman, Chapman, Kwapil, Eckblad, & Zinser, 1994) attempted to identify individuals at risk of psychosis by studying those with attenuated and isolated psychotic symptoms. They hypothesized that these symptoms confer a predisposition or diathesis to psychotic disorder. In addition to these "positive" psychotic phenomena, they also theorized that people who displayed physical and social anhedonia and impulsive non-conformity were also at risk. They developed questionnaires to measure these psychopathological symptoms (Chapman & Chapman, 1980; Chapman, Edell, & Chapman, 1980).

These researchers (Allen et al., 1987; Chapman & Chapman, 1987; Chapman et al., 1994) also noted the need to focus on people at or near the age of greatest risk for schizophrenia, that is late adolescence and early adulthood, and so studied college students. One sample of college students with high levels of self-reported "psychotic-like" symptoms was followed longitudinally over time and compared with a group of controls. At 10- to 15-year follow-up, students who scored highly on scales of perceptual abnormalities and magical thinking were more likely to have developed a psychotic disorder than comparison subjects. Social anhedonia, physical anhedonia and impulsive non-conformity were not predictive of psychotic disorder at follow-up, although high scores on the Social Anhedonia scale correlated with high levels of psychotic-like experiences at follow-up. The actual numbers of students who developed a psychotic disorder after 10 to 15 years was low: 11 out of 375 or 2.9%. This was not significantly higher than in the control group (2 of 159, or 1.3%). However, there was a trend for those in the group with high scores on the Perceptual Aberration and Magical Ideation scales to differ from controls, with 10 subjects out of 193 making the transition (5.2%, $p = .06$; Chapman et al., 1994). That is, those students with subthreshold forms of delusions and hallucinations seemed to be more at risk of subsequent full-blown psychotic disorder than those without these symptoms.

Nonetheless, many students with high levels of magical ideation and perceptual abnormalities did not develop a psychotic disorder. This finding is perhaps to be expected, given the seemingly large number of people in the general population who report psychotic-like experiences (Laurens et al., 2007; Poulton et al., 2000; van Os, Hanssen, Bijl, & Vollebergh, 2001; Yung et al., 2009).

To date, because of the low numbers developing a psychotic disorder, the high number of false positives and the long time frame of the follow-up, the psychosis-proneness research has not been used as the basis for any preventive intervention. However, the idea that mild or transitory psychotic-like experiences may increase risk for psychotic disorder has been expanded upon over the last 10–15 years with the development of the ultra high risk (UHR) strategy, discussed below.

Identifying the psychotic prodrome

An alternative to the genetic high risk, birth cohort and "psychosis proneness" approaches is to focus on help-seeking individuals who report symptoms that are known to occur prior to the onset of a psychotic disorder, that is, symptoms found in psychotic prodromes. In contrast to the above strategies, which study community samples of largely asymptomatic or at least non-help-seeking individuals, this strategy applies an initial filter of clinical need. This means that the person is likely to be at risk in the short term. An added criterion, as in some of the studies above, is age in adolescence and young adulthood, to further enrich degree of risk and reduce the period of follow-up required. Thus, this approach has the advantage of focusing on a short time period, rather than requiring several decades of follow-up.

There are different ways of approaching the recruitment of possibly prodromal individuals. Two broad methods have used the symptomatic approach to identify at-risk individuals: the basic symptoms method of the Bonn and Cologne groups (Klosterkötter, Hellmich, Steinmeyer, & Schultze-Lutter, 2001; Klosterkötter, Schultze-Lutter, Gross, Huber, & Steinmeyer, 1997) and the ultra high risk method developed in Melbourne, Australia (Yung et al., 1998, 2003; Yung, Phillips, Yuen, & McGorry, 2004), and adapted by other groups worldwide, including the large North American Prodrome Longitudinal Study (NAPLS) group (Cannon et al., 2008).

Basic symptoms as predictors

Researchers in Germany examined the predictive ability of basic symptoms in a tertiary psychiatric service, to which patients were referred if they had suspected schizophrenia (Klosterkötter et al., 2001; Klosterkötter, Schultze-Lutter et al., 1997). That is, in contrast to the psychosis-proneness research, the target population was a clinical one. Subjects were followed up on average eight years after initial assessment, and over this period over 50% of them had developed schizophrenia. Certain basic symptoms—disturbances of receptive speech, blocking of thoughts, visual perceptual disturbances, olfactory, gustatory and other sensory disturbances—were found significantly more often in the group which developed schizophrenia compared to the group which did not, suggesting that these symptoms may be predictors of schizophrenia.

From this study, the authors developed a checklist of nine symptoms suggestive of a schizophrenia prodrome, as measured by the Bonn Scale for the Assessment of Basic Symptoms (BSABS; Klosterkötter, Gross et al., 1997). High-risk criteria were then developed requiring the presence of at least two of these symptoms. The predictive validity of these criteria are currently being examined in a multi-site European study (Klosterkötter et al., 2005).

The ultra high risk approach

As has been found with the psychosis-proneness research, there are problems with using prodromal symptoms and signs alone to identify people thought to be at incipient risk of onset of psychotic disorder, even psychotic-like experiences, given the prevalence of these symptoms in the general population, especially in adolescents (see above). The false-positive rate would be high in a non-clinical sample, and any intervention provided may be done unnecessarily.

In an attempt to address these issues, a group in Melbourne, Australia, applied a "close in" strategy (Bell, 1992), which involved putting in place a number of different measures to concentrate the level of risk in the selected sample. That is, an individual must meet a number of conditions to be included in the high-risk sample rather than just one, as in the traditional genetic high-risk studies. In addition to help seeking, one of the required conditions was a recent change in mental state indicating risk of psychotic disorder in the near future (1–2 years). For example, recent functional decline and attenuated and isolated psychotic symptoms were included. Another risk factor required was age in adolescence and young adulthood as this represents the highest risk period for onset of psychotic disorder (Hafner et al., 1994). Individuals meeting these combinations of risk factors are called "ultra high risk" (UHR), the term "ultra" being added to distinguish these individuals from subjects in traditional genetic high risk studies (Yung & McGorry, 2007). The UHR criteria require that a young person be aged between 14 and 25, is referred for help to a clinical service and meets criteria for one or more of the following groups:

1   *Attenuated Psychotic Symptoms Group*: have experienced subthreshold, attenuated positive psychotic symptoms during the past year;
2   *Brief Limited Intermittent Psychotic Symptoms Group (BLIPS)*: have experienced episodes of frank psychotic symptoms that have not lasted longer than a week and have been spontaneously abated; or
3   *Trait and State Risk Factor Group*: have schizotypal personality disorder or a first-degree relative with a psychotic disorder and have experienced a significant decrease in functioning during the previous year.

The UHR criteria have been operationalized using specially designed instruments, the Comprehensive Assessment of At Risk Mental States (CAARMS; Yung et al., 2005) or the Structured Interview for Prodromal Symptoms (SIPS) and the Scale of Prodromal Symptoms (SOPS; Miller et al., 2003). The UHR criteria have been adapted and used in many sites around the world, and have been variably termed "clinical high risk" (CHR; Cornblatt, Lencz, & Obuchowski, 2002), At Risk Mental State (ARMS; Broome et al., 2005; Yung et al., 1996) or "prodromal" criteria (Cannon et al., 2008; T. Miller et al., 2002). Several longitudinal follow-up studies have assessed the predictive validity of the criteria (Cannon et al., 2008; Yung et al., 2003, 2004), with rates of UHR patients developing first-episode psychosis (FEP) within one year between 10 and 50% (Olsen & Rosenbaum, 2006), with an average across multiple studies of 36.7% (Ruhrmann, Schultze-Lutter, & Klosterkötter, 2003).

Recently, there has been a somewhat controversial proposal to include an adaptation of the UHR criteria as a diagnosis in the next version of the *Diagnostic and Statistical Manual of Mental Disorders* (5th ed.; DSM-V). Different terms have been suggested for this new diagnosis, including "psychosis risk syndrome", "risk syndrome for first psychosis", and, most recently, the "attenuated psychotic symptoms syndrome" (Carpenter, 2009; DSM-V Task Force, 2010). Some of the benefits of including the risk syndrome in DSM-V include: early intervention to delay or prevent later psychosis; encouraging attention and resources to be directed to an important clinical population; highlighting epidemiological work that demonstrates that attenuated psychotic symptoms are prevalent in the general population, and may be associated with both current morbidity and risk for illness; and aligning psychiatry more closely with other fields of medicine that identify risk factors for the purposes of instituting preventative interventions (Corcoran, First, & Cornblatt, 2010). Authors in favour of including the risk syndrome argue that a clinical need exists for these patients, as evidenced by the help-seeking behaviour of individuals and families. Furthermore, individuals with this syndrome may not attract a diagnosis under DSM-IV that adequately addresses their needs. Thus, they may have difficulty accessing care and receiving reimbursement under medical insurance schemes.

A number of points have been made against including the risk syndrome in DSM-V. First, there is the issue of the potentially high number of "false positives" diagnosed with the syndrome (Corcoran et al., 2010). The high number of "false positives" may be due to the inherent problem of "false positives" in those identified as being "at risk" compounded by the problem of misdiagnosis in "non-expert" settings (Corcoran et al., 2010). In addition, the base rate of psychosis may be lower in populations outside tertiary research settings, particularly in primary care and the general population, thus increasing the "false positive" rate (Drake & Lewis, 2010; Kaymaz & van Os, 2010; Yung, Buckby et al., 2006). This concern has led to the inclusion of a caveat that the attenuated psychotic symptoms must be associated with distress, disability, and help seeking. However, this addition is also problematic as help seeking is dependent on a number of non-illness factors, including availability of services and cultural and subcultural attitudes to seeking help.

The opponents of introducing the risk syndrome argue that the risk-benefit ratio of its inclusion is not favourable due to a number of possible unintended consequences: the high risk of stigma (both by self and other) and discrimination, including from health insurance companies (Yang, Wonpat-Borja, Opler, & Corcoran, 2010); the possibility of exacerbating the already evident trend of treatment with antipsychotic medications for patients with attenuated psychotic symptoms in the absence of good evidence for this (Corcoran et al., 2010); and the low benefits resulting from case identification given the lack of a clear evidence base for effective interventions (Corcoran et al., 2010; Drake & Lewis, 2010). It is also possible that the risk syndrome would suffer from the phenomenon of "diagnostic creep"—that is, the threshold for a diagnosis gradually shifting in response to clinical practice, political lobbying and other social forces. An example of this would be a scenario of a clinician providing a patient with a diagnosis of risk syndrome in order to access treatment and gain insurance coverage, even though the patient technically falls below the risk syndrome threshold.

Refining risk factors for psychosis in the UHR group

Although the rate of development of full-blown psychotic disorder in UHR groups is several hundred fold above that expected in the general population (Cannon et al., 2008), there are still high numbers of UHR individuals who do not become psychotic within a brief follow-up period. As can be seen from the above figures, this is at least 50%. Clearly what is needed is investigation of factors within the UHR group that further increase risk for onset of psychotic disorder.

Clinical and symptomatic predictors

Several symptoms and other clinical features have been found to increase risk of transition to psychosis within the UHR group. Negative symptoms such as impaired concentration and attention, subjectively abnormal emotional experiences, impaired energy and impaired tolerance to stress (Yung et al., 2005), marked impairment in role functioning, anhedonia and asociality (Mason et al., 2004), blunted affect (Mason et al., 2004; Yung et al., 2005) and social withdrawal (Haroun, Dunn, Haroun, & Cadenhead, 2006; Johnstone, Ebmeier, Miller, Owens, & Lawrie, 2005) are examples. These phenomena are of interest as they may reflect an underlying abnormality, particularly in schizophrenia, and may be associated with cognitive changes.

Depression has also been found to be a significant predictor of psychosis in UHR groups (Johnstone et al., 2005; Yung et al., 2003). Poor functioning at intake predicted onset of psychosis in several separate UHR cohorts (Mason et al., 2004; Yung et al., 2003; Yung, Stanford et al., 2006). This may indicate that a deterioration process, and actual onset of psychotic disorder, has already begun in those UHR subjects with poor functioning.

Can neuroscience help psychopathology?

In further attempting to refine risk factors within the UHR group neurocognitive and neurobiological factors have been examined.

Neurocognitive predictors

Cognitive deficits are recognized as one of the core features of schizophrenia and have been associated with functional outcome (Green, 1996). There has therefore been a large research effort to detect the presence of cognitive deficits prior to illness onset, as they may represent neurocognitive trait markers for schizophrenia. Initial studies (see Brewer et al., 2006, for a review) implicated frontal systems such as that underlying olfactory identification (Brewer et al., 2003), working memory (Wood et al., 2003) and rapid processing and efficient recall (Brewer et al., 2005). This focus on frontal lobe function, and working memory in particular, is unsurprising since this is consistently impaired throughout the course of the illness (Goldman-Rakic, 1994). Subsequent research has aimed to replicate and extend these findings, largely with great success. There is now evidence from a number of centres that the addition of neurocognitive variables such as impaired working memory and reduced speed of processing can improve the prediction of psychosis outcome (Pukrop et al., 2007; Riecher-Rössler et al., 2009). However, these reported impairments are cross-sectional snapshots of a clinical picture that may well change over time. There is evidence of progressive decline in certain cognitive domains over the transition to psychosis that further implicates speed of processing in the development of the illness (Wood et al., 2007), but further longitudinal cognitive data is required to confirm this.

Neurobiological predictors

HPA-axis dysfunction may play a role in the development of psychotic disorders (see Chapter 6, pp. 59–72). This is supported by the finding of higher cortisol levels (plasma, salivary or urinary) and abnormal circadian cortisol rhythms in patients with psychotic disorders compared to healthy control subjects (Kaneko et al., 1992).

We recently investigated HPA-axis functioning in 12 UHR subjects at the Personal Assessment and Crises Evaluation (PACE) clinic using the combined dexamethasone corticotrophin releasing hormone (DEX/CRH) test (Thompson et al., 2007). Over a two-year period, three of the 12 participants developed a psychosis. Analysis indicated that contrary to expectations, participants who did not make the transition to psychosis had on average higher cortisol levels, as well as a greater severity of depression and anxiety symptoms, than participants who subsequently developed psychosis. These preliminary results suggest that dysregulated HPA axis functioning in individuals at UHR for psychosis may be associated more with comorbid depression symptoms than factors specifically related to the process of emerging psychosis illness.

The pituitary gland contains corticotrophs, the cells that produce and secrete adrenocorticotropin hormone (ACTH), which in turn activates the secretion of cortisol. A recent study found increased pituitary volumes in FEP patients, while individuals with established schizophrenia of at least five years' duration had smaller pituitary volumes than controls (Pariante et al., 2004). This increased volume is thought to reflect an increase in the size and number of corticotrophs, and therefore activation of the HPA axis. Not only does this volume enlargement seem to occur prior to the development of the illness, but the greater the enlargement the shorter the period between assessment and the onset of frank psychotic symptoms (Garner et al., 2005). Taken together, these data suggest that alterations of the HPA axis may play a major role in the onset phase of psychotic disorders.

Studies of brain structure may also be relevant to the HPA dysfunction model of psychotic disorders. It is hypothesized that abnormal HPA-axis responses to stress might result in hippocampal damage, which may then compromise attention, memory and other cognitive skills and ultimately influence the development of positive psychotic symptoms.

While reductions in hippocampal volume are one of the most commonly reported features of schizophrenia (Shenton, Dickey, Frumin, & McCarley, 2001) hippocampal volumes of PACE UHR patients do not seem to be associated with a heightened risk of later developing psychosis (Velakoulis et al., 2006). Instead, a subtle increase in hippocampal perfusion seems to be a better predictor of outcome, although this needs to be replicated in a larger sample (Schobel et al., 2009).

In fact, there are few imaging measures that have any utility as predictive markers of later first-episode disorder (Wood et al., 2008). Regions which do seem to distinguish between those who do and do not make a transition include the insular cortex (Takahashi et al., 2009) and the corpus callosum (Walterfang, Yung et al., 2008), but these differences are at the group level only and do not provide a great deal of predictive power.

All the studies referred above were cross-sectional in design. However, as with detecting dementia, it is possible that change over time may turn out to be the most important metric with regard to the later onset of psychosis. The earliest such report was a small voxel-based morphometry study (Pantelis et al., 2003), which showed significant reductions in grey matter within medial temporal and orbitofrontal regions on the left, as well as the anterior cingulate bilaterally. These changes were not seen in patients who did not develop psychosis. These findings have since been supported by a study in a separate sample at another research centre (Borgwardt et al., 2008)—changes in frontal, temporal and parietal grey matter were seen in those who transitioned to psychosis, while no changes were seen in patients who did not.

Because of specific problems with these studies (not least that there was no statistically significant group-by-time interaction), we have since expanded our sample by 50% and used images with thinner slices. In this analysis (Sun et al., 2009), we were again able to show significant reductions of the right prefrontal cortex in patients who progressed to psychosis. However, importantly, we were able to show that these reductions were significantly greater than the changes seen in those who did not.

These changes are not limited to grey matter. In a similar approach to our initial study (Pantelis et al., 2003), we have shown that white matter also shows changes across the transition boundary (Walterfang, McGuire et al., 2008). Specifically, over the transition there were significant reductions in the volume of the left fronto-occipital fasciculus. In contrast, those who remained non-psychotic showed a significant *increase* in a region subjacent to the right inferior parietal lobule.

Taken together, these findings suggest that brain changes can occur during the process of transition to psychosis, and, if they can be detected over a sufficiently short period of time, could act as markers of impending illness onset. Furthermore, while the basis of the changes remains uncertain, there is the possibility that with sufficiently early treatment such changes could be minimized or prevented.

Conclusion

Progress has been made in detecting groups at risk of schizophrenia and other psychoses. Risk factors have been identified through general population cohorts, and enriched groups with added risk factors. Neuroscience plays an important and exciting role in attempting to explain the role of different factors: including epidemiological (such as migration, low socioeconomic status), developmental (delayed milestones) through to the general role of stress, as well as enhancing our ability to detect those most at risk within high-risk cohorts.

References

Allen, J. J., Chapman, L. J., Chapman, J. P., Vuchetich, J. P., & Frost, L. A. (1987). Prediction of psychotic-like symptoms in hypothetically psychosis-prone college students. *Journal of Abnormal Psychology, 96*(2), 83–88.

Aro, S., Aro, H., & Keskimaki, I. (1995). Socio-economic mobility among patients with schizophrenia or major affective disorder. A 17-year retrospective follow-up. *British Journal of Psychiatry, 166*(6), 759–767.

Asarnow, J. R. (1988). Children at risk for schizophrenia: Converging lines of evidence. *Schizophrenia Bulletin, 14*(4), 613–631.

Bell, R. Q. (1992). Multiple-risk cohorts and segmenting risk as solutions to the problem of false positives in risk for the major psychoses. *Psychiatry, 55*, 370–381.

Bendall, S., Jackson, H. J., Hulbert, C. A., & McGorry, P. D. (2008). Childhood trauma and psychotic disorders: A systematic, critical review of the evidence. *Schizophrenia Bulletin, 34*(3), 568–579.

Benes, F. M. (2003). Why does psychosis develop during adolescence and early adulthood? [editorial]. *Current Opinion in Psychiatry, 16*, 317–319.

Berton, O., McClung, C. A., DiLeone, R. J., Krishnan, V., Renthal, W., Russo, S. J., et al. (2006). Essential role of BDNF in the mesolimbic dopamine pathway in social defeat stress. *Science, 311*, 864–868.

Borgwardt, S. J., McGuire, P. K., Aston, J., Gschwandtner, U., Pfluger, M. O., Stieglitz, R. D., et al. (2008). Reductions in frontal, temporal and parietal volume associated with the onset of psychosis. *Schizophrenia Research, 106*(2–3), 108–114.

Boydell, J., van Os, J., Lambri, M., Castle, D., Allardyce, J., McCreadie, R. G., et al. (2003). Incidence of schizophrenia in south-east London between 1965 and 1997. *British Journal of Psychiatry, 182*, 45–49.

Brewer, W. J., Francey, S. M., Wood, S. J., Jackson, H. J., Pantelis, C., Phillips, L. J., et al. (2005). Memory impairments identified in people at ultra-high risk for psychosis who later develop first-episode psychosis. *American Journal of Psychiatry, 162*(1), 71–78.

Brewer, W. J., Wood, S. J., McGorry, P. D., Francey, S. M., Phillips, L. J., Yung, A. R., et al. (2003). Impairment of olfactory identification ability in individuals at ultra-high risk for psychosis who later develop schizophrenia. *American Journal of Psychiatry, 160*(10), 1790–1794.

Brewer, W. J., Wood, S. J., Phillips, L. J., Francey, S. M., Pantelis, C., Yung, A. R., et al. (2006). Generalised and specific cognitive performance in clinical high-risk cohorts: A review highlighting potential vulnerability markers for psychosis. *Schizophrenia Bulletin, 32*, 538–555.

Broome, M. R., Woolley, J. B., Johns, L. C., Valmaggia, L. R., Tabraham, P., Gafoor, R., et al. (2005). Outreach and support in south London (OASIS): Implementation of a clinical service for prodromal psychosis and the at risk mental state. *European Psychiatry, 20*(5–6), 372–378.

Cannon, T. D., Cadenhead, K., Cornblatt, B., Woods, S. W., Addington, J., Walker, E., et al. (2008). Prediction of psychosis in youth at high clinical risk: A multisite longitudinal study in North America. *Archives of General Psychiatry, 65*(1), 28–37.

Carpenter, W. T. (2009). Anticipating DSM-V: Should psychosis risk become a diagnostic class? *Schizophrenia Bulletin, 35*(5), 841–843.

Chapman, L. J., & Chapman, J. P. (1980). Scales for rating psychotic and psychotic-like experiences as continua. *Schizophrenia Bulletin, 6*(3), 476–489.

Chapman, L. J., & Chapman, J. P. (1987). The search for symptoms predictive of schizophrenia. *Schizophrenia Bulletin, 13*, 497–503.

Chapman, L. J., Chapman, J. P., Kwapil, T. R., Eckblad, M., & Zinser, M. C. (1994). Putatively psychosis-prone subjects 10 years later. *Journal of Abnormal Psychology, 103*(2), 171–183.

Chapman, L. J., Edell, W. S., & Chapman, J. P. (1980). Physical anhedonia, perceptual aberration, and psychosis proneness. *Schizophrenia Bulletin, 6*(4), 639–653.

Cirulli, F., Berry, A., & Alleva, E. (2003). Early disruption of the mother–infant relationship: Effects on brain plasticity and implications for psychopathology. *Neuroscience and Biobehavioral Reviews, 27*(1–2), 73–82.

Corcoran, C. M., First, M. B., & Cornblatt, B. (2010). The psychosis risk syndrome and its proposed inclusion in the DSM-V: A risk-benefit analysis. *Schizophrenia Research, 120*(1–3), 16–22.

Cornblatt, B., Lencz, T., & Obuchowski, M. (2002). The schizophrenia prodrome: Treatment and high-risk perspectives. *Schizophrenia Research, 54*, 177–186.

Cornblatt, B., & Obuchowski, M. (1997). Update of high-risk research: 1987–1997. *International Review of Psychiatry, 9*, 437–447.

Drake, R. J., & Lewis, S. W. (2010). Valuing prodromal psychosis: What do we get and what is the price? *Schizophrenia Research, 120*, 38–41.

DSM-V Task Force. (2010). *Proposed draft revisions to DSM disorders and criteria: Attenuated psychotic symptoms syndrome.* Washington, DC: American Psychiatric Association. (2010, updated 2010; cited 13 September 2010. Available from: http://www.dsm5.org/ProposedRevisions/Pages/proposedrevision.aspx?rid = 412)

Frangou, S., & Murray, R. M. (2000). *Schizophrenia.* London, UK: Informa.

Garner, B., Pariante, C. M., Wood, S. J., Velakoulis, D., Phillips, L., Soulsby, B., et al. (2005). Pituitary volume predicts future transition to psychosis in individuals at ultra-high risk of developing psychosis. *Biological Psychiatry, 58*(5), 417–423.

Geddes, J. R., & Lawrie, S. M. (1995). Obstetric complications, neurodevelopmental deviance and risk of schizophrenia. *Journal of Psychiatric Research, 21*, 413–421.

Golding, J., Pembrey, M., & Jones, R. (2001). ALSPAC—The Avon Longitudinal Study of Parents and Children. I. Study methodology. *Paediatric and Perinatal Epidemiology, 15*(1), 74–87.

Goldman-Rakic, P. S. (1994). Working memory in schizophrenia. *Journal of Neuropsychiatry and Clinical Neurosciences, 6*, 348–357.

Green, M. F. (1996). What are the functional consequences of neurocognitive deficits in schizophrenia? *American Journal of Psychiatry, 153*, 321–330.

Hafner, H., Maurer, K., Loffler, W., Fatkenheuer, B., An Der Heiden, W., Riecher-Rössler, A., et al. (1994). The epidemiology of early schizophrenia. Influence of age and gender on onset and early course. *British Journal of Psychiatry* (Suppl. 23), *164*, 29–38.

Hanssen, M., Bak, M., Bijl, R., Vollebergh, W., & van Os, J. (2005). The incidence and outcome of subclinical psychotic experiences in the general population. *British Journal of Clinical Psychology, 44*(2), 181–191.

Haroun, N., Dunn, L., Haroun, A., & Cadenhead, K. (2006). Risk and protection in prodromal schizophrenia: Ethical implications for clinical practice and future research. *Schizophrenia Bulletin, 32,* 166–178.

Heim, C., Newport, D. J., Mletzko, T., Miller, A. H., & Nemeroff, C. B. (2008). The link between childhood trauma and depression: Insights from HPA axis studies in humans. *Psychoneuroendocrinology, 33*(6), 693–710.

Hodges, A., Byrne, M., Grant, E., & Johnstone, E. C. (1999). People at risk of schizophrenia: Sample characteristics of the first 100 cases in the Edinburgh high-risk study. *British Journal of Psychiatry, 174,* 547–553.

Johnstone, E. C., Abukmeil, S. S., Byrne, M., Clafferty, R., Grant, E., Hodges, A., et al. (2000). Edinburgh high risk study—Findings after four years: Demographic, attainment and psychopathological issues. *Schizophrenia Research, 46,* 1–15.

Johnstone, E. C., Ebmeier, K. P., Miller, P., Owens, D. G., & Lawrie, S. M. (2005). Predicting schizophrenia: Findings from the Edinburgh high-risk study. *British Journal of Psychiatry, 186*(1), 18–25.

Jones, P., Rodgers, B., Murray, R., & Marmot, M. (1994). Child developmental risk factors for adult schizophrenia in the British 1946 birth cohort. *The Lancet, 344*(8934), 1398–1402.

Kaneko, M., Yokoyama, F., Hoshino, Y., Takahagi, K., Murata, S., Watanabe, M., et al. (1992). Hypothalamic-pituitary-adrenal axis function in chronic schizophrenia: Association with clinical features. *Neuropsychobiology, 25*(1), 1–7.

Kaymaz, N., & van Os, J. (2010). DSM-5 and the "psychosis risk syndrome": Babylonic confusion. *Psychosis: Psychological, Social and Integrative Approaches, 2*(2), 100–103.

Klosterkötter, J., Gross, G., Huber, G., Wieneke, A., Steinmeyer, E. M., & Schultze-Lutter, F. (1997). Evaluation of the "Bonn Scale for the Assessment of Basic Symptoms—BSABS" as an instrument for the assessment of schizophrenia proneness: A review of recent findings. *Neurology, Psychiatry and Brain Research, 5,* 137–150.

Klosterkötter, J., Hellmich, M., Steinmeyer, E. M., & Schultze-Lutter, F. (2001). Diagnosing schizophrenia in the initial prodromal phase. *Archives of General Psychiatry, 58,* 158–164.

Klosterkötter, J., Ruhrmann, S., Schultze-Lutter, F., Salokangas, R. K., Linszen, D., Birchwood, M., et al. (2005). The European Prediction of Psychosis Study (EPOS): Integrating early recognition and intervention in Europe. *World Psychiatry, 4*(3), 161–167.

Klosterkötter, J., Schultze-Lutter, F., Gross, G., Huber, G., & Steinmeyer, E. M. (1997). Early self-experienced neuropsychological deficits and subsequent schizophrenic diseases: An 8-year average follow-up prospective study. *Acta Psychiatrica Scandinavica, 95,* 396–404.

Laurens, K. R., Hodgins, S., Maughan, B., Murray, R. M., Rutter, M. L., & Taylor, E. A. (2007). Community screening for psychotic-like experiences and other putative antecedents of schizophrenia in children aged 9–12 years. *Schizophrenia Research, 90*(1–3), 130–146.

Mason, O., Startup, M., Halpin, S., Schall, U., Conrad, A., & Carr, V. (2004). Risk factors for transition to first episode psychosis among individuals with "at-risk mental states". *Schizophrenia Research, 71*(2–3), 227–237.

McGee, R., Williams, S., Poulton, R., & Moffitt, T. (2000). A longitudinal study of cannabis use and mental health from adolescence to early adulthood. *Addiction*, *95*(4), 491–503.

McNaught, A. S., Jeffreys, S. E., Harvey, C. A., Quayle, A. S., King, M. B., & Bird, A. S. (1997). The Hampstead schizophrenia survey 1991. II: Incidence and migration in inner London. *British Journal of Psychiatry*, *170*, 307–311.

McNeil, T. F. (1995). Perinatal risk factors and schizophrenia: Selective review and methodological concerns. *Epidemiologic Reviews*, *17*(1), 107–112.

Mednick, S. A., Parnas, J., Schulsinger, F., & Mednick, B. (1987). The Copenhagen high-risk project, 1962–1986. *Schizophrenia Bulletin*, *13*, 485–496.

Miller, P. M., Byrne, M., Hodges, A., Lawrie, S. M., & Johnstone, E. C. (2002). Childhood behaviour, psychotic symptoms and psychosis onset in young people at high risk of schizophrenia: Early findings from the Edinburgh high risk study. *Psychological Medicine*, *32*(1), 173–179.

Miller, T. J., McGlashan, T. H., Rosen, J. L., Cadenhead, K., Ventura, J., McFarlane, W., et al. (2003). Prodromal assessment with the structured interview for prodromal syndromes and the scale of prodromal symptoms: Predictive validity, interrater reliability, and training to reliability. *Schizophrenia Bulletin*, *29*(4), 703–715.

Miller, T. J., McGlashan, T. H., Rosen, J. L., Somjee, L., Markovich, P. J., Stein, K., et al. (2002). Prospective diagnosis of the initial prodrome for schizophrenia based on the Structured Interview for Prodromal Syndromes: Preliminary evidence of interrater reliability and predictive validity. *American Journal of Psychiatry*, *159*(5), 863–865.

Morgan, D., Grant, K. A., Gage, D., Mach, R. H., Kaplan, J. R., Prioleau, O., et al. (2002). Social dominance in monkeys: Dopamine D2 receptors and cocaine self-administration. *Nature Neuroscience*, *5*, 169–174.

Mortensen, P. B., Pedersen, C. B., Westergaard, T., Wohlfahrt, J., Ewald, H., Mors, O., et al. (1999). Effects of family history and place and season of birth on the risk of schizophrenia. *New England Journal of Medicine*, *340*(8), 603–608.

Myin-Germeys, I., van Os, J., Schwartz, J. E., Stone, A. A., & Delespaul, P. A. (2001). Emotional reactivity to daily life stress in psychosis. *Archives of General Psychiatry*, *58*(12), 1137–1144.

Olsen, K. A., & Rosenbaum, B. (2006). Prospective investigations of the prodromal state of schizophrenia: Review of studies. *Acta Psychiatrica Scandinavica*, *113*, 247–272.

Pantelis, C., Velakoulis, D., McGorry, P. D., Wood, S. J., Suckling, J., Phillips, L. J., et al. (2003). Neuroanatomical abnormalities before and after onset of psychosis: A cross-sectional and longitudinal MRI comparison. *Lancet*, *361*(9354), 281–288.

Pariante, C. M., Vassilopoulou, K., Velakoulis, D., Phillips, L., Soulsby, B., Wood, S. J., et al. (2004). Pituitary volume in psychosis. *British Journal of Psychiatry*, *185*(1), 5–10.

Phillips, L. J., McGorry, P. D., Garner, B., Thompson, K. N., Pantelis, C., Wood, S. J., et al. (2006). Stress, the hippocampus and the hypothalamic-pituitary-adrenal axis: Implications for the development of psychotic disorders. *Australian and New Zealand Journal of Psychiatry*, *40*(9), 725–741.

Poulton, R., Caspi, A., Moffitt, T. E., Cannon, M., Murray, R., & Harrington, H. (2000). Children's self-reported psychotic symptoms and adult schizophreniform disorder: A 15-year longitudinal study. *Archives of General Psychiatry*, *57*(11), 1053–1058.

Pukrop, R., Ruhrmann, S., Schultze-Lutter, F., Bechdolf, A., Brockhaus-Dumke, A., & Klosterkötter, J. (2007). Neurocognitive indicators for a conversion to psychosis: Comparison of patients in a potentially initial prodromal state who did or did not convert to a psychosis. *Schizophrenia Research*, *92*(1–3), 116–125.

Riecher-Rössler, A., Pflueger, M. O., Aston, J., Borgwardt, S. J., Brewer, W. J., Gschwandtner, U., et al. (2009). Efficacy of using cognitive status in predicting psychosis: A 7-year follow-up. *Biological Psychiatry, 66*(11), 1023–1030.

Ruhrmann, S., Schultze-Lutter, F., & Klosterkötter, J. (2003). Early detection and intervention in the initial prodromal phase of schizophrenia. *Pharmacopsychiatry, 36*(Suppl. 3), S162–S167.

Schobel, S. A., Lewandowski, N. M., Corcoran, C. M., Moore, H., Brown, T., Malaspina, D., et al. (2009). Differential targeting of the CA1 subfield of the hippocampal formation by schizophrenia and related psychotic disorders. *Archives of General Psychiatry, 66*(9), 938–946.

Selten, J.-P., & Cantor-Graae, E. (2007). Hypothesis: Social defeat is a risk factor for schizophrenia? *British Journal of Psychiatry, 51*(Suppl.), 9–12.

Shenton, M. E., Dickey, C. C., Frumin, M., & McCarley, R. W. (2001). A review of MRI findings in schizophrenia. *Schizophrenia Research, 49*, 1–52.

Spataro, J., Mullen, P. E., Burgess, P. M., Wells, D. L., & Moss, S. A. (2004). Impact of child sexual abuse on mental health: Prospective study in males and females. *British Journal of Psychiatry, 184*, 416–421.

Spauwen, J., Krabbendam, L., Lieb, R., Wittchen, H.-U., & van Os, J. (2006). Evidence that the outcome of developmental expression of psychosis is worse for adolescents growing up in an urban environment. *Psychological Medicine, 36*(3), 407–415.

Sun, D., Phillips, L., Velakoulis, D., Yung, A., McGorry, P. D., Wood, S. J., et al. (2009). Progressive brain structural changes mapped as psychosis develops in "at risk" individuals. *Schizophrenia Research, 108*(1–3), 85–92.

Takahashi, T., Wood, S. J., Yung, A. R., Phillips, L. J., Soulsby, B., McGorry, P. D., et al. (2009). Insular cortex gray matter changes in individuals at ultra-high-risk of developing psychosis. *Schizophrenia Research, 111*(1–3), 94–102.

Thompson, K., Berger, G., Phillips, L., Komesaroff, P., Purcell, R., & McGorry, P. D. (2007). HPA axis functioning associated with transition to psychosis: Combined DEX/CRH test. *Journal of Psychiatric Research, 41*(5), 446–450.

Tidey, J. W., & Miczek, K. A. (1996). Social defeat stress selectively alters mesocorticolimbic dopamine release: An in vivo microdialysis study. *Brain Research, 721*, 140–149.

Torrey, E. F., Miller, J., Rawlings, R., & Yolken, R. H. (1997). Seasonality of births in schizophrenia and bipolar disorder: A review of the literature. *Schizophrenia Research, 28*(1), 1–38.

van Os, J. (2004). Does the urban environment cause psychosis? *British Journal of Psychiatry, 184*(4), 287–288.

van Os, J., Hanssen, M., Bijl, R. V., & Vollebergh, W. (2001). Prevalence of psychotic disorder and community level of psychotic symptoms: An urban–rural comparison. *Archives of General Psychiatry, 58*(7), 663–668.

van Os, J., Hanssen, M., de Graaf, R., & Vollebergh, W. (2002). Does the urban environment independently increase the risk for both negative and positive features of psychosis? *Social Psychiatry & Psychiatric Epidemiology, 37*(10), 460–464.

van Os, J., & McGuffin, P. (2003). Can the social environment cause schizophrenia? *British Journal of Psychiatry, 182*(4), 291–292.

Velakoulis, D., Walterfang, M., Mocellin, R., Pantelis, C., & McLean, C. (2009). Frontotemporal dementia presenting as schizophrenia-like psychosis in young people: Clinicopathological series and review of cases. *British Journal of Psychiatry, 194*(4), 298–305.

Velakoulis, D., Wood, S. J., Wong, M. T., McGorry, P. D., Yung, A., Phillips, L., et al. (2006). Hippocampal and amygdala volumes according to psychosis stage and diagnosis:

A magnetic resonance imaging study of chronic schizophrenia, first-episode psychosis, and ultra-high-risk individuals. *Archives of General Psychiatry, 63*(2), 139–149.

Walterfang, M., McGuire, P. K., Yung, A. R., Phillips, L. J., Velakoulis, D., Wood, S. J., et al. (2008). White matter volume changes in people who develop psychosis. *British Journal of Psychiatry, 193*(3), 210–215.

Walterfang, M., Yung, A., Wood, A. G., Reutens, D. C., Phillips, L., Wood, S. J., et al. (2008). Corpus callosum shape alterations in individuals prior to the onset of psychosis. *Schizophrenia Research, 103*(1–3), 1–10.

Warner, R. (2001). The prevention of schizophrenia: What interventions are safe and effective? *Schizophrenia Bulletin, 27*(4), 551–562.

Wood, S. J., Brewer, W. J., Koutsouradis, P., Phillips, L. J., Francey, S. M., Proffitt, T. M., et al. (2007). Cognitive decline following psychosis onset: Data from the PACE clinic. *British Journal of Psychiatry, 51*(Suppl.), s52–57.

Wood, S. J., Pantelis, C., Proffitt, T., Phillips, L. J., Stuart, G. W., Buchanan, J. A., et al. (2003). Spatial working memory ability is a marker of risk-for-psychosis. *Psychological Medicine, 33*(7), 1239–1247.

Wood, S. J., Pantelis, C., Velakoulis, D., Yucel, M., Fornito, A., & McGorry, P. D. (2008). Progressive changes in the development toward schizophrenia: Studies in subjects at increased symptomatic risk. *Schizophrenia Bulletin, 34*(2), 322–329.

Yang, L. H., Wonpat-Borja, A. J., Opler, M. G., & Corcoran, C. M. (2010). Potential stigma associated with inclusion of the psychosis risk syndrome in the DSM-V: An empirical question. *Schizophrenia Research, 120*(1–3), 42–48.

Yung, A. R., Buckby, J. A., Cotton, S. M., Cosgrave, E. M., Killackey, E. J., Stanford, C., et al. (2006). Psychotic-like experiences in nonpsychotic help-seekers: Associations with distress, depression, and disability. *Schizophrenia Bulletin, 32*(2), 352–359.

Yung, A. R., & McGorry, P. D. (2007). Prediction of psychosis: Setting the stage. *British Journal of Psychiatry, 51*(Suppl.) s1–s8.

Yung, A. R., McGorry, P. D., McFarlane, C. A., Jackson, H. J., Patton, G. C., & Rakkar, A. (1996). Monitoring and care of young people at incipient risk of psychosis. *Schizophrenia Bulletin, 22*(2), 283–303.

Yung, A. R., Nelson, B., Baker, K., Buckby, J. A., Baksheev, G., & Cosgrave, E. M. (2009). Psychotic-like experiences in a community sample of adolescents: Implications for the continuum model of psychosis and prediction of schizophrenia. *Australian and New Zealand Journal of Psychiatry, 43*(2), 118–128.

Yung, A. R., Phillips, L. J., McGorry, P. D., McFarlane, C. A., Francey, S., Harrigan, S., et al. (1998). Prediction of psychosis: A step towards indicated prevention of schizophrenia. *British Journal of Psychiatry, 172*(Suppl. 33), 14–20.

Yung, A. R., Phillips, L. J., Yuen, H. P., Francey, S. M., McFarlane, C. A., Hallgren, M., et al. (2003). Psychosis prediction: 12-month follow up of a high-risk ("prodromal") group. *Schizophrenia Research, 60*(1), 21–32.

Yung, A. R., Phillips, L. J., Yuen, H. P., & McGorry, P. D. (2004). Risk factors for psychosis in an ultra high-risk group: Psychopathology and clinical features. *Schizophrenia Research, 67*(2–3), 131–142.

Yung, A. R., Stanford, C., Cosgrave, E., Killackey, E., Phillips, L., Nelson, B., et al. (2006). Testing the ultra high risk (prodromal) criteria for the prediction of psychosis in a clinical sample of young people. *Schizophrenia Research, 84*, 57–66.

Yung, A. R., Yuen, H. P., McGorry, P. D., Phillips, L. J., Kelly, D., Dell'Olio, M., et al. (2005). Mapping the onset of psychosis: The Comprehensive Assessment of At-Risk Mental States. *Australian and New Zealand Journal of Psychiatry, 39*(11–12), 964–971.

4   Genetic determinants of the vulnerability to psychosis: Findings from twin studies

Marco Picchioni and Timothea Toulopoulou

Introduction

One of the few areas of agreement between proponents of the biological and psychodynamic origins of schizophrenia is that many of its roots lie within the family (Rosenthal, 1960). Indeed Kraepelin's earliest observations of abnormalities in patients' unaffected relatives, suggested a familial component to this disorder. Familiality, however, can arise from common (or shared) environmental factors, as much as genetic causes. Studies of unaffected relatives can not separate these competing factors and twin studies offer the only experimental design that can separate and quantify the genetic and common environmental and, indeed, unique environmental influences that act on complex traits. To achieve this, studies must adopt specific statistical approaches that demand adequately sized samples, often a major failing in twin studies in schizophrenia.

Epidemiology

Twin studies can only be truly informative about schizophrenia if twins are not themselves at inherently greater risk of developing the disorder (Jackson, 1960; Lidz, Schafer, Fleck, Cornelison, & Terry, 1962). While the majority of studies have found no evidence of this for schizophrenia (Allen & Pollin, 1970; Hoffer & Pollin, 1970; Kringlen, 1967; Nathan & Guttman, 1984; Rosenthal, 1960; Sirugo, Ashenbrenner, Odunsi, Morakinyo, & Page, 2004; Tienari, 1963), two large national surveys (Klaning, 1999; Klaning, Mortensen, & Kyvik, 1996) did report an increased risk in dizygotic (DZ) twins alone. Theories for this link implicate shared genetic risk for both DZ twinning and schizophrenia, though competing hypotheses suggest other confounding factors, such as obstetric complications (Lewis, 1996) or increasing parental age, link the two (Crow, 1999; Malaspina et al., 2001).

Sullivan (Sullivan, Kendler, & Neale, 2003) in a recent meta-analysis of the 12 independent twin studies in schizophrenia, highlighted their methodological heterogeneity, but was still able to report a heritability estimate of over 80% for schizophrenia, proposing that the most important aetiological influences were additive genetic and, more contentiously, common environmental factors. By way of contrast, two national studies, one using the Finnish cohort, the other the Maudsley Twin Series, applied biometrical model fitting techniques (Cannon, Kaprio, Lönnqvist, Huttunen, & Koskenvuo, 1998; Cardno et al., 1999) and concluded that the most parsimonious and, indeed, more widely accepted, aetiological model incorporated additive genetic and unique environmental effects.

The heterogeneity in the early twin studies in part reflected their methodological inconsistencies. They recruited differently, from national population surveys, to studies of psychiatric in-patients and even US Army recruits, each population with their own biases and morbidity levels (Sadrzadeh, Treloar, van Baal, & Lambalk, 2001). The diagnostic criteria they applied also varied conspicuously, with a direct impact on reported concordance rates both for schizophrenia (Farmer, McGuffin, & Gottesman, 1987; Franzek & Beckmann, 1998; McGuffin, Farmer, Gottesman, Murray, & Reveley, 1984) and other disorders (Gatz, Pedersen, Crowe, & Fiske, 2000). Crucially, Cardno (Cardno, Rijsdijk, Sham, Murray, & McGuffin, 2002; Cardno, Sham, Murray, & McGuffin, 2001) was able to challenge the Kraepelinian psychotic dichotomy, in the national Maudsley Psychotic Twin Series of consecutive admissions to that hospital. They were able to report, for the first time, that schizophrenia, schizoaffective disorder and mania share genetic risk and suggested that as diagnostic criteria are broadened, concordance rates peak. In a subsequent factor analysis the same authors concluded that the disorganized dimension, analogous to schizophrenia's hebephrenic subtype, was the most genetically determined, with little evidence of a genetic contribution to the positive symptom dimension as a whole.

Thus, assuming multi-factorial inheritance, the best fitting aetiological models for schizophrenia propose additive genetic and non-shared environmental affects (Gervil, Ulrich, Kaprio, & Russell, 2001).

Environmental mechanisms

Dermatoglyphics

Dermatoglyphic abnormalities hypothetically offer a time-sensitive marker of ectodermal development. Studies in twins with schizophrenia have tended to be small and, by implication, underpowered. Bracha (Bracha, Torrey, Bigelow, Lohr, & Linington, 1991) found evidence of abnormal development early in the second trimester of pregnancy in probands with schizophrenia and concluded that this was evidence of the action of an aetiologically important environmental agent during that developmental stage. All but one of several other studies (Bracha, Torrey, Gottesman, Bigelow, & Cunniff, 1992; Davis & Bracha, 1996; Kelly et al., 2004; van Oel et al., 2001; van Os, Fananas, Cannon, Macdonald, & Murray, 1997) reported reduced a–b ridge count correlations within discordant compared to control pairs, though only two (Davis & Bracha, 1996; Kelly et al., 2004) actually detected greater numbers of abnormalities in the probands themselves, thus providing only limited evidence to support their specificity for schizophrenia.

The two studies that assessed finger ridge fluctuating asymmetry (FA) in psychotic twins reached strikingly different conclusions. The failure of many of these studies to detect significant differences between the probands and their well co-twins appears to directly undermine their usefulness as an index of aetiologically relevant unique environmental insult.

Two studies assessed ridge dissociation in twins (Rosa, Fananas, Bracha, Torrey, & van Os, 2000; van Os et al., 1997), both detected more abnormalities in the patients. However one (van Os et al., 1997) detected greater rates in concordant compared to discordant pairs, while the other (Rosa et al., 2000), detected more abnormalities in probands compared to their well co-twins in discordant pairs.

The evidence from twin studies of abnormal ectodermal development in psychosis is mixed. There is some dermatoglyphic evidence to suggest the presence of early developmental divergence in monozygotic (MZ) pairs who later become discordant for schizophrenia and this divergence may be present from as early as the first 15 weeks of life in utero. However the presence of these markers, albeit at attenuated levels in the well co-twins as well, necessarily undermines their validity as markers of the unique environmental insult responsible for schizophrenia. Thus it seems more likely that these markers may reflect abnormal ectodermal development in utero, but that they give little indication of the underlying aetiology.

Obstetric complications

By way of contrast obstetric complications (OCs), in particular perinatal hypoxia, are themselves hypothetical environmental risk factors for schizophrenia. Notwithstanding that they are almost always retrospectively assessed, are frequently shared within twin pairs and that twins, as with all multiple pregnancies are inherently at greater risk of OCs, including prematurity and low birth weight, several attempts have been made to explore their association with schizophrenia in twins.

Early evidence suggested that OCs are overrepresented in discordant twins. Two small highly selected cohorts (Fuller Torry & Bowler, 1994; Lewis, Chitkara, Reveley, & Murray, 1987) detected greater birth weight discordance in discordant pairs, with the lighter twin more likely to develop schizophrenia. Some (McNeil, Cantor-Graae, & Sjöström, 1994) have reported a reducing gradient of peri- and neonatal complications in MZ discordant through MZ concordant to MZ control pairs. However, others (Fischer, 1973; Kringlen, 1967; Onstad, Skre, Torgersen, & Kringlen, 1992) could not replicate these findings, nor detect any evidence of an increased risk of OCs in MZ discordant and concordant pairs. Gilmore (Gilmore et al., 1996) used ultrasound to detect greater mean parietal diameter differences in MZ than DZ pairs and suggested that environmental factors, acting through the placenta had caused divergent brain development, in at least a portion of the MZ twins. The same NIMH sample (Cantor-Graae et al., 1994) demonstrated an association between early pregnancy complications and minor physical anomalies in the MZ discordant group, though these were detected both in the probands and the well co-twins. The study also used unvalidated markers of chorionic status to suggest that the environmental agent may have been an infectious agent (Davis & Phelps, 1995; Davis, Phelps, & Bracha, 1995). A related study (McNeil, Cantor-Graae, & Weinberger, 2000) explored the link between obstetric complications and brain structure, reporting reduced hippocampal volume and increased lateral ventricular volume with more OCs. However, this finding was in the discordant group as a whole, not just the patients. It also reported that the length of labour predicted hippocampal volume and raised the suggestion that a complicated delivery, through hypoxia might induce brain changes in regions implicated in the pathophysiology of schizophrenia.

Neuropsychological findings

Twin neuropsychological studies in schizophrenia have evolved from the simple deficits detection, to the identification and quantification of shared genetic risk driving such cognitive deficiencies.

Goldberg et al. (1990, 1993, 1995) originally reported in the NIMH twin sample, that the probands from MZ discordant pairs underperformed compared to their genetically identical but unaffected co-twins on tests of vigilance, concept formation, learning and memory. The authors could report only limited evidence for genetic effects however (Goldberg et al., 1995), as the unaffected co-twins showed relatively minor deficits of memory and executive function, implicating unique environmental factors in determining the patients' deficits. Subsequently and by way of contrast, Reichenberg et al. (2000) examined premorbid function in a national twin cohort and detected evidence to suggest familial deficits in some aspects of cognition in schizophrenia. The twins who would later develop schizophrenia scored worse than controls, with no significant differences in premorbid cognitive or behavioural scores between the members of the future discordant pairs.

Two studies contrasted MZ and DZ discordant pairs (Docherty & Gottesman, 2000; Pardo et al., 2000) and focused on specific cognitive tasks. They reported a genetic contribution to perseverative errors (Pardo et al., 2000) and intrusive missing information references (Docherty & Gottesman, 2000), on the basis of greater deficits in the unaffected co-twins from MZ than DZ pairs.

Cannon (Cannon et al., 2000) in a large representative national population cohort used a comprehensive structured cognitive battery to examine the heritability of the neurocognitive deficits in schizophrenia. They concluded that several cognitive domains, including spatial working memory, divided attention, intrusions during recall and choice reaction time were linked to the genetic load for schizophrenia, while spatial working memory and recall intrusions were genetically determined. In contrast, verbal and visual episodic memory were more impaired in the ill than the well MZ co-twins, suggesting unique environmental effects. The same group (Johnson et al., 2003) reported that cognitive function was linked specifically to schizotypal symptoms in those at genetic risk and that in the absence of schizotypal traits, there were no or minimal cognitive deficits.

The authors suggested that future genetic studies should model this bivariate phenotype of cognitive deficits and schizotypy to improve power. Furthermore as spatial working memory seemed to be uniquely associated with genetic load for schizophrenia but not schizotypy, it could be used as a separate linkage marker. Most recently Toulopoulou et al. (2007), using a large carefully phenotyped psychotic twin series and full genetic modelling techniques, highlighted the significant correlation between intelligence, as well as working memory and schizophrenia and most importantly that shared genetic variance accounted for a large proportion of the covariance between the two.

Thus twin studies of cognition in schizophrenia have suggested that specific cognitive markers may be able to act as sensitive markers of the genetic risk for schizophrenia, with particular emphasis on intelligence, working memory and divided attention, intrusions during recall of a word list and choice reaction time to visual targets, as the most likely targets to warrant further investigation.

Neuroimaging brain structure: CT, MRI

Whole brain volume

Structural imaging studies of twins with schizophrenia have in the main to date been hampered by their relatively small sample sizes and limited statistical power. Only one has so far been sufficiently powered to implement full genetic modelling and so to tease apart genetic and common environmental influences on the structures under investigation.

Two qualitative studies (Noga, Bartley, Jones, Torrey, & Weinberger, 1996; Suddath, Christison, Torrey, Casanova, & Weinberger, 1990), used overlapping MZ discordant cohorts, but failed to agree on the presence of significant differences between patients and their well co-twins. Two later studies, used the same sample (Narr, Cannon et al., 2002; Narr, van Erp et al., 2002) and reported no differences in intracranial, grey or white matter volume between patients and either their healthy co-twins or controls.

In contrast, later, larger studies, including up to 15 discordant pairs, have shown reduced whole brain volume (WBV) in discordant pairs compared to controls (Baaré et al., 2001; Hulshoff Pol et al., 2004) and that within these pairs, patients had lower WBV than their well co-twins (Noga et al., 1996; van Haren et al., 2004). These results suggested genetically or common environmentally driven deficits in WBV with additional unique environmental effects driving the further volume loss in the patients. This finding was substantiated by Rijsdijk et al. (2005), who reported on a large combined Maudsley Family and Twin sample. The authors reported that WBV in schizophrenia was heritable, but perhaps more importantly that there was evidence of a significant genetic correlation with schizophrenia, and thus that some of the genes that cause or are linked to schizophrenia also reduce WBV. When grey and white matter volumes are segmented (Hulshoff Pol et al., 2004), white matter reductions were detected in the discordant group, suggesting common genetic or familial effects, with the grey matter deficits appearing to be more specific to the probands, implying unique environmental effects on this tissue class. Intra-class correlation coefficients (ICCs) for whole brain, grey and white matter volumes (Baaré et al., 2001; Hulshoff Pol et al., 2004; Narr, van Erp et al., 2002; van Haren et al., 2004) have been consistently greater in MZ compared to DZ twins, irrespective of their concordance for schizophrenia, consistent with the data from healthy control twins, that prominent genetic or common environmental effects act on all these volumes.

The most sophisticated image analysis methods applied so far to cortical grey matter in discordant twins (Cannon et al., 2002) used a novel mapping algorithm to produce estimates of the location and magnitude of illness/unshared environmental and genetically driven deficits over the entire cortical surface in schizophrenia. Non-genetic effects were found particularly in the dorso-lateral prefrontal cortex, superior and middle temporal gyrus, parietal association and motor cortex. By contrast, genetic effects were particularly localized to a region in the frontal cortex.

Brans et al. (2008) utilized a twin modelling approach in a unique longitudinal study that rescanned many of the original Utrecht cohort (Baaré et al., 2001), approximately five years after their original scan. This careful methodological approach has resulted in the only magnetic resonance imaging (MRI) follow-up study in twins in schizophrenia and yielded results that suggest that accelerated loss of brain volume was a feature of both schizophrenia and its genetic risk and that the genetic correlation, for example with loss of whole brain volume, was over 60%.

Taken as a whole, the majority of these results strongly suggest that genetic mechanisms central to the risk for schizophrenia have an impact on total cerebral volume and grey and possibly white matter volumes specifically and perhaps more contentiously that these genes may contribute to accelerated loss of tissue volume over the lifespan.

Regions of interest

Region of interest studies can help to address the anatomical specificity of the tissue loss described in the previous section. Increased lateral ventricular volume is perhaps the most robust imaging finding in schizophrenia. In MZ discordant twin pairs, lateral ventricular volume is greater in patients than their healthy co-twins, controls (Ohara et al., 1998; Reveley, Reveley, Clifford, & Murray, 1982; Reveley, Reveley, & Murray, 1984), and even than in patients from concordant pairs (van Haren et al., 2004), suggesting a greater sensitivity to environmental insult in the patients from pairs. However, Styner et al. (2005) have shown that despite the presence of the illness, lateral ventricular volume and shape can remain highly conserved, even within MZ discordant pairs, confirming that strong genetic or common environmental influences continue to act on this structure.

Only two studies have assessed brain volumes in relation to environmental agents in twins with schizophrenia. The first (Reveley et al., 1984) found a relationship between obstetric complications and increased lateral ventricular volume, but only in healthy controls, and that a positive family history for schizophrenia was associated with smaller lateral ventricular volumes in patients. The second (McNeil et al., 2000) reported that perinatal complications were associated with smaller hippocampi and larger lateral ventricular volumes in patients. These results suggest that obstetric complications and in particular perinatal hypoxia, may represent an environmental insult that in genetically vulnerable individuals, leads to enlarged ventricles and smaller hippocampi, while genetic risk alone leads to more subtle structural changes.

Medial temporal lobe structural differences have been detected in both members of discordant pairs compared to controls (Baaré et al., 2001; Narr, van Erp et al., 2002), but with no additional deficits in the patients, while others (McNeil et al., 2000; Suddath et al., 1990; van Erp et al., 2004) have found further illness-specific volume loss in the patients from MZ discordant pairs and that these deficits were correlated with cognitive performance, including verbal working memory (Goldberg, Torrey, Berman, & Weinberger, 1994). The only study to reliably assess hippocampal subregions reported that volume loss may be greatest posteriorly. Only one twin study applied genetic model-fitting techniques to pairs with schizophrenia (van Erp et al., 2004) and produced heritability estimates for hippocampal volume of 71% in controls and 42% in discordant twins.

Two studies (Casanova et al., 1990; Narr, Cannon et al., 2002) assessed the corpus callosum in MZ discordant twin pairs. Both agreed that there was no evidence of abnormalities in length or area but found that there was an upwards displacement of the structure in probands, while the latter study also found this effect in the well co-twins when compared to healthy controls, suggesting a common genetic or environmental effect in schizophrenia, possibly acting primarily through changes in lateral ventricular volume or shape.

Two studies have assessed thalamic volumes in twins. The first and smaller study (Bridle et al., 2002) assessed thalamic and caudate volume and reported no significant differences between controls and MZ discordant or concordant pairs for thalamic volume, while probands had larger caudates than their co-twins, but not controls. By way of contrast the second and larger study Ettinger et al. (2007) detected reduced thalamic volume in MZ concordant pairs compared to controls, with a gradient of volume reduction from MZ concordant, through MD discordant ill and discordant well twins to the MZ healthy controls. Perhaps contentiously the finding was interpreted as evidence of a sliding scale of genetic load across these pairs.

Finally, a selective case report (Lewis, Harvey, Ron, Murray, & Reveley, 1990) reported greater structural abnormalities in the unaffected co-twin from an MZ discordant pair and made the point that selective brain structural changes may actually either have little to do with the pathophysiology of the illness or perhaps even be protective.

Voxel-based morphometry

Only two studies have so far examined the brains of twins with schizophrenia using a whole brain voxel-based approach. Both the Utrecht and Maudsley studies examined samples that overlapped with their respective WBV studies described above (Baaré et al., 2001; van Haren et al., 2004). Neither were sufficiently powered to implement full genetic modelling, but were only able to use regression approaches to detect significant group differences that were then ascribed to genetic and environmental sources.

The first (Hulshoff Pol et al., 2006) included moderately large MZ and DZ discordant samples. However, despite the earlier evidence of unique environment effects leading to grey matter volume deficits in the patients, it was only able to detect a significant difference between the discordant twins and controls, irrespective of zygosity and illness status. The region implicated was the left orbitofrontal gyrus, corresponding to a reduction in tissue density in the discordant twins. The second (Borgwardt et al., 2010) did not include any DZ twins but did include MZ concordant pairs. The authors detected no differences between twins with schizophrenia from concordant and discordant pairs. Similarly, they found no evidence of focal grey matter deficits between the MZ discordant well and the healthy control twins. However, unique environmental differences were detected in particular in the insula and the superior temporal gyrus, as well as the cingulate gyrus in the twins with schizophrenia.

Functional imaging

Despite a wealth of functional imaging studies to date few have focused on twins with schizophrenia, reflecting significant recruitment difficulties. One functional MRI study examined lateralization for word tasks in MZ discordant and control twins (Sommer, Ramsey, Mandl, van Oel, & Kahn, 2004). It reported an increase in activity in right-sided language structures, in both members of discordant pairs in comparison to healthy controls and interpreted this as evidence of genetically determined abnormal language lateralization in schizophrenia. In contrast, a case report of a single MZ discordant pair (Spaniel et al., 2003) highlighted the non-genetic nature of a very similar deficit detected only in the patient, with no lateralization impairment in the well co-twin, the authors linked the patient's deficit to abnormal hippocampal function detected at spectroscopy. The same group (Spaniel et al., 2005) reported further illness-specific deficits in the structural integrity of the globus pallidus detected using MR relaxometry.

A larger study (Berman, Torrey, Daniel, & Weinberger, 1992) used radio-labelled xenon to measure regional cerebral blood flow and reported localized frontal- but no temporal-lobe deficits in the patients of MZ discordant pairs compared both to their well co-twins and healthy controls, findings that were only apparent during a frontal-lobe functional challenge. In particular there was no evidence of functional deficits in the well co-twins. These data thus suggested that the frontal-lobe deficits were illness specific and reflected the impact of unique environmental factors. In a secondary analysis the same authors (Weinberger, Berman, Suddath, & Torrey, 1992) demonstrated that within-pair differences in hippocampal volume, measured using structural MRI predicted these frontal-lobe blood-flow deficits and interpreted this finding as evidence of illness-specific abnormalities in a distributed cortical–subcortical network. In contrast, a later study (Hirvonen et al., 2005), examined only the well co-twins from MZ and DZ discordant pairs and detected increases in genetically determined caudate D2 receptor density that reflected each individual's genetic risk for the disorder as defined by their genetic proximity to their proband. A single proton magnetic resonance spectroscopy study has been conducted in a modest mixed-zygosity subsample of the Finnish twin cohort (Lutkenhoff et al., 2010). The authors were still able to detect evidence of genetically determined mesial prefrontal cortical glutamate reductions, with additional disease-specific elevations in hippocampal N-acetylaspartate, creatine and glycerophosphocholine. This preliminary data supports a genetically determined model of glutamate dysfunction in schizophrenia.

Other biological markers

Electrophysiology

To date, five studies have examined electrophysiological function in MZ twins with schizophrenia (Hall et al., 2007; Stassen et al., 1999; Weisbrod, Hill, Niethammer, & Sauer, 1999; Weisbrod et al., 2004), all with modest sample sizes.

Weisbrod et al. (1999) reported reduced P300 amplitude in both patients and their well co-twins in MZ discordant pairs and concluded that this reflected the genetically determined vulnerability to schizophrenia. Two other studies, one by the same group (Stassen et al., 1999; Weisbrod et al., 2004), contrasted EEG coherence in concordant and discordant MZ twin pairs and healthy control twins, however their reported findings and conclusions contrasted with the earlier report. They noted that pairs with at least one ill member had much lower within-pair EEG concordance, leading to the conclusion that this represented a change in cortical activity driven by illness and thus by unique environmental effects. Furthermore, both studies, after discriminant analysis, identified a single parameter that could reliably distinguish the ill twins from their unaffected co-twins, suggesting its use as a disease marker. Specifically these studies suggest, given the electrophysiological sensitivity to illness, that these measures were unsuitable as endophenotype markers.

Two other studies have used cognitive challenges to manipulate the EEG signal in twins. In the first, Bachman et al. (2008) demonstrated, in a small subsample of the Finnish twin cohort, that impaired spatial working memory and its electrophysiological correlate, event-related synchronization (ERS), acted as markers for the genetic risk for schizophrenia. A second study in the same sample (Ahveninen et al., 2006) and a study in the London twins (Hall et al., 2007) progressively improved the statistical techniques employed. These culminated in the quantification of phenotypic and genetic correlation of selected electrophysiological markers and schizophrenia, identifying P50 suppression as the best candidate endophenotype marker for schizophrenia.

Thus, while much of the earlier work is mixed, the emerging evidence from the newest electrophysiological studies, which have included the largest, but still modest, numbers of subjects, is that selected electrophysiological measures offer scope as candidate endophenotype markers, though this needs further replication.

Eye movements

Two landmark Scandinavian studies examined eye-tracking abnormalities between MZ and DZ discordant pairs, though did not compare within-twin pairs, nor include any control twins. The studies were consistent, detecting smooth pursuit abnormalities in the well co-twins and that the MZ pairs were more similar than DZ pairs, whether assessed qualitatively (Holzman, Kringlen, Levy, Proctor, & Haberman, 1978) or quantitatively (Holzman et al., 1977). The authors concluded that eye-tracking deficits could serve as genetic markers for schizophrenia and that these deficits were more penetrant than schizophrenia's clinical phenotype. Two studies (Litman et al., 1997; Torrey & Gottesman, 1994) contentiously failed to reproduce these results (Holzman, Levy, Matthysse, & Abel, 1997). The Holzman et al. study in particular used more advanced recording techniques, but adopted a different statistical model, which could have contributed to this inconsistency. Both, however, found that the well co-twins were not significantly impaired compared to controls and rejected a genetic model for smooth pursuit abnormalities in schizophrenia. By way of contrast, in the Maudsley cohort (Ettinger et al., 2006), contrasting relatively modest MZ discordant and control twin samples produced evidence of genetically determined deficits in antisaccade gain and latency that were consistent with similar deficits in a familial risk cohort.

Neurological soft signs

Neurological soft signs (NSS) are well recognized in patients with schizophrenia and their unaffected relatives. Mosher (Mosher, Pollin, & Stabenau, 1971), studying MZ discordant pairs, detected a qualitative increase in NSS in probands but no increase in their co-twins, while Kelly (Kelly et al., 2004) could not detect any difference between probands and their well co-twins. The remaining studies (Picchioni et al., 2006; Rosenthal & Kety, 1968; Torrey & Gottesman, 1994), reported that the well co-twins from MZ discordant pairs occupy a position midway between probands and healthy controls. One (Picchioni et al., 2006) reported no difference between patients from MZ concordant and discordant pairs and a genetically determined dose–response effect driving NSS in schizophrenia, with additional unique environmental effects. The only environmental factor explored in twins with schizophrenia in relation to NSS were obstetric complications (OCs; Cantor-Graae et al., 1994; Mosher et al., 1971). Results suggested that OCs, particularly those in the perinatal period, increased the risk of NSS in the patients.

Three studies (Boklage, 1977; Lewis, Chitkara, & Reveley, 1989; Luchins, Pollin, & Wyatt, 1980) have explored laterality and handedness (Crow, 1999) in twins with schizophrenia from a clinical perspective. The evidence is mixed but suggests that in twin pairs with at least one left-handed member, the proband is more likely to be left handed, though because of limited power these studies could not further explore the aetiology of this as an indicator of aberrant neurodevelopment.

Discussion

Twin studies have over many years significantly influenced thought about the aetiology and pathophysiology of schizophrenia. From the early concordance studies to today's advanced genetic modelling this remains the case. Over the last decade the methodology underpinning twin research in schizophrenia has advanced considerably and sample sizes have slowly increased.

The early, generally small and highly selected, twin studies established the presence of deficits in the patients and their co-twins suggesting the familiarity of this disorder. Qualitatively similar but quantitatively less marked deficits for many traits in the MZ and DZ unaffected co-twins supported a familial and furthermore a genetic effect, though these studies often did not have the statistical power or technology to discriminate between and quantify the genetic and shared-environmental effects. It is only more recently with the larger national and, indeed, international twins studies, that have successfully recruited sufficiently large samples from across the effected spectrum and that are able to deploy the latest genetic-modelling techniques, that we have started to be able to quantify the genetic links between deficits and schizophrenia. At present there are two linked international collaborations underway, the Schizophrenia Twin and Family (STaR) consortium involving Utrecht, Jena, Helsinki and London and the EUTwins Network, sponsored by the European Union through a Marie Curie Training Network grant that extends to nine European centres. It is only through such international collaborations that we will truly be able to evaluate the usefulness of any of these markers as intermediate endophenotype markers of the genetic risk of schizophrenia. It is only by applying the most advanced statistical modelling techniques to these truly unique datasets that the full power of the twin model can be realized.

References

Ahveninen, J., Jaaskelainen, I. P., Osipova, D., Huttunen, M. O., Ilmoniemi, R. J., Kaprio, J., et al. (2006). Inherited auditory-cortical dysfunction in twin pairs discordant for schizophrenia. *Biological Psychiatry*, *60*(6), 612–620.

Allen, M. G., & Pollin, W. (1970). Schizophrenia in twins and diffuse ego boundary hypothesis. *American Journal of Psychiatry*, *127*(4), 437–442.

Baaré, W. F. C., van Oel, C. J., Hulshoff Pol, H. E., Schnack, H. G., Durston, S., Sitskoorn, M. M., et al. (2001). Volumes of brain structures in twins discordant for schizophrenia. *Archives of General Psychiatry*, *58*(1), 33–40.

Bachman, P., Kim, J., Yee, C. M., Therman, S., Manninen, M., Lönnqvist, J., et al. (2008). Abnormally high EEG alpha synchrony during working memory maintenance in twins discordant for schizophrenia. *Schizophrenia Research, 103*(1–3), 293–297.

Berman, K. F., Torrey, E. F., Daniel, D. G., & Weinberger, D. R. (1992). Regional cerebral blood-flow in monozygotic twins discordant and concordant for schizophrenia. *Archives of General Psychiatry, 49*(12), 927–934.

Boklage, C. E. (1977). Schizophrenia, brain asymmetry development and twinning—Cellular relationship with etiological and possibly prognostic implications. *Biological Psychiatry, 12*(1), 19–35.

Borgwardt, S. J., Picchioni, M. M., Ettinger, U., Toulopoulou, T., Murray, R., & McGuire, P. K. (2010). Regional gray matter volume in monozygotic twins concordant and discordant for schizophrenia. *Biological Psychiatry, 67*(10), 956–964.

Bracha, H. S., Torrey, E. F., Bigelow, L. B., Lohr, J. B., & Linington, B. B. (1991). Subtle signs of prenatal maldevelopment of the hand ectoderm in schizophrenia—A preliminary monozygotic twin study. *Biological Psychiatry, 30*(7), 719–725.

Bracha, H. S., Torrey, E. F., Gottesman, I. I., Bigelow, L. B., & Cunniff, C. (1992). 2nd trimester markers of fetal size in schizophrenia—A study of monozygotic twins. *American Journal of Psychiatry, 149*(10), 1355–1361.

Brans, R., van Haren, N., van Baal, G. C., Schnack, H. G., Kahn, R. S., & Hulshoff Pol, H. E. (2008). Heritability of changes in brain volume over time in twin pairs discordant for schizophrenia. *Archives of General Psychiatry, 65*(11), 1259–1268.

Bridle, N., Pantelis, C., Wood, S. J., Coppola, R., Velakoulis, D., McStephen, M., et al. (2002). Thalamic and caudate volumes in monozygotic twins discordant for schizophrenia. *Australian and New Zealand Journal of Psychiatry, 36*(3), 347–354.

Cannon, T. D., Huttunen, M. O., Lonnqvist, J., Tuulio-Henriksson, A., Pirkola, T., Glahn, D., et al. (2000). The inheritance of neuropsychological dysfunction in twins discordant for schizophrenia. *American Journal of Human Genetics, 67*(2), 369–382.

Cannon, T. D., Kaprio, J., Lönnqvist, J., Huttunen, M., & Koskenvuo, M. (1998). The genetic epidemiology of schizophrenia in a Finnish twin cohort—A population-based modeling study. *Archives of General Psychiatry, 55*(1), 67–74.

Cannon, T. D., Thompson, P. M., van Erp, T. G., Toga, A. W., Poutanen, V. P., Huttunen, M., et al. (2002). Cortex mapping reveals regionally specific patterns of genetic and disease-specific gray-matter deficits in twins discordant for schizophrenia. *Proceedings of the National Academy of Sciences of the United States of America, 99*(5), 3228–3233.

Cantor-Graae, E., McNeil, T. F., Torrey, E. F., Quinn, P., Bowler, A., Sjöström, K., et al. (1994). Link between pregnancy complications and minor physical anomalies in monozygotic twins discordant for schizophrenia. *American Journal of Psychiatry, 151*(8), 1188–1193.

Cardno, A. G., Marshall, E. J., Coid, B., Macdonald, A. M., Ribchester, T. R., Davies, N. J., et al. (1999). Heritability estimates for psychotic disorders—The Maudsley Twin Psychosis Series. *Archives of General Psychiatry, 56*(2), 162–168.

Cardno, A. G., Rijsdijk, F. V., Sham, P. C., Murray, R. M., & McGuffin, P. (2002). A twin study of genetic relationships between psychotic symptoms. *American Journal of Psychiatry, 159*(4), 539–545.

Cardno, A. G., Sham, P. C., Murray, R. M., & McGuffin, P. (2001). Twin study of symptom dimensions in psychoses. *British Journal of Psychiatry, 179*, 39–45.

Casanova, M. F., Sanders, R. D., Goldberg, T. E., Bigelow, L. B., Christison, G., Torrey, E. F., et al. (1990). Morphometry of the corpus callosum in monozygotic twins discordant for schizophrenia—A magnetic-resonance-imaging study. *Journal of Neurology Neurosurgery and Psychiatry, 53*(5), 416–421.

Crow, T. J. (1999). Twin studies of psychosis and the genetics of cerebral asymmetry. *British Journal of Psychiatry, 175,* 399–401.

Davis, J. O., & Bracha, H. S. (1996). Prenatal growth markers in schizophrenia: A monozygotic co-twin control study. *American Journal of Psychiatry, 153*(9), 1166–1172.

Davis, J. O., & Phelps, J. A. (1995). Twins with schizophrenia—Genes or germs. *Schizophrenia Bulletin, 21*(1), 13–18.

Davis, J. O., Phelps, J. A., & Bracha, H. S. (1995). Prenatal development of monozygotic twins and concordance for schizophrenia. *Schizophrenia Bulletin, 21*(3), 357–366.

Docherty, N. M., & Gottesman, I. I. (2000). A twin study of communication disturbances in schizophrenia. *Journal of Nervous and Mental Disease, 188*(7), 395–401.

Ettinger, U., Picchioni, M., Hall, M. H., Schulze, K., Toulopoulou, T., Landau, S., et al. (2006). Antisaccade performance in monozygotic twins discordant for schizophrenia: The Maudsley twin study. *American Journal of Psychiatry, 163*(3), 543–545.

Ettinger, U., Picchioni, M., Landau, S., Matsumoto, K., van Haren, N. E., Marshall, N., et al. (2007). Magnetic resonance imaging of the thalamus and adhesio interthalamica in twins with schizophrenia. *Archives of General Psychiatry, 64*(4), 401–409.

Farmer, A. E., McGuffin, P., & Gottesman, I. I. (1987). Twin concordance for DSM-III schizophrenia—Scrutinizing the validity of the definition. *Archives of General Psychiatry, 44*(7), 634–641.

Fischer, M. (1973). Genetic and environmental factors in schizophrenia. A study of schizophrenic twins and their families. *Acta Psychiatrica Scandinavica, 238*(Suppl.), 9–142.

Franzek, E., & Beckmann, H. (1998). Different genetic background of schizophrenia spectrum psychoses: A twin study. *American Journal of Psychiatry, 155*(1), 76–83.

Fuller Torry, E., & Bowler, A. E. (1994). *Schizophrenia and manic-depressive disorder: The biological roots of mental illness as revealed by the landmark study of identical twins.* New York, NY: Basic Books.

Gatz, M., Pedersen, N. L., Crowe, M., & Fiske, A. (2000). Defining discordance in twin studies of risk and protective factors for late life disorders. *Twin Research, 3*(3), 159–164.

Gervil, M., Ulrich, V., Kaprio, J., & Russell, M. B. (2001). Is the genetic liability in multifactorial disorders higher in concordant than discordant monozygotic twin pairs? A population-based family twin study of migraine without aura. *European Journal of Neurology, 8*(3), 231–235.

Gilmore, J. H., Perkins, D. O., Kliewer, M. A., Hage, M. L., Silva, S. G., Chescheir, N. C., et al. (1996). Fetal brain development of twins assessed in utero by ultrasound: Implications for schizophrenia. *Schizophrenia Research, 19*(2–3), 141–149.

Goldberg, T. E., Ragland, J. D., Torrey, E. F., Gold, J. M., Bigelow, L. B., & Weinberger, D. R. (1990). Neuropsychological assessment of monozygotic twins discordant for schizophrenia. *Archives of General Psychiatry, 47*(11), 1066–1072.

Goldberg, T. E., Torrey, E. F., Berman, K. F., & Weinberger, D. R. (1994). Relations between neuropsychological performance and brain morphological and physiological measures in monozygotic twins discordant for schizophrenia. *Psychiatry Research – Neuroimaging, 55*(1), 51–61.

Goldberg, T. E., Torrey, E. F., Gold, J. M., Bigelow, L. B., Ragland, R. D., Taylor, E., et al. (1995). Genetic risk of neuropsychological impairment in schizophrenia—A study of monozygotic twins discordant and concordant for the disorder. *Schizophrenia Research*, *17*(1), 77–84.

Goldberg, T. E., Torrey, E. F., Gold, J. M., Ragland, J. D., Bigelow, L. B., & Weinberger, D. R. (1993). Learning and memory in monozygotic twins discordant for schizophrenia. *Psychological Medicine*, *23*(1), 71–85.

Hall, M. H., Rijsdijk, F., Picchioni, M., Schulze, K., Ettinger, U., Toulopoulou, T., et al. (2007). Substantial shared genetic influences on schizophrenia and event-related potentials. *American Journal of Psychiatry*, *164*(5), 804–812.

Hirvonen, J., van Erp, T. G. M., Huttunen, J., Aalto, S., Någren, K., Huttunen, M., et al. (2005). Increased caudate dopamine D-2 receptor availability as a genetic marker for schizophrenia. *Archives of General Psychiatry*, *62*(4), 371–378.

Hoffer, A., & Pollin, W. (1970). Schizophrenia in nas-nrc panel of 15,909 veteran twin pairs. *Archives of General Psychiatry*, *23*(5), 469–477.

Holzman, P. S., Kringlen, E., Levy, D. L., Proctor, L. R., & Haberman, S. (1978). Smooth pursuit eye-movements in twins discordant for schizophrenia. *Journal of Psychiatric Research*, *14*(1–4), 111–120.

Holzman, P. S., Kringlen, E., Levy, D. L., Proctor, L. R., Haberman, S. J., & Yasillo, N. J. (1977). Abnormal-pursuit eye-movements in schizophrenia. *Archives of General Psychiatry*, *34*(7), 802–805.

Holzman, P. S., Levy, D. L., Matthysse, S. W., & Abel, L. A. (1997). Smooth pursuit eye tracking in twins—A critical commentary. *Archives of General Psychiatry*, *54*(5), 429–431.

Hulshoff Pol, H. E., Brans, R. G. H., van Haren, N. E., Schnack, H. G., Langen, M., Baaré, W. F., et al. (2004). Gray and white matter volume abnormalities in monozygotic and same-gender dizygotic twins discordant for schizophrenia. *Biological Psychiatry*, *55*(2), 126–130.

Hulshoff Pol, H. E., Schnack, H. G., Mandl, R. C., Brans, R. G., van Haren, N. E., Baaré, W. F., et al. (2006). Gray and white matter density changes in monozygotic and same-sex dizygotic twins discordant for schizophrenia using voxel-based morphometry. *NeuroImage*, *31*(2), 482–488.

Jackson, D. D. (Ed.). (1960). *The etiology of schizophrenia*. New York, NY: Basic Books.

Johnson, J. K., Tuulio-Henriksson, A., Pirkola, T., Huttunen, M. O., Lönnqvist, J., Kaprio, J., et al. (2003). Do schizotypal symptoms mediate the relationship between genetic risk for schizophrenia and impaired neuropsychological performance in co-twins of schizophrenic patients? *Biological Psychiatry*, *54*(11), 1200–1204.

Kelly, B. D., Cotter, D., Denihan, C., Larkin, D., Murphy, P., Kinsella, A., et al. (2004). Neurological soft signs and dermatoglyphic anomalies in twins with schizophrenia. *European Psychiatry*, *19*(3), 159–163.

Klaning, U. (1999). Greater occurrence of schizophrenia in dizygotic but not monozygotic twins—Register-based study. *British Journal of Psychiatry*, *175*, 407–409.

Klaning, U., Mortensen, P. B., & Kyvik, K. O. (1996). Increased occurrence of schizophrenia and other psychiatric illnesses among twins. *British Journal of Psychiatry*, *168*(6), 688–692.

Kringlen, E. (1967). *Heredity and environment in the functional psychoses*. Oslo, Norway: Universitetsforlaget.

Lewis, S. (1996). Schizophrenia in twins. *British Journal of Psychiatry*, *169*(4), 522–523.

Lewis, S. W., Chitkara, B., & Reveley, A. M. (1989). Hand preference in psychotic twins. *Biological Psychiatry*, *25*(2), 215–221.

Lewis, S. W., Chitkara, B., Reveley, A. M., & Murray, R. M. (1987). Family history and birth-weight in monozygotic twins concordant and discordant for psychosis. *Acta Geneticae Medicae et Gemellologiae, 36*(2), 267–273.

Lewis, S. W., Harvey, I., Ron, M., Murray, R., & Reveley, A. (1990). Can brain-damage protect against schizophrenia—A case-report of twins. *British Journal of Psychiatry, 157*, 600–603.

Lidz, T., Schafer, S., Fleck, S., Cornelison, A., & Terry, D. (1962). Ego differentiation and schizophrenic symptom formation in identical twins. *Journal of the American Psychoanalytic Association, 10*(1), 74–90.

Litman, R. E., Torrey, E. F., Hommer, D. W., Radant, A. R., Pickar, D., & Weinberger, D. R. (1997). A quantitative analysis of smooth pursuit eye tracking in monozygotic twins discordant for schizophrenia. *Archives of General Psychiatry, 54*(5), 417–426.

Luchins, D., Pollin, W., & Wyatt, R. J. (1980). Laterality in monozygotic schizophrenic twins—Alternative hypothesis. *Biological Psychiatry, 15*(1), 87–93.

Lutkenhoff, E. S., van Erp, T. G., Thomas, M. A., Therman, S., Manninen, M., Huttunen, M. O., et al. (2010). Proton MRS in twin pairs discordant for schizophrenia. *Molecular Psychiatry, 15*(3), 308–318.

Malaspina, D., Harlap, S., Fennig, S., Heiman, D., Nahon, D., Feldman, D., et al. (2001). Advancing paternal age and the risk of schizophrenia. *Archives of General Psychiatry, 58*(4), 361–367.

McGuffin, P., Farmer, A. E., Gottesman I. I., Murray, R. M., & Reveley, A. M. (1984). Twin concordance for operationally defined schizophrenia—Confirmation of familiality and heritability. *Archives of General Psychiatry, 41*(6), 541–545.

McNeil, T. F., Cantor-Graae, E., & Sjöström, K. (1994). Obstetric complications as antecedents of schizophrenia—Empirical effects of using different obstetric complication scales. *Journal of Psychiatric Research, 28*(6), 519–530.

McNeil, T. F., Cantor-Graae, E., & Weinberger, D. R. (2000). Relationship of obstetric complications and differences in size of brain structures in monozygotic twin pairs discordant for schizophrenia. *American Journal of Psychiatry, 157*(2), 203–212.

Mosher, L. R., Pollin, W., & Stabenau, J. R. (1971). Identical twins discordant for schizophrenia—Neurologic findings. *Archives of General Psychiatry, 24*(5), 422–430.

Narr, K. L., Cannon, T. D., Woods, R. P., Thompson, P. M., Kim, S., Asunction, D., et al. (2002). Genetic contributions to altered callosal morphology in schizophrenia. *Journal of Neuroscience, 22*(9), 3720–3729.

Narr, K. L., van Erp, T. G. M., Cannon, T. D., Woods, R. P., Thompson, P. M., Jang, S., et al. (2002). A twin study of genetic contributions to hippocampal morphology in schizophrenia. *Neurobiology of Disease, 11*(1), 83–95.

Nathan, M., & Guttman, R. (1984). Similarities in test-scores and profiles of kibbutz twins and singletons. *Acta Geneticae Medicae et Gemellologiae, 33*(2), 213–218.

Noga, J. T., Bartley, A. J., Jones, D. W., Torrey, E. F., & Weinberger, D. R. (1996). Cortical gyral anatomy and gross brain dimensions in monozygotic twins discordant for schizophrenia. *Schizophrenia Research, 22*(1), 27–40.

Ohara, K., Xu, H. D., Matsunaga, T., Xu, D. S., Huang, X. Q., Gu, G. F., et al. (1998). Cerebral ventricle–brain ratio in monozygotic twins discordant and concordant for schizophrenia. *Progress in Neuro-Psychopharmacology & Biological Psychiatry, 22*(6), 1043–1050.

Onstad, S., Skre, I., Torgersen, S., & Kringlen, E. (1992). Birth-weight and obstetric complications in schizophrenic twins. *Acta Psychiatrica Scandinavica, 85*(1), 70–73.

Pardo, P. J., Knesevich, M. A., Vogler, G. P., Pardo, J. V., Towne, B., Cloninger, C. R., et al. (2000). Genetic and state variables of neurocognitive dysfunction in schizophrenia: A twin study. *Schizophrenia Bulletin*, *26*(2), 459–477.

Picchioni, M. M., Toulopoulou, T., Landau, S., Davies, N., Ribchester, T., & Murray, R. M. (2006). Neurological abnormalities in schizophrenic twins. *Biological Psychiatry*, *59*(4), 341–348.

Reichenberg, A., Rabinowitz, J., Weiser, M., Mark, M., Kaplan, Z., & Davidson, M. (2000). Premorbid functioning in a national population of male twins discordant for psychoses. *American Journal of Psychiatry*, *157*(9), 1514–1516.

Reveley, A. M., Reveley, M. A., Clifford, C. A., & Murray, R. M. (1982). Cerebral ventricular size in twins discordant for schizophrenia. *Lancet*, *1*(8271), 540–541.

Reveley, A. M., Reveley, M. A., & Murray, R. M. (1984). Cerebral ventricular enlargement in non-genetic schizophrenia—A controlled twin study. *British Journal of Psychiatry*, *144*, 89–93.

Rijsdijk, F. V., van Haren, N. E. M., Picchioni, M. M., McDonald, C., Toulopoulou, T., Hulshoff Pol, H. E., et al. (2005). Brain MRI abnormalities in schizophrenia: Same genes or same environment? *Psychological Medicine*, *35*(10), 1399–1409.

Rosa, A., Fananas, L., Bracha, H. S., Torrey, E. F., & van Os, J. (2000). Congenital dermatoglyphic malformations and psychosis: A twin study. *American Journal of Psychiatry*, *157*(9), 1511–1513.

Rosenthal, D. (1960). Confusion of identity and the frequency of schizophrenia in twins. *Archives of General Psychiatry*, *3*(3), 297–304.

Rosenthal, D., & Kety, S. S. (Eds.). (1968). *The transmission of schizophrenia*. Oxford, UK: Pergamon Press.

Sadrzadeh, S., Treloar, S. A., van Baal, G. C., & Lambalk, C. B. (2001). Potential bias regarding birth weight in historical and contemporary twin data bases. *Twin Research*, *4*(5), 332–336.

Sirugo, G., Ashenbrenner, J., Odunsi, K., Morakinyo, O., & Page, G. (2004). No evidence of association between the genetic predisposition for dizygotic twinning and schizophrenia in West Africa. *Schizophrenia Research*, *70*(2–3), 343–344.

Sommer, I. E. C., Ramsey, N. F., Mandl, R. C., van Oel, C. J., & Kahn, R. S. (2004). Language activation in monozygotic twins discordant for schizophrenia. *British Journal of Psychiatry*, *184*, 128–135.

Spaniel, F., Hajek, T., Tintera, J., Harantová, P., Dezortová, M., & Hájek, M. (2003). Differences in fMRI and MRS in a monozygotic twin pair discordant for schizophrenia (case report). *Acta Psychiatrica Scandinavica*, *107*(2), 155–157.

Spaniel, F., Herynek, V., Hajek, T., Dezortova, M., Horacek, J., Hajek, M., et al. (2005). Magnetic resonance relaxometry in monozygotic twins discordant and concordant for schizophrenia. *European Psychiatry*, *20*(1), 41–44.

Stassen, H. H., Coppola, R., Gottesman, I. I., Torrey, E. F., Kuny, S., Rickler, K. C., et al. (1999). EEG differences in monozygotic twins discordant and concordant for schizophrenia. *Psychophysiology*, *36*(1), 109–117.

Styner, M., Lieberman, J. A., McClure, R. K., Weinberger, D. R., Jones, D. W., & Gerig, G. (2005). Morphometric analysis of lateral ventricles in schizophrenia and healthy controls regarding genetic and disease-specific factors. *Proceedings of the National Academy of Sciences of the United States of America*, *102*(13), 4872–4877.

Suddath, R. L., Christison, G. W., Torrey, E. F., Casanova, M. F., & Weinberger, D. R. (1990). Anatomical abnormalities in the brains of monozygotic twins discordant for schizophrenia. *New England Journal of Medicine*, *322*(12), 789–794.

Sullivan, P. F., Kendler, K. S., & Neale, M. C. (2003). Schizophrenia as a complex trait—Evidence from a meta-analysis of twin studies. *Archives of General Psychiatry, 60*(12), 1187–1192.

Tienari, P. (1963). Psychiatric illnesses in identical-twins. *Acta Psychiatrica Scandinavica, 39*, 1–145.

Torrey, E. F., & Gottesman, I. I. (1994). *Schizophrenia and manic depressive disorder: The biological roots of mental illness as revealed by a landmark study of identical twins.* New York, NY: Basic Books.

Toulopoulou, T., Picchioni, M., Rijsdijk, F., Hua-Hall, M., Ettinger, U., Sham, P., et al. (2007). Substantial genetic overlap between neurocognition and schizophrenia: Genetic modeling in twin samples. *Archives of General Psychiatry, 64*(12), 1348–1355.

van Erp, T. G. M., Saleh, P. A., Huttunen, M., Lönnqvist, J., Kaprio, J., Salonen, O., et al. (2004). Hippocampal volumes in schizophrenic twins. *Archives of General Psychiatry, 61*(4), 346–353.

van Haren, N. E. M., Picchioni, M. M., McDonald, C., Marshall, N., Davis, N., Ribchester, T., et al. (2004). A controlled study of brain structure in monozygotic twins concordant and discordant for schizophrenia. *Biological Psychiatry, 56*(6), 454–461.

van Oel, C. J., Baare, W. F. C., Hulshoff Pol, H. E., Haag, J., Balazs, J., Dingemans, A., et al. (2001). Differentiating between low and high susceptibility to schizophrenia in twins: The significance of dermatoglyphic indices in relation to other determinants of brain development. *Schizophrenia Research, 52*(3), 181–193.

van Os, J., Fananas, L., Cannon, M., Macdonald, A., & Murray, R. (1997). Dermatoglyphic abnormalities in psychosis: A twin study. *Biological Psychiatry, 41*(5), 624–626.

Weinberger, D. R., Berman, K. F., Suddath, R., & Torrey, E. F. (1992). Evidence of dysfunction of a prefrontal-limbic network in schizophrenia—A magnetic-resonance-imaging and regional cerebral blood-flow study of discordant monozygotic twins. *American Journal of Psychiatry, 149*(7), 890–897.

Weisbrod, M., Hill, H., Niethammer, R., & Sauer, H. (1999). Genetic influence on auditory information processing in schizophrenia: P300 in monozygotic twins. *Biological Psychiatry, 46*(5), 721–725.

Weisbrod, M., Hill, H., Sauer, H., Niethammer, R., Guggenbühl, S., Hell, D., et al. (2004). Nongenetic pathologic developments of brain-wave patterns in monozygotic twins discordant and concordant for schizophrenia. *American Journal of Medical Genetics Part B-Neuropsychiatric Genetics, 125B*(1), 1–9.

5 Stress and cortisol in the pre-psychotic phases

Fern Day and Carmine Pariante

Background

Stress is a key feature of many aetiological models of psychosis (e.g., Corcoran et al., 2003; Walker & Diforio, 1997; Zubin & Spring, 1977). According to stress-vulnerability models, stressful experiences throughout life interact in a dynamic way with trait vulnerability for psychosis, inducing psychological and biological changes, which may then result in the expression of psychotic symptoms or disorder. There is considerable empirical evidence implicating stress in the development of psychosis. Increased rates of exposure to stressful or traumatic events, such as sexual and physical abuse, along with increased emotional and behavioural reactivity to stress, have been reported in people with psychosis (e.g., Morgan & Fisher, 2007; Read, van Os, Morrison, & Ross, 2005; van Winkel, Stefanis, & Myin-Germeys, 2008) and a functional disturbance in the body's principal stress response system (the hypothalamic-pituitary-adrenal, or HPA, axis) has been observed during acute episodes of psychosis (Corcoran et al., 2003; Phillips et al., 2006). Moreover, several studies have found associations between stress and psychosis-like experiences in the general population (e.g., Bebbington et al., 2004; Janssen et al., 2004; Spauwen, Krabbendam, Lieb, Wittchen, & van Os, 2006) and increased stress sensitivity in people with a genetic predisposition for psychosis (Myin-Germeys & van Os, 2007). Despite widespread acceptance of a role for stress in the onset of psychosis, the precise nature of this role remains unclear, as do the underlying neurobiological mechanisms. In recent years, research has been directed towards investigating stress during the pre-psychotic phases. This chapter will review the findings of such research and discuss how it has contributed to current understanding of the role of stress in the development of psychosis.

What is stress?

Stress is an elusive concept that is defined differently in different contexts. Early conceptualizations of stress define it as the physiological reaction of an organism to a threatening stimulus (the "stressor"). The physiological stress response is similar across mammalian species and involves activation of two key systems: the

HPA axis and the sympathetic branch of the autonomic nervous system. Activation of these systems allows the organism to respond to the threat in an adaptive way. Stress is also defined as a psychological concept, in which cognitive appraisal of threatening stimuli occurs, resulting in the activation of a coping response (Lazarus & Folkman, 1984). Stress is also commonly used in everyday language to indicate a variety of subjective mental states, including feelings of anxiety, frustration and inability to cope with demands, in addition to its use as a euphemism for more serious mental health problems. In this chapter, stress is defined broadly, including any event or experience that provokes feelings of distress, mental strain, or physiological symptoms of stress.

The HPA axis

The HPA axis is the principal mediator of the body's response to stress and its activation results in an elevation of glucocorticoids in the circulation (O'Brien, 1997). Threatening or stressful stimuli are perceived by the organism, triggering the release of corticotrophin-releasing hormone (CRH) from the paraventricular nucleus of the hypothalamus. CRH in turn stimulates secretion of adreno-corticotropic hormone (ACTH) from corticotroph cells within the anterior region of the pituitary gland, which then enters the circulation and induces release of glucocorticoids, including cortisol, from the adrenal cortex. Cortisol acts at a variety of peripheral targets throughout the body, inducing physiological and behavioural changes that enable the organism to respond adaptively to the stimulus. Circulating cortisol inhibits further activation of the HPA axis through negative feedback at both pituitary and hypothalamic level and also via the hippocampus (Jacobson & Sapolsky, 1991). In addition to the hippocampus, several other brain areas provide regulatory influence over HPA axis function, while the HPA axis itself also leads to changes in activity of various pathways within the brain (Corcoran et al., 2003; Lopez, Akil, & Watson, 1999; Walker & Diforio, 1997). Of particular relevance to psychosis are the reciprocal interactions between the HPA axis and dopaminergic pathways, like the mesolimbic dopamine system (Corcoran et al., 2003; Walker & Diforio, 1997).

Neurobiological mechanisms linking stress and psychosis

While HPA axis activity is adaptive in the short term, chronic activation of the HPA axis, resulting in persistent elevation of circulating cortisol, can lead to sensitization to stress and various undesirable neurobiological and cognitive changes. These include neurotoxicity and neuronal atrophy in glucocorticoid receptor dense areas, decreased neurogenesis and suppression of long-term potentiation in the hippocampus and cognitive impairment (Corcoran et al., 2003). These effects in turn damage the regulatory control over HPA axis activity, particularly the negative feedback input from the hippocampus, leading to further glucocorticoid release and the establishment of a "vicious cycle" known as the stress cascade (Sapolsky, Krey, & McEwen, 1985).

There is evidence from animal and human studies that early stress or glucocorticoid exposure, even before birth, can have long-term effects on the function and responsivity of the HPA axis (see Walker & Diforio, 1997, for a review). Such long-term changes in HPA axis activity could explain the stress sensitivity and altered HPA responses to challenge found in people experiencing psychosis and it has been suggested that excessive activation of the HPA axis might underlie some of the hippocampal alterations and cognitive disturbances observed in psychosis (Corcoran et al., 2003; Phillips et al., 2006). Stress and glucocorticoid administration is associated with increased activation of the mesolimbic dopamine system in both animals and humans and administration of antipsychotic drugs has been found to normalize HPA axis dysregulation in psychosis (see Walker & Diforio, 1997, for a review). These findings have been integrated into the neural diathesis-stress model proposed by Walker and Diforio (1997), providing a possible neurobiological mechanism linking psychosocial stress and early environmental insults with HPA axis disturbance and abnormal mesolimbic dopamine activity. Increased HPA axis activity and initiation of the stress cascade leads to increased activation and sensitization of the mesolimbic dopamine system, resulting in the subsequent expression of psychotic symptoms and disorder in vulnerable individuals (Walker & Diforio, 1997). Genetic liability is thought to be manifested in the neurobiological and behavioural response to stress, with increasing genetic vulnerability being associated with greater likelihood of sensitization of the HPA axis and dopamine systems to repeated exposure to stress (van Winkel et al., 2008).

How can stress be measured?

Psychosocial stressors are typically assessed using structured interviews or self-report questionnaires, in which individuals are asked to report particular events occurring over a specific period of time (Phillips, Francey, Edwards, & McMurray, 2007). Reported events can range from mild feelings of "everyday" stress and minor hassles (e.g., running late), through significant life events (e.g., the end of a serious relationship), to traumatic events (e.g., sexual abuse). Current stress can also be assessed using the Experience Sampling Method (ESM), a technique that allows in-the-moment measurement of an individual's environment, activities and feelings repeatedly and at random over a given period of time (Myin-Germeys et al., 2009). Given that stress is such a vaguely defined concept and there is considerable inter- and intra-individual variability in the subjective experience of stress, there are methodological limitations in its accurate assessment and the variety of methods used to measure stress make comparison of findings across studies problematic (Norman & Malla, 1993b; Phillips et al., 2007). Some instruments focus on "objective" measures of exposure to specific events, e.g., being assaulted, assuming that such events will indeed be stressful to all respondents, while others concentrate on the more personal, subjective experience of stress, e.g., feeling unable to cope, which is likely influenced by a variety of factors like personality and mental health. Other relevant issues are the timing, frequency and duration of stressful events, as well as previous experience of psychosocial stress, which are thought to moderate the impact of the stressful experience. Most measures of psychosocial stress rely primarily on retrospective self-report and are thus susceptible to recall and other forms of bias, which is even more problematic if it occurs differentially across participant groups.

The activity of the HPA axis can also be measured under normal conditions and in response to awakening, pharmacological challenge and exposure to psychosocial stress. Basal levels of cortisol (and other HPA hormones) can be measured easily in plasma, saliva, urine, or cerebrospinal fluid, however there is considerable inter-individual variation in diurnal cortisol release, so the time of sampling is an important factor to consider and it is desirable to collect samples across several time-points (Corcoran et al., 2003). The dexamethasone suppression test (DST) assesses HPA axis function by measuring the suppression of cortisol release following administration of a synthetic glucocorticoid, with non-suppression indicating impaired negative feedback control within the HPA axis. Psychosocial stress tests, like the Trier Social Stress Test, allow measurement of both psychological and physiological stress before, during and after performance of stressful tasks such as a speech in front of an audience. Psychological stress is typically measured using visual analogue scales and physiological stress is assessed using cortisol levels and heart rate. Given the distress associated with invasive sampling procedures like taking blood, saliva sampling is considered a superior method in stress research (Corcoran et al., 2003). It also provides a better reflection of the levels of the biologically active, "free" form of cortisol in circulation than plasma samples (Hellhammer, Wust, & Kudielka, 2009). The pituitary gland shows dynamic changes in volume over time and it is suggested that its volume, as measured using magnetic resonance imaging (MRI), can be used as an indicator of HPA axis activity, with a larger volume corresponding to hyperactivity within the system (Pariante et al., 2004).

How can stress be measured in the pre-psychotic phases?

At present, it is not possible to identify the individuals within a population who will go on to develop psychosis until they actually do, when, of course, it is too late to measure the levels of stress they experienced during the pre-psychotic phase. An ideal approach to this problem is to perform prospective studies in large numbers of participants sampled from the general population, in which both stress exposure and psychosis-like experiences or onset of psychotic disorder are assessed repeatedly over the lifespan, although the costliness of such large longitudinal studies limits their use. Instead, the majority of research investigating stress and HPA-axis function before the onset of psychosis has been conducted in smaller populations identified as being at increased risk of developing the disorder. This includes participants with "trait" vulnerability—indicated by their fulfilling criteria for schizotypal personality disorder (SPD), or by having high genetic risk on account of having at least one first-degree relative with a psychotic disorder— and those with "state" vulnerability—indicated by presence of psychosis-like experiences or more severe attenuated psychotic symptoms—or a combination of both. The "ultra-high-risk" (UHR) criteria are used to identify individuals at imminent risk of developing psychosis based on such "state and trait" vulnerability factors—the UHR group is associated with high rates of transition to psychosis (25–40%) within the following two years (Yung, Phillips, Yuen, & McGorry, 2004). Studies in such populations have great advantages over studies of people with first-episode or chronic psychosis as they allow assessment *before* the onset of the disorder. However, this approach identifies a high number of "false positives", as the majority of people with psychosis-like experiences or a family member with psychosis do not develop psychosis and often such studies do not have sufficient statistical power to make useful comparisons between those who do develop psychosis and those who do not. Other factors worth considering when interpreting findings in such populations are the possible confounding effect of intervention, as well as the generalizability of findings, given that high-risk groups are typically comprised of "help-seeking" individuals who are unlikely to be representative of all those at high risk of developing psychosis.

Psychosocial stressors

Trauma

A high prevalence of trauma, including physical and sexual abuse, is commonly reported in people with psychotic disorders (see Read et al., 2005; Morgan & Fisher, 2007, for reviews) and, conversely, positive symptoms of psychosis, such as hallucinations and delusions, are often found in people with a diagnosis of post-traumatic stress disorder (PTSD; Butler, Mueser, Sprock, & Braff, 1996). Several large studies have found an association between traumatic experiences, such as physical abuse, sexual abuse and bullying and psychotic symptoms or disorder in adults (e.g., Bebbington et al., 2004; Shevlin, Dorahy, & Adamson, 2007) and this association has also been observed during adolescence (e.g., Kelleher et al., 2008; Lataster et al., 2006). However, the design of these studies was cross-sectional and retrospective and the occurrence of the relevant traumatic event in relation to the onset of psychotic symptoms or psychosis was not always established. It cannot, therefore, be assumed that the traumatic events occurred in the pre-psychotic phase, nor can firm conclusions be drawn regarding causality. Support for a causal association comes from the results of the Netherlands Mental Health Survey and Incidence Study (NEMESIS; Janssen et al., 2004) in The Netherlands and the Early Developmental Stages of Psychopathology (EDSP) study in Germany (Spauwen et al., 2006). These prospective cohort studies assessed childhood abuse (emotional, physical and sexual; NEMESIS) and lifetime trauma (including sexual and physical abuse; EDSP) at baseline and found that exposure to abuse significantly increased the risk of subsequent development of psychotic symptoms.

To date, only two studies have examined the prevalence of traumatic experiences in people at UHR for psychosis and high rates of exposure to trauma were found in both studies. Out of 30 participants, 27 had experienced at least one traumatic event (Thompson et al., 2009). Physical, sexual and emotional abuse were reported by 83, 27 and 67% of the sample, respectively. While the rates of reported trauma appear high, it was not clear whether or not this was exceptional for an inner-city area, as no information was collected from a geographically matched control sample, although an association between trauma history and presenting symptoms was reported (Thompson et al., 2009). However, this high rate of exposure to trauma was replicated in a more recent study by Bechdolf et al. (2010), in which traumatic experiences were assessed in a sample of 92 people at UHR for psychosis. Of these participants, 70% had a history of trauma, as assessed by their care manager, with 26, 28 and 24% reporting physical abuse, sexual abuse and neglect, respectively. Exposure to childhood sexual abuse was found to be associated with transition to psychosis over a mean 615-day follow-up, after controlling for other clinical factors related to transition. These studies provide further support for early trauma as a risk factor for psychosis.

Life events and minor stressors

Several studies have reported that individuals with psychosis experienced more life events in the period leading up to a psychotic episode (e.g., Bebbington et al., 1993; Brown & Birley, 1968), suggesting that stressful life events might serve to precipitate the emergence of psychotic symptoms. However, this finding has not been replicated in all studies (e.g., Chung, Langeluddecke, & Tennant, 1986) and there has been some general criticism of the methods used to assess life events (Phillips et al., 2007). Malla and Norman (1992) reported that it was the number of minor stressors, rather than life events, experienced by people with schizophrenia that correlated with their level of distress, suggesting that chronic exposure to everyday stress might be more relevant to psychotic symptoms than major stressful events (Norman & Malla, 1993a).

The two studies that investigated life events and "hassles" in the UHR group do not provide support for a role of such stressors in expression of psychotic symptoms in the pre-psychotic phase and the subsequent transition to psychosis. Experience of recent stressful life events in a sample of 74 UHR participants was not associated with the development of psychosis (Mason et al., 2004) and life events did not appear to be related to symptomatology in a smaller sample ($n = 13$; Thompson, Phillips et al., 2007). A significant correlation was found between the number of hassles experienced by 18 UHR participants and scores on the Brief Psychiatric Rating Scale, but no association was found with the positive symptom subscale, which suggests that any effect may be nonspecific, although the sample size in this case was also small (Thompson, Phillips et al., 2007).

In contrast, an association between psychotic-like symptoms and lifetime experience of major stressors was found in a large sample ($n = 155$) of participants at genetic high-risk for psychosis (Miller et al., 2001), but whether such experiences were related to subsequent development of psychosis is not known. Interestingly, the association between psychotic experiences and stress was also present in the comparison group of participants with no genetic predisposition to psychosis. The discrepancy between these studies in high-risk populations regarding the association between life events and psychotic symptomatology could be due to the time-scale of assessment: no association was found when only recent life events were recorded (Mason et al., 2004; Thompson, Phillips et al., 2007), but a dose–response relationship was reported for experience of stressful events over the lifetime and severity of symptoms (Miller et al., 2001), or possibly due to limited power to detect any associations in the UHR samples, for which the experience of psychosis-like symptoms itself was a selection criterion.

Myin-Germeys, van Os, Schwartz, Stone, and Delespaul (2001) investigated how people with varying levels of genetic liability for psychosis (participants with psychosis, their first-degree relatives and control participants) responded to minor stressors encountered in daily life using the Experience Sampling Method (ESM). The study revealed differential emotional reactivity to stress across the three groups. Participants in the psychosis group displayed greater increases in negative affect and decreases in positive affect compared with the control group, while first-degree relatives responded with intermediate changes in affect. This suggests that vulnerability to psychosis might be manifested in subtle changes in the way people respond to stressful events. In a subsequent study using the same technique (Myin-Germeys, Delespaul, & van Os, 2005), behavioural sensitization, in the form of increased intensity of psychotic experiences, was observed in response to activity-related stress in the first-degree relatives of participants with psychosis, but not in control participants.

Summary

The evidence described above provides support for the view that early traumatic experiences constitute a risk factor for the development of psychosis, although more research, utilizing stronger methods, is needed in high-risk populations to shed further light on this matter. The evidence regarding the role of stress at later stages, proximal to the onset of psychosis, is less consistent and it seems that chronic exposure to minor stressors might be more important than life events in terms of symptom severity and associated distress. However, the validity of using life-event exposure as an index of stress has been questioned and the considerable methodological variation between studies attempting to address this question could account for some of mixed findings (Phillips et al., 2007). Another important issue rarely addressed in such studies is the independence of the stressful experiences from the individual's behaviour. Psychotic symptoms can be extremely distressing or even traumatic and it is not difficult to imagine how behavioural responses to such experiences might actually increase the risk of certain life events, e.g., serious problems with significant others or becoming unemployed. Further research in larger high-risk samples, involving repeated measurements of stress and psychotic symptoms over time, would be of great value in clarifying the precise nature of the role of stress at this stage. It would also be advantageous to assess exposure to lifetime stressful events, trauma, recent life events and minor stressors, along with neurobiological measures, in the same individuals, as this would allow for clarification of their relative contributions to psychosis risk and investigation of the putative mechanisms involved.

Cortisol and HPA-axis function

Findings in psychosis

Evidence from studies using several methodological techniques is suggestive of a dysregulation of the HPA axis in psychosis, although there have been some inconsistent findings. Elevated cortisol levels in people experiencing acute psychosis were first reported by Sachar, Kanter, Buie, Engle, and Mehlman in 1970. Subsequent research has shown increased cortisol levels and diurnal cortisol disturbances in people with psychosis, even during the first episode and before treatment (e.g., Mondelli et al., 2009; Ryan, Collins, & Thakore, 2003). Furthermore, rates of non-suppression in the DST are higher in people with psychosis compared with control participants in most studies (e.g., Tandon et al., 1991). Several, but not all (e.g., Nicolo et al., 2010), structural magnetic resonance imaging (MRI) studies have shown an increased volume of the pituitary gland in people experiencing a first psychotic episode compared to control participants (Pariante et al., 2004, 2005). As these differences were present in antipsychotic-naive individuals but not in people with chronic illness, they may be specifically related to the experience of acute psychosis, although exposure to typical antipsychotics appears to induce additional enlargement of the gland (Pariante, 2008). Interestingly, the HPA axis might actually be involved in the response to pharmacological intervention in acute psychosis. A recent study of people with a first episode of psychosis found that those with larger pituitary gland volume displayed a poorer response to subsequent antipsychotic medication, in terms of improvement of psychotic symptoms (Garner et al., 2009). While these studies demonstrate that acute psychosis is associated with abnormalities of HPA-axis function, they do not provide any evidence as to whether such abnormalities are present before the onset and are thus implicated in the development of psychosis, or occur in response to the experience of psychotic symptoms, which are often distressing and potentially traumatic (McGorry et al., 1991).

Findings in the pre-psychotic phases

In recent years, there have been several studies that attempted to address this issue by investigating HPA-axis function in people who had not developed psychosis, but were at UHR of doing so. Garner et al. (2005) measured the pituitary gland in a sample of 94 UHR individuals (all of whom were antipsychotic-naive) and found that the participants who went on to develop psychosis had larger pituitary gland volumes than those who did not. Interestingly, they reported a negative correlation between pituitary volume and the time between MRI and psychosis onset. Pituitary gland volume is thought to be an index of HPA-axis activity and so these findings suggest that the HPA-axis dysregulation observed in psychosis might actually precede the first psychotic episode, with greater hyperactivity of the system as the individual approaches the onset of psychosis (Pariante, 2008). A recent study found enlarged volume of the pituitary gland in unaffected relatives of people with psychosis, compared to control participants, with the greatest enlargement observed in participants with more than one affected relative (Mondelli et al., 2008). These findings raise the possibility that pituitary enlargement in psychosis might be an indicator of a genetic predisposition towards hyperactivity of the HPA axis.

The results of other studies investigating HPA-axis function through different methods in high-risk groups provide further evidence indicating abnormal cortisol levels. Elevated saliva cortisol levels have been found in adolescent participants with SPD, an indicator of trait vulnerability for the development of psychosis, compared with healthy control participants (Walker, Walder, & Reynolds, 2001; Weinstein, Diforio, Schiffman, Walker, & Bonsall, 1999). Heightened cortisol at baseline was associated with severity of schizotypal symptoms at follow-up 18–24 months later (Walker et al., 2001). Another study in this group found a correlation between morning cortisol and minor physical abnormalities, which are thought to be indicators of abnormal foetal development, suggesting the possibility that elevated cortisol constitutes a bio-risk marker for psychosis (Mittal, Dhruv, Tessner, Walder, & Walker, 2007). A more recent longitudinal study of a group of 56 adolescent individuals at UHR of developing psychosis examined changes in morning saliva cortisol levels at up to three occasions over a 12-month period (Walker et al., 2010). Higher cortisol levels were observed at follow-up assessments in those participants who made a transition to psychosis than those who did not, indicating that HPA-axis activity is indeed altered prior to the onset of psychosis (Walker et al., 2010).

Not all studies in people with elevated psychosis risk have reported results consistent with a disturbance of HPA-axis function. Blood samples were collected at 0800 hours in a small sample ($n = 18$) of UHR individuals, and these were then analysed to give plasma cortisol levels and number of glucocorticoid receptors (Thompson, Phillips et al., 2007). No difference in glucocorticoid receptor number between those who subsequently developed psychosis and those who did not was found, but lower morning cortisol levels were observed in the subgroup that went on to become psychotic (Thompson, Phillips et al., 2007). Another study examined the cortisol and ACTH response in 12 UHR participants to administration of CRH following administration of dexamethasone the previous night (the DEX/CRH test; Thompson, Berger et al., 2007). The small sample size precluded any statistical analysis, although qualitative information regarding elevated cortisol in the subgroup that did not go on to develop psychosis was reported (Thompson, Berger et al., 2007). The cortisol response to a metabolic stressor (injection of 2-deoxyglucose) was measured in participants at elevated risk of psychosis on account having a first-degree relative with a psychotic disorder, but no difference was found when compared with control participants (Marcelis, Cavalier, Gielen, Delespaul, & van Os, 2004).

Summary

The findings presented above, from studies of individuals with SPD or high genetic risk, suggest that predisposition towards HPA-axis hyperactivity, as indexed by elevated cortisol (Mittal et al., 2007) and enlargement of the pituitary gland (Mondelli et al., 2008), might be a characteristic of trait vulnerability for psychosis. Further support comes from findings that HPA-axis activity (Walker et al., 2001) and exposure to stress (Miller et al., 2001) are associated with the severity of psychotic symptoms in these groups. The results of studies in individuals at UHR for psychosis, ascertained primarily on the basis of experiencing attenuated psychotic symptoms, are less clear with regard to the role of the HPA axis at this stage, although the results of the two largest studies are consistent with findings in established psychosis (Garner et al., 2005; Walker et al., 2010). Enlargement of the pituitary gland predicting subsequent psychosis onset provides strong support for hypothesis that hyperactivity of the HPA axis drives the development of psychosis (Garner et al., 2005), which is further supported by a recent study showing an elevation in cortisol over time before the development of psychosis (Walker et al., 2010). Not all studies in UHR groups support an association between HPA-axis activity and psychotic symptoms or disorder (Thompson, Berger et al., 2007; Thompson, Phillips et al., 2007). However, the sample sizes in these studies were small, thus statistical power may have been insufficient to detect any changes. To elucidate the nature of HPA-axis function and the role it plays in the onset of psychosis, more research, investigating multiple indices of HPA axis activity, is needed in larger samples of clinical and genetic high-risk individuals. Repeated-measures designs would be of value in determining whether HPA-axis activity fluctuates over time with psychotic symptoms, particularly during the emergence of a full psychotic episode. Given the high rates of depression and anxiety in the UHR group and the well-known disturbances in HPA-axis function in depression, comorbidity, as well as the effects of psychotropic medication on HPA-axis activity, are important factors to consider in future research.

General summary

The studies reviewed in this chapter represent the early stages of research examining stress in the pre-psychotic phases and the findings provide justification for continued research in this area. However, there are considerable methodological issues to be addressed before any firm conclusions can be drawn regarding stress as a risk factor and HPA-axis dysfunction as a mediating mechanism in the development of psychosis. Improved understanding of the role of stress in the onset of psychosis will be acquired through studies that integrate multiple, repeated measures of stress and HPA-axis activity in high-risk individuals to assess how these vary over time with psychotic symptomatology and other relevant neurobiological factors, such as hippocampal structure and function and dopaminergic activity.

References

Bebbington, P., Wilkins, S., Jones, P., Foerster, A., Murray, R., Toone, B., et al. (1993). Life events and psychosis. Initial results from the Camberwell Collaborative Psychosis Study. *British Journal of Psychiatry*, *162*, 72–79.

Bebbington, P. E., Bhugra, D., Brugha, T., Singleton, N., Farrell, M., Jenkins, R., et al. (2004). Psychosis, victimisation and childhood disadvantage: Evidence from the second British National Survey of Psychiatric Morbidity. *British Journal of Psychiatry*, *185*, 220–226.

Bechdolf, A., Thompson, A., Nelson, B., Cotton, S., Simmons, M. B., Amminger, G. P., et al. (2010). Experience of trauma and conversion to psychosis in an ultra-high-risk (prodromal) group. *Acta Psychiatrica Scandinavica*, *121*(5), 377–384.

Brown, G. W., & Birley, J. L. (1968). Crises and life changes and the onset of schizophrenia. *Journal of Health and Social Behavior*, *9*, 203–214.

Butler, R. W., Mueser, K. T., Sprock, J., & Braff, D. L. (1996). Positive symptoms of psychosis in posttraumatic stress disorder. *Biological Psychiatry*, *39*, 839–844.

Chung, R. K., Langeluddecke, P., & Tennant, C. (1986). Threatening life events in the onset of schizophrenia, schizophreniform psychosis and hypomania. *British Journal of Psychiatry*, *148*, 680–685.

Corcoran, C., Walker, E., Huot, R., Mittal, V., Tessner, K., Kestler, L., et al. (2003). The stress cascade and schizophrenia: Etiology and onset. *Schizophrenia Bulletin*, *29*, 671–692.

Garner, B., Berger, G. E., Nicolo, J. P., Mackinnon, A., Wood, S. J., Pariante, C. M., et al. (2009). Pituitary volume and early treatment response in drug-naive first-episode psychosis patients. *Schizophrenia Research*, *113*, 65–71.

Garner, B., Pariante, C. M., Wood, S. J., Velakoulis, D., Phillips, L., Soulsby, B., et al. (2005). Pituitary volume predicts future transition to psychosis in individuals at ultra-high risk of developing psychosis. *Biological Psychiatry*, *58*, 417–423.

Hellhammer, D. H., Wust, S., & Kudielka, B. M. (2009). Salivary cortisol as a biomarker in stress research. *Psychoneuroendocrinology*, *34*, 163–171.

Jacobson, L., & Sapolsky, R. (1991). The role of the hippocampus in feedback regulation of the hypothalamic-pituitary-adrenocortical axis. *Endocrine Reviews*, *12*, 118–134.

Janssen, I., Krabbendam, L., Bak, M., Hanssen, M., Vollebergh, W., de Graaf, R., et al. (2004). Childhood abuse as a risk factor for psychotic experiences. *Acta Psychiatrica Scandinavica*, *109*, 38–45.

Kelleher, I., Harley, M., Lynch, F., Arseneault, L., Fitzpatrick, C., & Cannon, M. (2008). Associations between childhood trauma, bullying and psychotic symptoms among a school-based adolescent sample. *British Journal of Psychiatry*, *193*, 378–382.

Lataster, T., van Os, J., Drukker, M., Henquet, C., Feron, F., Gunther, N., et al. (2006). Childhood victimisation and developmental expression of non-clinical delusional ideation and hallucinatory experiences: Victimisation and non-clinical psychotic experiences. *Social Psychiatry and Psychiatric Epidemiology*, *41*, 423–428.

Lazarus, R. S., & Folkman, S. (1984). *Stress, appraisal and coping*. New York, NY: Springer.

Lopez, J. F., Akil, H., & Watson, S. J. (1999). Neural circuits mediating stress. *Biological Psychiatry*, *46*, 1461–1471.

Malla, A. K., & Norman, R. M. (1992). Relationship of major life events and daily stressors to symptomatology in schizophrenia. *The Journal of Nervous and Mental Disease*, *180*, 664–667.

Marcelis, M., Cavalier, E., Gielen, J., Delespaul, P., & van Os, J. (2004). Abnormal response to metabolic stress in schizophrenia: Marker of vulnerability or acquired sensitization? *Psychological Medicine, 34*, 1103–1111.

Mason, O., Startup, M., Halpin, S., Schall, U., Conrad, A., & Carr, V. (2004). Risk factors for transition to first episode psychosis among individuals with "at-risk mental states". *Schizophrenia Research, 71*, 227–237.

McGorry, P. D., Chanen, A., McCarthy, E., Van Riel, R., McKenzie, D., & Singh, B. S. (1991). Posttraumatic stress disorder following recent-onset psychosis. An unrecognized postpsychotic syndrome. *The Journal of Nervous and Mental Disease, 179*, 253–258.

Miller, P., Lawrie, S. M., Hodges, A., Clafferty, R., Cosway, R., & Johnstone, E. C. (2001). Genetic liability, illicit drug use, life stress and psychotic symptoms: Preliminary findings from the Edinburgh study of people at high risk for schizophrenia. *Social Psychiatry and Psychiatric Epidemiology, 36*, 338–342.

Mittal, V. A., Dhruv, S., Tessner, K. D., Walder, D. J., & Walker, E. F. (2007). The relations among putative biorisk markers in schizotypal adolescents: Minor physical anomalies, movement abnormalities and salivary cortisol. *Biological Psychiatry, 61*, 1179–1186.

Mondelli, V., Dazzan, P., Gabilondo, A., Tournikioti, K., Walshe, M., Marshall, N., et al. (2008). Pituitary volume in unaffected relatives of patients with schizophrenia and bipolar disorder. *Psychoneuroendocrinology, 33*, 1004–1012.

Mondelli, V., Dazzan, P., Hepgul, N., Di Forti, M., Aas, M., D'Albenzio, A., et al. (2009). Abnormal cortisol levels during the day and cortisol awakening response in first-episode psychosis: The role of stress and of antipsychotic treatment. *Schizophrenia Research, 116*(2–3), 234–242.

Morgan, C., & Fisher, H. (2007). Environment and schizophrenia. Environmental factors in schizophrenia: Childhood trauma—A critical review. *Schizophrenia Bulletin, 33*, 3–10.

Myin-Germeys, I., Delespaul, P., & van Os, J. (2005). Behavioural sensitization to daily life stress in psychosis. *Psychological Medicine, 35*, 733–741.

Myin-Germeys, I., Oorschot, M., Collip, D., Lataster, J., Delespaul, P., & van Os, J. (2009). Experience sampling research in psychopathology: Opening the black box of daily life. *Psychological Medicine, 39*, 1533–1547.

Myin-Germeys, I., & van Os, J. (2007). Stress-reactivity in psychosis: Evidence for an affective pathway to psychosis. *Clinical Psychology Review, 27*, 409–424.

Myin-Germeys, I., van Os, J., Schwartz, J. E., Stone, A. A., & Delespaul, P. A. (2001). Emotional reactivity to daily life stress in psychosis. *Archives of General Psychiatry, 58*, 1137–1144.

Nicolo, J. P., Berger, G. E., Garner, B. A., Velakoulis, D., Markulev, C., Kerr, M., et al. (2010). The effect of atypical antipsychotics on pituitary gland volume in patients with first-episode psychosis: A longitudinal MRI study. *Schizophrenia Research, 116*(1), 49–54.

Norman, R. M., & Malla, A. K. (1993a). Stressful life events and schizophrenia. I: A review of the research. *British Journal of Psychiatry, 162*, 161–166.

Norman, R. M., & Malla, A. K. (1993b). Stressful life events and schizophrenia. II: Conceptual and methodological issues. *British Journal of Psychiatry, 162*, 166–174.

O'Brien, J. T. (1997). The "glucocorticoid cascade" hypothesis in man. *British Journal of Psychiatry, 170*, 199–201.

Pariante, C. M. (2008). Pituitary volume in psychosis: The first review of the evidence. *Journal of Psychopharmacology, 22*, 76–81.

Pariante, C. M., Dazzan, P., Danese, A., Morgan, K. D., Brudaglio, F., Morgan, C., et al. (2005). Increased pituitary volume in antipsychotic-free and antipsychotic-treated patients of the AEsop first-onset psychosis study. *Neuropsychopharmacology, 30,* 1923–1931.

Pariante, C. M., Vassilopoulou, K., Velakoulis, D., Phillips, L., Soulsby, B., Wood, S. J., et al. (2004). Pituitary volume in psychosis. *British Journal of Psychiatry, 185,* 5–10.

Phillips, L. J., Francey, S. M., Edwards, J., & McMurray, N. (2007). Stress and psychosis: Towards the development of new models of investigation. *Clinical Psychology Review, 27,* 307–317.

Phillips, L. J., McGorry, P. D., Garner, B., Thompson, K. N., Pantelis, C., Wood, S. J., et al. (2006). Stress, the hippocampus and the hypothalamic-pituitary-adrenal axis: Implications for the development of psychotic disorders. *Australian and New Zealand Journal of Psychiatry, 40,* 725–741.

Read, J., van Os, J., Morrison, A. P., & Ross, C. A. (2005). Childhood trauma, psychosis and schizophrenia: A literature review with theoretical and clinical implications. *Acta Psychiatrica Scandinavica, 112,* 330–350.

Ryan, M. C., Collins, P., & Thakore, J. H. (2003). Impaired fasting glucose tolerance in first-episode, drug-naive patients with schizophrenia. *American Journal of Psychiatry, 160,* 284–289.

Sachar, E. J., Kanter, S. S., Buie, D., Engle, R., & Mehlman, R. (1970). Psychoendocrinology of ego disintegration. *American Journal of Psychiatry, 126,* 1067–1078.

Sapolsky, R. M., Krey, L. C., & McEwen, B. S. (1985). Prolonged glucocorticoid exposure reduces hippocampal neuron number: Implications for aging. *Journal of Neuroscience, 5,* 1222–1227.

Shevlin, M., Dorahy, M. J., & Adamson, G. (2007). Trauma and psychosis: An analysis of the National Comorbidity Survey. *American Journal of Psychiatry, 164,* 166–169.

Spauwen, J., Krabbendam, L., Lieb, R., Wittchen, H. U., & van Os, J. (2006). Impact of psychological trauma on the development of psychotic symptoms: Relationship with psychosis proneness. *British Journal of Psychiatry, 188,* 527–533.

Tandon, R., Mazzara, C., DeQuardo, J., Craig, K. A., Meador-Woodruff, J. H., Goldman, R., et al. (1991). Dexamethasone suppression test in schizophrenia: Relationship to symptomatology, ventricular enlargement and outcome. *Biological Psychiatry, 29,* 953–964.

Thompson, J. L., Kelly, M., Kimhy, D., Harkavy-Friedman, J. M., Khan, S., Messinger, J. W., et al. (2009). Childhood trauma and prodromal symptoms among individuals at clinical high risk for psychosis. *Schizophrenia Research, 108,* 176–181.

Thompson, K. N., Berger, G., Phillips, L. J., Komesaroff, P., Purcell, R., & McGorry, P. D. (2007). HPA axis functioning associated with transition to psychosis: Combined DEX/CRH test. *Journal of Psychiatric Research, 41,* 446–450.

Thompson, K. N., Phillips, L. J., Komesaroff, P., Yuen, H. P., Wood, S. J., Pantelis, C., et al. (2007). Stress and HPA-axis functioning in young people at ultra high risk for psychosis. *Journal of Psychiatric Research, 41,* 561–569.

van Winkel, R., Stefanis, N. C., & Myin-Germeys, I. (2008). Psychosocial stress and psychosis. A review of the neurobiological mechanisms and the evidence for gene–stress interaction. *Schizophrenia Bulletin, 34,* 1095–1105.

Walker, E. F., Brennan, P. A., Esterberg, M., Brasfield, J., Pearce, B., & Compton, M. T. (2010). Longitudinal changes in cortisol secretion and conversion to psychosis in at-risk youth. *Journal of Abnormal Psychology, 119,* 401–408.

Walker, E. F., & Diforio, D. (1997). Schizophrenia: A neural diathesis-stress model. *Psychological Review, 104,* 667–685.

Walker, E. F., Walder, D. J., & Reynolds, F. (2001). Developmental changes in cortisol secretion in normal and at-risk youth. *Development and Psychopathology*, *13*, 721–732.

Weinstein, D. D., Diforio, D., Schiffman, J., Walker, E., & Bonsall, R. (1999). Minor physical anomalies, dermatoglyphic asymmetries and cortisol levels in adolescents with schizotypal personality disorder. *American Journal of Psychiatry*, *156*, 617–623.

Yung, A. R., Phillips, L. J., Yuen, H. P., & McGorry, P. D. (2004). Risk factors for psychosis in an ultra high-risk group: Psychopathology and clinical features. *Schizophrenia Research*, *67*, 131–142.

Zubin, J., & Spring, B. (1977). Vulnerability—A new view of schizophrenia. *Journal of Abnormal Psychology*, *86*, 103–126.

6 Neurocognitive indicators of high-risk states for psychosis

Ralf Pukrop and Stephan Ruhrmann

Neurocognitive abnormalities across a wide range of functions are considered to be central to the pathophysiology of psychosis. Some cognitive deficits may be stable trait-related vulnerability markers observable very early in the development of individuals who later become psychotic, or in relatives of these individuals who *will not ever* become psychotic. Some other cognitive deficits may vary with illness progression, emerging or intensifying only in certain stages of development such as childhood antecedents, prodromal signs long or immediately before transition to acute psychosis, during a first psychotic episode or more chronic conditions of the illness.

Three major strategies have been adopted to investigate cognitive deficits prior to illness onset. First, clinical high-risk approaches try to identify help-seeking adolescents or young adults who do not yet have manifest psychosis, but subthreshold schizophrenia-like symptoms or some other putatively prodromal signs. Most widely used clinical criteria sets comprise ultra high-risk criteria (UHR; attenuated or transient psychotic symptoms or genetic risk plus decline in psychosocial functioning; Yung, Phillips, Yuen, & McGorry, 2004), basic symptoms (subtle self-experienced cognitive or affective disturbances; Klosterkötter, Hellmich, Steinmeyer, & Schultze-Lutter, 2001), DSM-IV criteria of schizotypal personality disorder, negative symptoms or more general psychopathological symptoms (Table 6.1). Second, follow-ups or follow-backs of large birth cohorts incorporating individuals who eventually develop psychosis spectrum disorders in the future usually include some general assessments of cognitive functions. Third, genetic high-risk studies longitudinally assess cognitive functioning in young family members of individuals with psychosis or psychosis spectrum disorders, who have not yet passed the period of maximum risk. The following sections will briefly summarize results obtained by these three approaches with a major focus on clinical high-risk (HR) studies (see Table 6.1 for an overview of studies).

Cross-sectional baseline assessments in clinical HR samples

The following overview of baseline comparisons between clinically identified HR samples with an unclear conversion-to-psychosis status and normal controls has been ordered by neurocognitive domains. It should be kept in mind, however, that

Table 6.1 Basic characteristics of studies with neurocognitive baseline or follow-up assessments in clinically defined high-risk (HR) samples

Reference (date)	Project/site	At risk criteria	HR (n)	HR (mean age in years)	HR (% male)	HR converters (n)
Parnas et al. (2001)	Copenhagen (DEN)	ICD-10 STD; BS	10	28	33	—
Brewer et al. (2003)	PACE, Melbourne (AUS)	UHR	81	20	53–58	34
Wood et al. (2003)			98	19	48–56	9
Brewer et al. (2005)			70	19	44–56	12
Francey et al. (2005)			43	20	40–58	20
Hawkins et al. (2004)	PRIME, multi-site	UHR	36	20	64	—
Keefe et al. (2006)			37	21	54	11
Hoffman et al. (2007)			43	—	—	12
Hawkins et al. (2008)			37	18	65	21
Silverstein et al. (2006)	PAS, Newcastle (AUS)	UHR	70	17	66	24
Pukrop et al. (2006)	FETZ, Cologne (GER)	BS; UHR	128	24	63	—
Pukrop et al. (2007)			83	24	67	44
Koethe et al. (2009)			22	26	82	—
Gschwandtner et al. (2006)	FEPSY, Basel (CH)	DSM-III/ BPRS; UHR	40	27	50	—
Pflüger et al. (2007)			60	27	57	—
Riecher-Rössler et al. (2009)			53	26	60	21
Smith et al. (2006)	RAP, New York (USA)	UHR; NS	8	16	100	—
Lencz et al. (2006)			38	17	58	12

Trotman et al. (2006)	EUADP, New York (USA)	DSM-IV, STPD	34	14	68	—
Walder et al. (2008)			37	14	65	12
Niendam et al. (2006)	CAPPS, UCLA (USA)	UHR	45	18	64	—
Niendam et al. (2007)			35	18	60	—
Simon et al. (2007)	BEPS, Basel (CH)	UHR; BS	93	21	59	—
Keri & Benedek (2007)	Budapest	UHR	16	—	—	—
Eastvold et al. (2007)	CARE, San Diego (USA)	UHR; NS	40	21	51	5
Chung et al. (2008)	Seoul (SCOR)	UHR	33	21	58	—
Özgürdal et al. (2009)	BoFit, Bochum (GER)	UHR; BS	54	25	63	—
Frommann et al. (2010)	Multi-site, (GER)	UHR; BS	205	25	60–66	—

Notes: BS = basic symptoms; UHR = ultra high-risk; STD = schizotypal disorder; STPD = schizotypal personality disorder; BPRS = Brief Psychiatric Rating Scale.

there is no clear mapping of single neuropsychological tests to clearly circumscribed functional domains. Different authors rather subsume identical tests under diversely labelled domains and define the same cognitive domain by quite different tests. At first sight the impression of a more or less generalized neurocognitive deficit profile in clinically identified HR subjects is received (Table 6.2), because there is at least some evidence of abnormal functioning across all investigated domains. However, when the focus is shifted from significant abnormalities to negative findings of missing differences to controls, conclusions become much less clear.

Perceptual (preattentive) abilities

Perceptual abilities are usually viewed as demanding no or small amounts of attentive processing. Silverstein et al. (2006) did not find any differences between 70 HR subjects and controls in a perceptual organization task in terms of reaction time and accuracy. The authors concluded that abnormal perceptual organization is not a feature of risk status, but is linked to chronicity in schizophrenia and maybe to neuroleptic medication. More evidence of intact pattern recognition functions in 128 HR subjects was reported by Pukrop et al. (2006) for a visual backward masking task using four different stimulus conditions.

Table 6.2 Published journal articles with neurocognitive baseline assessments for the comparison of clinical high-risk (HR) samples with an unknown conversion-to-psychosis status and normal controls (NC)

Neurocognitive function	Test(s)	Significant abnormalities (HR ≠ NC)	Negative findings (HR = NC)
Perception	Perceptual organization; VBM; visual binding; BODI; MCPT	Keri & Benedek (2007) Koethe et al. (2009) Parnas et al. (2001)	Pukrop et al. (2007) Silverstein et al. (2006)
Psychomotor functions	Reaction time; TMT-A; Pegboard; Finger Tapping; fine motor control	Frommann et al. (2010) Gschwandtner et al. (2006) Lencz et al. (2006) Niendam et al. (2006)	Brewer et al. (2005) Chung et al. (2008) Hawkins et al. (2004) Keefe et al. (2006) Parnas et al. (2001)
Attention	Continuous Performance Test	Francey et al. (2005) Frommann et al. (2010) Gschwandtner et al. (2006) Hawkins et al. (2004) Lencz et al. (2006) Pflüger et al. (2007) Pukrop et al. (2006)	Frommann et al. (2010) Keefe et al. (2006) Pflüger et al. (2007) Pukrop et al. (2006)
	Stroop Colour Word; TAP; global/local	Chung et al. (2008) Hawkins et al. (2004) Simon et al. (2007)	Brewer et al. (2005) Özgürdal et al. (2009) Parnas et al. (2001) Simon et al. (2007)
Working Memory (WM)	Verbal WM: span tasks; TAP; DMTS; SOPT	Eastvold et al. (2007) Frommann et al. (2010) Gschwandtner et al. (2006) Hawkins et al. (2004) Lencz et al. (2006) Pflüger et al. (2007) Pukrop et al. (2006) Simon et al. (2007)	Chung et al. (2008) Frommann et al. (2010) Keefe et al. (2006) Niendam et al. (2007) Wood et al. (2003)
	Spatial WM: HT; SL; Dot test; DRT	Chung et al. (2008) Smith et al. (2006) Wood et al. (2003)	Hawkins et al. (2004) Keefe et al. (2006) Parnas et al. (2001) Pukrop et al. (2006)
Verbal long-term memory	Word lists (A/C/H/RVLT)	Eastvold et al. (2007) Frommann et al. (2010) Hawkins et al. (2004) Lencz et al. (2006) Niendam et al. (2006) Pukrop et al. (2006) Simon et al. (2007)	Brewer et al. (2005) Chung et al. (2008) Keefe et al. (2006) Özgürdal et al. (2009)

	Wechsler Memory Scale	Lencz et al. (2006) Niendam et al. (2006)	Brewer et al. (2005) Trotman et al. (2006)
Visual long-term memory	Wechsler Memory Scale; ROFT	Brewer et al. (2005)	Chung et al. (2008) Hawkins et al. (2004) Lencz et al. (2006) Niendam et al. (2006) Pukrop et al. (2006)
Executive functions	Verbal fluency	Frommann et al. (2010) Hawkins et al. (2004) Keefe et al. (2006) Pukrop et al. (2006) Simon et al. (2007)	Brewer et al. (2005) Chung et al. (2008) Özgürdal et al. (2009)
	WCST; ToH; Matrix Reasoning	Eastvold et al. (2007) Gschwandtner et al. (2006) Pflüger et al. (2007) Simon et al. (2007)	Chung et al. (2008) Gschwandtner et al. (2006) Niendam et al. (2006) Özgürdal et al. (2009) Pukrop et al. (2006)
Processing speed	Digit Symbol Coding Test	Brewer et al. (2005) Frommann et al. (2010) Hawkins et al. (2004) Keefe et al. (2006)	
	TMT-B	Chung et al. (2008) Frommann et al. (2010) Hawkins et al. (2004) Niendam et al. (2006) Simon et al. (2007)	Brewer et al. (2005) Özgürdal et al. (2009)
	Stroop – Colour Naming; Go/Nogo	Chung et al. (2008) Eastvold et al. (2007) Gschwandtner et al. (2006) Pflüger et al. (2007)	
IQ	Premorbid IQ: NART; MCVT; WRAT	Gschwandtner et al. (2006) Lencz et al. (2006) Pflüger et al. (2007) Simon et al. (2007)	Brewer et al. (2005) Frommann et al. (2010) Keefe et al. (2006) Özgürdal et al. (2009) Silverstein et al. (2006) Simon et al. (2007) Wood et al. (2003)

(continued)

Table 6.2 Continued.

Full-scale IQ: WAIS-R; LPS; Raven	Brewer et al. (2005) Eastvold et al. (2007) Gschwandtner et al. (2006) Lencz et al. (2006)	Chung et al. (2008) Hawkins et al. (2004) Niendam et al. (2006) Özgürdal et al. (2009) Parnas et al. (2001) Pflüger et al. (2007) Smith et al. (2006) Trotman et al. (2006)

Notes: VBM = Visual Backward Masking; BODI = Binocular Depth Inversion; MCPT = Magnocellular Pathway Test; TMT-A/B = Trailmaking Test A/B; TAP = Testbatterie zur Aufmerksamkeitsprüfung (Test Battery for Attention); DMTS = Delayed-matching-to-sample; SOPT = Subject Ordered Pointing Task; HT = Hidden Tokens; SL = Spatial Location; DRT = Delayed Response Task; A/C/H/RVLT = Auditory/California/Hopkins/Rey Verbal Learning Test; ROFT = Rey Osterrieth Figure Test; WCST = Wisconsin Card Sorting Test; ToH = Tower of Hanoi; NART = National Adult Reading Test; MCVT = Multiple Choice Vocabulary Test; WRAT = Wide Range Achievement Test; WAIS-R = Wechsler Adult Intelligence Scale–Revised; LPS = Leistungsprüfsystem (performance test system).

On the other hand, Parnas et al. (2001) identified enhanced Gestalt extraction in an HR sample ($n = 10$) in two out of three visual binding tasks. The authors suggest an obtrusive, conspicuous and salient appearance of objects and a degraded, faded sense of context information as a particular perceptual style during prodromal phases of the illness. This finding was supported by a study demonstrating elevated contrast sensitivity during a magnocellular visual pathway test but not a parvocellular pathway test (Keri & Benedek, 2007) in 16 HR subjects. Results suggest hyper-reactive magnocellular pathways being responsible for abnormal intensity perception of environmental stimuli. More evidence of disturbed visual perception comes from a study using the binocular depth inversion illusion test demonstrating higher illusion scores in 22 HR subjects (Koethe et al., 2009).

Psychomotor functions

The Trailmaking Test A (TMT-A) is often used to test psychomotor function because of its very low cognitive load. Three studies reported no abnormalities in HR subjects using the TMT-A (Brewer et al., 2005; Chung, Kang, Shin, Yoo, & Kwon, 2008; Hawkins et al., 2004). Further negative evidence was provided by a finger oscillation test (Keefe et al., 2006) and a simple reaction-time task (Parnas et al., 2001).

A positive finding was reported by Lencz et al. (2006) for a motor speed component defined by TMT-A, Finger Tapping and a Pegboard Test in 38 HR subjects. Consistently, abnormalities could be observed by a Finger Tapping Test (Niendam et al., 2006) and the TMT-A (Frommann et al., 2010). Applying a more comprehensive battery for testing fine motor functions revealed abnormalities in three out of five indexes (dexterity and two velocity parameters; Gschwandtner et al., 2006; $n = 60$). Thus, despite mixed evidence, psychomotor functions should be considered for more detailed analysis in future studies.

Attention

It should be noted that attentional capacities cannot be measured exclusively, but are always linked to other cognitive abilities such as working-memory functions. Most frequently, the Continuous Performance Test (CPT; Cornblatt, 1996) has been used to capture sustained and selective attention functions. HR subjects performed both significantly worse than controls in CPT parameters (Francey et al., 2005; Gschwandtner et al., 2006; Hawkins et al., 2004; Lencz et al., 2006; Pflüger, Gschwandtner, Stieglitz, & Riecher-Rössler, 2007) and at a normal level of functioning (Keefe et al., 2006; Özgürdal et al., 2009). Three studies subdividing large HR samples of 205, 128 and 93 subjects into early and late prodromal states found CPT or similarly measured abnormalities only for the late prodromal state (defined by attenuated or brief psychotic symptoms), but not for the early prodrome predominantly defined by basic symptoms (Frommann et al., 2010; Pukrop et al., 2006; Simon et al., 2007).

Other than CPT measures of attention revealing negative findings in HR samples were a selective attention task and a global local test (Parnas et al., 2001) or the Stroop Colour and Word test (Brewer et al., 2005; Özgürdal et al., 2009), although the latter one also provided positive evidence (Chung et al., 2008; Hawkins et al., 2004). Thus, at least for HR subjects defined by UHR criteria, there is ample evidence that attention measures such as the CPT or the Stroop test can indicate an increased clinical risk for psychosis.

Verbal (and nonspatial) working-memory functions

Working-memory functions are frequently tested by verbal material or by information that can be verbally represented. The material must be held online for a short period of time to reproduce it from short-term-memory storage, or it is required to manipulate the information in some way. Most frequently, the Letter-Number Span (LNS), simple Digit Span tests or initial learning trials of standard word lists were applied demonstrating both clear abnormalities (Eastvold, Heaton, & Cadenhead, 2007; Frommann et al., 2010; Hawkins et al., 2004; Pukrop et al., 2006; Simon et al., 2007) and no differences to controls (Chung et al., 2008; Frommann et al., 2010; Keefe et al., 2006; Niendam et al., 2006). A working-memory index defined by two-back tasks revealed further significant differences to controls (Gschwandtner et al., 2006; Pflüger et al., 2007). Moreover, this index was the best discriminating parameter within a larger test battery (Pflüger et al., 2007). Selective deficits within the cognitive performance profile were also reported by Lencz et al. (2006) using a composite score for working memory/ executive functions (LNS, Digit Span, Wisconsin Card Sorting Test, verbal and figural fluency, TMT-B).

Two less frequently used tests produced inconsistent results. A delayed matching-to-sample task revealed an overall group difference, but post hoc tests did not become significant ($n = 98$ HR subjects; Wood et al., 2003). Moreover, subjects supposed to be in a late prodromal state scored abnormally on the Subject Ordered Pointing Task (SOPT), but not those in an early prodromal state as defined by the presence of basic symptoms (Frommann et al., 2010).

Spatial working-memory functions

There is some evidence for spatial working-memory malfunctions using a simple visual span task (Wood et al., 2003), a spatial location task (Chung et al., 2008), or the number of errors (but not a strategy score) when hidden tokens should be located (Wood et al., 2003). Furthermore, a delayed-response task revealed significant differences to controls in a small sample of 8 HR subjects (Smith, Park, & Cornblatt, 2006).

On the other hand, there are clear negative findings on working-memory tasks emphasizing spatial processing. Using a similar delayed response task as Smith et al., in an HR sample of 128 subjects no abnormalities could be observed (Pukrop et al., 2006). Moreover, a Dot test (Hawkins et al., 2004; Keefe et al., 2006) and a position test (Parnas et al., 2001) did not indicate any norm deviances.

Verbal memory and learning

Either standard word lists (California/Auditory/Rey/Hopkins Verbal Learning Test) or subscales of the Wechsler Memory Scale in its revised version (WMS-R) have been used to investigate long-term verbal memory functions. There is strong evidence for clear abnormalities in word-learning tests (Eastvold et al., 2007; Frommann et al., 2010; Hawkins et al., 2004; Pukrop et al., 2006; Simon et al., 2007). Moreover, Lencz et al. (2006) and Niendam et al. (2006) found significant impairments using a composite of a verbal-learning test and the WMS-R, indicating even a selective impairment when contrasted with other cognitive domains (Lencz et al., 2006) and being significantly correlated with social functioning in HR subjects (Niendam et al., 2006).

However, a number of authors also reported no significant abnormalities in HR subjects with an unclear conversion status both for word lists (Brewer et al., 2005; Chung et al., 2008; Keefe et al., 2006; Özgürdal et al., 2009) and the WMS-R (Brewer et al., 2005; Trotman, McMillan, & Walker, 2006). Nevertheless, in particular, word-list learning seems to be a promising risk indicator.

Visual memory

Visual memory functions are usually measured by the visual reproduction subtests of the WMS-R consistently providing negative results (Hawkins et al., 2004; Lencz et al., 2006; Niendam et al., 2006). Further negative evidence stems from two studies (Chung et al., 2008; Pukrop et al., 2006) applying the Rey Osterrieth Figure Test. The only available positive finding for visual memory deficits in clinical HR samples was reported by Brewer et al. (2005) administering the WMS-R subscales.

Verbal executive functions (verbal fluency)

Using lexical or semantic verbal fluency tasks more positive findings (Frommann et al., 2010; Hawkins et al., 2004; Keefe et al., 2006; Pukrop et al., 2006; Simon et al., 2007) than negative ones (Brewer et al., 2005; Chung et al., 2008; Özgürdal et al., 2009) were provided. Moreover, a figural fluency test also indicated abnormal performance in HR subjects (Hawkins et al., 2004).

Executive functions

There is mixed evidence for the frequently used Wisconsin Card Sorting Test (WCST). Norm deviances in WCST performance could be demonstrated by some authors (Eastvold et al., 2007; Gschwandtner et al., 2006; Pflüger et al., 2007; Simon et al., 2007), but not by others (Chung et al., 2008; Özgürdal et al., 2009; Pukrop et al., 2006). Other measures used for the broad cognitive domain of executive functioning were the Tower of Hanoi with one positive (Pflüger et al., 2007) and one negative finding (Gschwandtner et al., 2006) and the Matrix Reasoning Test indicating no differences to controls (Niendam et al., 2006). In sum, when used as single measures, these tests do not seem to be reliable risk indicators.

Processing speed

Tests such as the Trailmaking Test-B (TMT-B) and the Digit Symbol Coding Test (DST), which have to be executed under time pressure and do not demand too much cognitive load, can serve as measures for the speed of cognitive processing. For the TMT-B there is strong evidence for abnormal functioning in HR samples (Chung et al., 2008; Frommann et al., 2010; Hawkins et al., 2004; Niendam et al., 2006; Simon et al., 2007), but also two negative findings have been reported (Brewer et al., 2005; Özgürdal et al., 2009). Exclusively positive evidence has been revealed for the DST (Brewer et al., 2005; Frommann et al., 2010; Hawkins et al., 2004; Keefe et al., 2006) the Stroop Colour Naming (Chung et al., 2008; Eastvold et al., 2007) and a Go/Nogo test (Gschwandtner et al., 2006; Pflüger et al., 2007). Moreover, Frommann et al. (2010) reported a processing speed compound measure (TMT-A and B, DST, verbal fluency) being selectively disturbed in the early prodrome defined by basic symptoms. Taking all findings together, processing speed seems to be a quite consistent marker of increased risk status.

Intellectual functions

Many studies used short tests of premorbid (verbal) intellectual capacity as a proxy for full-scale IQ, usually integrated as a covariate in the analyses of other neuropsychological functions. Whereas most authors did not report significant abnormalities (Brewer et al., 2005; Frommann et al., 2010; Keefe et al., 2006;

Özgürdal et al., 2009; Silverstein et al., 2006; Simon et al., 2007, for basic symptom criteria; Wood et al., 2003), others found HR subjects to present significantly low premorbid (verbal) IQ (Gschwandtner et al., 2006; Lencz et al., 2006; Pflüger et al., 2007; Simon et al., 2007, for UHR criteria).

The Wechsler Adult Intelligence Scale in its revised version (WAIS-R) was used for more comprehensive assessment of IQ. However, different compositions of subtests make it difficult to compare these results. Brewer et al. (2005) found clear abnormalities in performance IQ (and less in verbal IQ), that went back to the subtests Block Design and Digit Symbol. Further significant deviances were reported by Lencz et al. (2006; although HR subjects scored within the normal range), Eastvold et al. (2007) and Gschwandtner et al. (2006). Others failed to find norm deviances using the WAIS-R (Chung et al., 2008; Hawkins et al., 2004; Niendam et al., 2006; Smith et al., 2006; Trotman et al., 2006) or other standardized intelligence measures (Özgürdal et al., 2009; Parnas et al., 2001; Pflüger et al., 2007).

Social cognition and emotional processing

Chung et al. (2008) reported abnormalities in two tasks measuring theory of mind (ToM) related abilities in 33 HR subjects. Another hint stems from a genetic HR study (Marjoram et al., 2006) demonstrating significant ToM abnormalities in 12 symptomatic HR subjects, but not in 13 nonsymptomatic HR subjects. Tasks measuring facial emotion identification and discrimination observed both emotion identification deficits in $n = 86$ HR subjects (Addington, Penn, Woods, Addington, & Perkins, 2008) and intact emotion processing in $n = 19$ clinical HR individuals (Pinkham, Penn, Perkins, Graham, & Seigel, 2007).

Summary evaluation of cross-sectional studies with clinical HR samples

Summarizing the above presented evidence (Table 6.2) from baseline assessments in clinically defined HR samples for whom the true prodromal state is not yet clear, most convincing results have been collected for measures of processing speed (Digit Symbol Coding, TMT-B, Stroop Colour Naming, Go/Nogo). Moreover, significant abnormalities could be demonstrated rather consistently for the Continuous Performance Test, verbal (but not spatial) working-memory measures, long-term verbal (but not visual) memory and learning, verbal fluency (but not other executive function tests) and perceptual contrast sensitivity, though negative findings have also been reported in every instance. Only a few studies also reported effect sizes. Tests demanding the processing of verbal material in long-term or working memory under executive control usually produced the highest effect sizes from 0.74 up to 1.59 standard deviation units (Lencz et al., 2006; Simon et al., 2007). In terms of Cohen's *d* median effect sizes for HR samples across different cognitive domains were 0.49 (Brewer et al., 2005), $d = 0.34$ (Pukrop et al., 2006, for the late prodrome) and as low as 0.15 (Özgürdal et al., 2009).

Longitudinal follow-up assessments in clinical HR samples

The central problem of all cross-sectional baseline assessments is the high but unknown number of false-positive cases who cannot be considered as true prodromals. Thus, it is necessary to have long-term follow-up data to compare subjects who later convert to psychosis with those who do not convert after a sufficient observation period to obtain conversion indicators instead of increased risk indicators. Studies with follow-up data can be identified in Table 6.1 by the sample sizes listed for HR subjects who had converted to psychosis. An overview of results from long-term investigations is given in Table 6.3.

One analysis strategy is to calculate regression models within samples of converters and nonconverters to find out which neurocognitive functions significantly contribute to the prediction of psychosis outcome. Four longitudinal studies could be identified applying this methodological approach. Lencz et al. (2006) found low verbal memory performance, using the California Verbal Learning Test (CVLT) and Wechsler Memory Scale (WMS), together with positive symptom severity to be significant predictors for a transition to psychosis in samples of 12 converters and 21 nonconverters after six months to a maximum of five years observation period. This is rather consistent with data published by Pukrop et al. (2007) identifying verbal memory by means of the Auditory Verbal Learning Test (AVLT), premorbid verbal IQ and Digit Symbol Coding as significant predictors for a sample of 44 converters who developed psychosis within a median interval of 10 months when compared to sociodemographically matched 39 nonconverters (median observation period of three years).

A third prediction model has been calculated by Keefe et al. (2006) using neurocognitive data from 11 converters and 17 nonconverters after a one-year observation period. These authors found poor CPT performance and high scores on Digit Symbol Coding to be significant predictors. This suggests a combination of poor vigilance and a high processing speed making HR subjects particularly vulnerable. Moreover, nonconverters improved significantly over time whereas converters stayed at the baseline level. Finally, Riecher-Rössler et al. (2009) identified premorbid verbal IQ and a Go/Nogo speed of processing test together with positive symptoms (suspiciousness) and negative symptoms (anhedonia/asociality) as significant predictors in 21 converters and 32 nonconverters after a median interval of 10 months (up to a maximum of seven years). Fit values were rather similar across all four studies (sensitivity 0.75–0.83; specificity 0.79 for all models). Neurocognitive variables, that did not enter the prediction models can be derived from Table 6.3 (negative evidence).

A second strategy is to search for significant baseline differences between HR subjects who converted to psychosis and those who did not convert. The biggest sample of converters published so far ($n = 44$; Pukrop et al., 2007) differed from normal controls in all neurocognitive measures (visual backward masking, LNS, SOPT, dual tasking, verbal and visual memory, TMT-B, Digit Symbol, verbal fluency and premorbid verbal IQ), except for WCST, CPT and spatial working memory (delayed response task). The median effect size across all domains was

Table 6.3 Published journal articles with neurocognitive follow-up assessments for the comparison of clinical high-risk (HR) subjects converting to psychosis and HR subjects not converting

Neurocognitive function	Test(s)	Positive evidence	Negative evidence
Perception	Perceptual organization; VBM; olfactory identification	Brewer et al. (2003)	Pukrop et al. (2007) Silverstein et al. (2006)
Psychomotor functions	TMT-A; Finger Tapping		Brewer et al. (2005) Hawkins et al. (2004) Keefe et al. (2006)
Attention	Continuous Performance Test	Keefe et al. (2006)	Brewer et al. (2005) Hawkins et al. (2004) Pukrop et al. (2007) Riecher-Rössler et al. (2009)
	Stroop Colour Word; Dual Tasking		Brewer et al. (2005) Pukrop et al. (2007
Working Memory (WM)	Verbal WM: span tasks; TAP; DMTS; SOPT	Pukrop et al. (2007)	Hawkins et al. (2004) Keefe et al. (2006) Lencz et al. (2006) Pukrop et al. (2007) Riecher-Rössler et al. (2009) Walder et al. (2008) Wood et al. (2003)
	Spatial WM: HT; SL; Dot test; DRT		Keefe et al. (2006) Pukrop et al. (2007) Wood et al. (2003)
Verbal memory	Word lists (A/C/H/ RVLT)	Lencz et al. (2006) Pukrop et al. (2007)	Brewer et al. (2005) Hawkins et al. (2004) Keefe et al. (2006)
	Wechsler Memory Scale	Brewer et al. (2005) Lencz et al. (2006)	Walder et al. (2008)
Visual memory	Wechsler Memory Scale; ROFT	Brewer et al. (2005)	Hawkins et al. (2004) Pukrop et al. (2007) Walder et al. (2008)
Executive functions	Verbal fluency	Pukrop et al. (2007)	Brewer et al. (2005) Hawkins et al. (2004) Keefe et al. (2006) Lencz et al. (2006) Pukrop et al. (2007)

	WCST; ToH		Hawkins et al. (2004) Lencz et al. (2006) Pukrop et al. (2007) Riecher-Rössler et al. (2009)
Processing speed	Digit Symbol Coding Test	Keefe et al. (2006) Pukrop et al. (2007)	Hawkins et al. (2004)
	TMT-B	Pukrop et al. (2007)	Brewer et al. (2005) Hawkins et al. (2004) Lencz et al. (2006) Pukrop et al. (2007)
	Go/Nogo	Riecher-Rössler et al. (2009)	
IQ	Premorbid IQ: NART; MCVT	Pukrop et al. (2007) Riecher-Rössler et al. (2009)	Wood et al. (2003)
	Full-scale IQ: WAIS-R; LPS		Brewer et al. (2005) Lencz et al. (2006) Riecher-Rössler et al. (2009) Walder et al. (2008)

Notes: VBM = Visual Backward Masking; TMT-A/B = Trailmaking Test A/B; TAP = Testbatterie zur Aufmerksamkeitsprüfung (Test Battery for Attention); DMTS = Delayed-matching-to-sample; SOPT = Subject Ordered Pointing Task; HT = Hidden Tokens; SL = Spatial Location; DRT = Delayed Response Task; A/C/H/RVLT = Auditory/California/Hopkins/Rey Verbal Learning Test; ROFT = Rey Osterrieth Figure Test; WCST = Wisconsin Card Sorting Test; ToH = Tower of Hanoi; NART = National Adult Reading Test; MCVT = Multiple Choice Vocabulary Test; WAIS-R = Wechsler Adult Intelligence Scale-Revised; LPS = Leistungsprüfsystem (performance test system).

$d = 0.74$ with highest values for premorbid verbal IQ (1.06), Digit Symbol Coding (1.01) and TMT-B (0.93). When compared with nonconverters ($n = 39$) those HR subjects who transited to psychosis showed significantly worse performance in processing speed measures (TMT-B, Digit Symbol Coding), working memory (SOPT), verbal memory (AVLT) and verbal fluency, but not in the other measures listed above. Highest effect sizes for the comparison between converters and nonconverters were obtained for Digit Symbol (0.88) and verbal IQ (0.67).

Brewer et al. (2005) found significantly worse long-term-memory performance for verbal and visual material (WMS) in 34 converters after one to three years. There were no differences to nonconverters in full-scale IQ (WAIS), verbal learning and memory by word lists, attention (Stroop test), verbal fluency, processing speed (TMT-B), psychomotor functions (TMT-A) and CPT as revealed in a separate study (Francey et al., 2005). Those who developed a schizophrenia spectrum psychosis had a median effect size of 0.39 across domains when compared with healthy controls with strongest effects for the WMS index (0.79), premorbid verbal IQ (0.76) and performance IQ (0.70). The same research team (Brewer et al., 2003) reported significantly impaired olfactory identification for those who converted to schizophrenia spectrum psychosis (*n* = 12), when compared to healthy controls, nonconverters and converters to psychoses other than schizophrenia spectrum psychoses.

Another piece of positive evidence stems from Hoffman et al. (2007), who noted a tendency to extract spurious, message-like meaning from meaningless noise measured by word length of speech illusions *being significantly* more pronounced in nonmedicated HR subjects when compared to HR subjects on neuroleptic medication (*n* = 43). Moreover, the word-length variable was significantly associated with conversion to psychosis (*n* = 12). Niendam et al. (2007) found improvement in social and role functioning, after eight months in *n* = 35 HR subjects, to be associated with neurocognitive improvement in a processing speed compound measure (TMT-A, TMT-B, verbal fluency, Digit Symbol Coding) and in visual memory performance (WMS). Eastvold et al. (2007) reported remarkably high effect sizes for a small group of converters (*n* = 5) relative to healthy controls at baseline for verbal memory (*d* = 1.34) and IQ (Vocabulary subtest; *d* = 1.28).

Mostly negative findings of missing differences between converters and nonconverters were provided by the following authors: Hawkins et al. (2008) collected follow-up data from 21 HR subjects converting within 12 months, who did not differ significantly from nonconverters across all neurocognitive domains: psychomotor functions, CPT, visual and verbal working memory (LNS), verbal and figural fluency, verbal learning and memory (CVLT), visual memory (WMS), processing speed (Digit Symbol, Stroop, TMT-B) and executive functions (WCST). Moreover, neither treatment with antipsychotics nor conversion to psychosis yielded a significant impact on neuropsychological functioning. Wood et al. (2003) found no significant differences between nine converters when compared with nonconverters after a 12–34 months observation period in spatial and other working-memory measures and in premorbid verbal IQ. However, spatial working-memory performance was significantly correlated with negative symptoms in the later-psychotic group.

Furthermore, a neurocognitive summary score did not differ from first-episode schizophrenia anymore after conversion had taken place in 11 HR subjects, but there were no differences to nonconverters at baseline. Using a perceptual organization task, Silverstein et al. (2006) did not find any differences between converters to psychosis (*n* = 24) and those HR subjects who developed mood disorders after two years. Finally, Walder, Mittal, Trotman, McMillan, and Walker (2008) could not identify significantly different baseline assessments for converters (*n* = 12) and nonconverters after four years in full-scale IQ (WAIS), verbal and visual memory (WMS) and verbal working memory (LNS).

Summarizing long-term studies in clinical HR samples, conclusions must be handled cautiously because of the few studies available with bigger sample sizes (Table 6.1). Measures of processing speed and of verbal memory (and premorbid verbal IQ) seem to be most promising so far in predicting conversion to psychosis in clinical HR samples. Particularly, standard word lists or the Wechsler Memory Scale for verbal memory and the Digit Symbol Coding or a Go/Nogo test for processing speed can be recommended for prediction purposes. This conclusion fits nicely with a recent meta-analysis on neurocognitive abnormalities in patients with schizophrenia and their non-affected siblings (Dickinson, Ramsey, & Gold, 2007). These authors identified the Digit Symbol Coding as producing the largest effect sizes in both schizophrenia patients and siblings followed by verbal memory and learning measures. Together with extensive use of the frontotemporal networks involved in verbal memory tasks (and maybe also in verbal IQ tests), speed of processing may be a useful indicator of risk for conversion to psychosis within the next few months or years. These findings are consistent with the recent North American Prodrome Longitudinal Study (NAPLS) Group paper on neuropsychological predictors of transition to psychosis (Seidman et al., 2010).

Longitudinal follow-up assessments in birth-cohort studies

Birth-cohort studies follow up large epidemiological samples from infancy, childhood or adolescence to adulthood until they have passed through the period of risk for onset of psychosis. Usually neurocognitive assessments have been limited to measures of general intellectual functioning because of high time and effort investment.

Within the National Collaborative Perinatal Project (Cannon, Bearden, & Hollister, 2000; Niendam et al., 2003), 46 patients with schizophrenia or schizoaffective disorder identified by chart-review-based DSM-IV diagnoses and their 33 unaffected siblings performed significantly worse than 5127 controls on the Stanford-Binet Intelligence Scale and the Wechsler Intelligence Scale for Children (WISC) at ages 4 and 7, respectively, after adjustment for sociodemographic differences. However, patients and their unaffected siblings did not differ from each other at both childhood assessments. Because there was no intra-individual decline between age 4 and age 7, premorbid cognitive dysfunction was viewed as representing a relatively stable indicator of vulnerability in this study. Moreover, there was a linear relationship between IQ at ages 4 and 7 and diagnostic outcome in adulthood, suggesting that dysfunction was not restricted to a risk subgroup at the lowest performance level. A further analysis of seven WISC subtests at age 7 in 32 subjects who later developed schizophrenia revealed significant differences to normal controls for Picture Arrangement, Vocabulary and Digit Symbol Coding and to their healthy siblings only in the Digit Symbol Coding subtest.

Investigating another subsample of the same US national project ($n = 547$), Kremen et al. (1998) reported that IQ decline between ages 4 and 7 and not low IQ at age 7 itself was a significant predictor for psychotic symptoms at age 23. Seidman, Buka, Goldstein, and Tsuang (2006) could retest 26 subjects from this sample who finally were diagnosed with schizophrenia and compare them with 59 controls at age 35. Patients with schizophrenia had significantly lower full-scale IQ scores at age 7 (and on WISC subtests Digit Symbol Coding, Digit

Span and Information with effects of > 0.6 *SD*s). Moreover, there was a significant decline from age 7 to age 35 of about 10 points in full-scale IQ.

For a British birth cohort (*n* = 5362), Jones and Rodgers (1994) reported significantly lower test scores for educational tests at ages 8, 11 and 15 in 30 cases who later developed schizophrenia. Again, increased risk was not confined to a subgroup with very low scores. Similar results were obtained from a Swedish birth-cohort study including 18-year-old male army conscripts (*n* = 49,968) finding a linear relationship between general IQ and risk for schizophrenia (*n* = 192 patients) up to 13 years later (David, Malmberg, Brandt, Allebeck, & Lewis, 1997). Those subjects developing schizophrenia and nonpsychotic comparison subjects differed in subtests for verbal abilities and mechanical knowledge, but not in visuospatial abilities and general knowledge.

Finally, in an Israeli historical prospective study the cognitive assessment of males at ages 16 to 17 was significantly related to hospitalization because of schizophrenia in adulthood. Schizophrenia cases (*n* = 509) differed from sociodemographically matched 9215 subjects without a psychiatric history on general IQ measures (Davidson et al., 1999). Together with social functioning and organizational abilities, intellectual functioning reached a sensitivity of 75% and a specificity of 100%. A later reanalysis of an even bigger sample of 1856 patients with hospitalization for schizophrenia demonstrated that a lower than expected IQ at age 17 (defined by a discrepancy between premorbid reading/spelling abilities and actual IQ) was the strongest predictor with high specificity for schizophrenia: lower than expected IQ was not associated with bipolar disorder, depression or anxiety disorders (Reichenberg et al., 2005).

In sum, results from birth-cohort studies consistently demonstrated reduced intellectual functioning in childhood and adolescence for those cohort members who later developed schizophrenia in adulthood. Particularly, further decline and lower IQ than expected from more unaffected functions were the strongest and most specific predictors of schizophrenia outcome. Moreover, on a subtest level, the strongest predictive evidence has been collected for the Digit Symbol Coding and for tests measuring verbal abilities. The latter finding corresponds well with results from clinical HR research favouring the Digit Symbol Coding, verbal memory and premorbid verbal IQ measures as transition indicators. However, results from birth-cohort studies would imply that these indicators can be abnormal since infancy or childhood and may show further decline later on.

Longitudinal follow-up assessments in genetic HR studies

In genetic HR research the offspring or other relatives of psychotic patients are investigated, who have not yet passed the period of risk. Major problems with this approach are the length of follow-up period and the limited representativeness, because only about 10 to 15% of first-episode patients have a positive family history. There is one study testing the joint effects of genetic risk (*n* = 98) and clinical risk status (*n* = 113) demonstrating that these two risk factors exert independent effects on neurocognitive deficits and that genetic risk has a broader impact than clinical status (Myles-Worsley et al., 2007). Thus, neurocognitive impairments can be genetically mediated and occur in genetically vulnerable individuals regardless of clinical symptoms indicating the possibility of different aetiologies for genetically and clinically defined HR states.

Similar to clinical HR samples, there is again evidence from cross-sectional assessments for abnormalities across a wide range of neurocognitive functions in genetically defined HR subjects, which has been summarized in numerous reviews (Cornblatt & Obuchowski, 1997; Keshavan, Diwadkar, Montrose, Rajarethinam, & Sweeney, 2005; Niemi, Suvisaari, Tuulio-Henriksson, & Lönnqvist, 2003; Owens-Cunningham & Johnstone, 2006; Seidman et al., 2006). Therefore, the present review will focus on studies that have followed through to the period of maximum illness risk in adulthood and that used more comprehensive neuropsychological test batteries that had been applied at baseline.

The Edinburgh High-Risk Study concentrated on young adults between 16 and 25 years who have at least two close relatives with schizophrenia and followed them up for 10 years. In more recent publications covering the full 10-year duration of the study, 118 subjects at familial HR of schizophrenia, subdivided into those with no symptoms at all ($n = 49$), those experiencing at least one psychotic symptom ($n = 56$) and subjects who later developed schizophrenia ($n = 13$), were compared with 30 healthy controls (Byrne et al., 2003; Cosway et al., 2002; Johnstone, Ebmeier, Miller, Owens, & Lawrie, 2005; O'Connor et al., 2009; Whyte et al., 2006). Contrasts between controls and the total HR sample became significant for the majority of neuropsychological measures revealing a medium effect size of 0.56. However, symptomatic and never-symptomatic HR subjects did not differ from each other and from those who transited to psychosis on all measures (premorbid verbal IQ, Rivermead Behavioural Memory Test, Hayling Sentence Completion Test, Digit Symbol Coding, WMS-visual memory, CPT, Stroop test, full-scale IQ, verbal fluency, spatial working memory and Tower-of-London). The only exception was verbal memory (AVLT) revealing a difference between those developing schizophrenia and the other two HR samples. Furthermore, there was no clear pattern of deterioration over time indicating rather stable trait deficits in the total HR sample. The authors conclude that neuropsychological deficits mainly represent a genetic vulnerability present in all relatives independent of the level of genetic liability. Thus, the cognitive decline observed in manifest schizophrenia may be attributable to processes occurring in childhood or adolescence rather than a prodromal period close to psychosis onset.

The New York High-Risk Project recruited 79 offspring of parents with schizophrenia, 57 offspring of affectively ill parents and 133 offspring of normal controls who had complete neurocognitive data at age 9 and could be followed up during six rounds of clinical evaluations (Erlenmeyer-Kimling et al., 2000). Sixteen subjects developed schizophrenia-related psychosis assessed at age 31 and their mean performance on all tasks (CPT, Digit Span/Attention Span, fine and gross motor skills) was worse than in the two offspring control groups at age 9. Path analyses revealed significant relationships between attention (CPT), verbal working memory (Digit and Attention Span) and gross (but not fine) motor skills and onset of schizophrenia-related psychosis but not with other major axis I disorders. Sensitivity and specificity for identifying future development of schizophrenia-related psychoses were 83% and 72% for working memory and 58% and 82% for attention, respectively. Moreover, attention and working-memory deficits were stable in subjects with schizophrenia-like symptoms or manifest schizophrenia across several evaluations from age 9 to age 26 (Cornblatt, Obuchowski, Roberts, Pollack, & Erlenmeyer-Kimling, 1999). The authors suggest these neurobehavioural measures being rather specific phenotypic indicators of the genetic liability to schizophrenia that together with offspring-of-schizophrenic-parents status are significant predictors of future development of schizophrenia. On the other hand, general intelligence (WISC) at age 9 and WCST performance at age 26 could not be related to adulthood schizophrenia at age 31 (Ott et al., 1998; Wolf, Cornblatt, Roberts, Shapiro, & Erlenmeyer-Kimling, 2002). However, similar to the Israeli birth-cohort study (Reichenberg et al., 2005), the difference between IQ subtest Vocabulary and all other subtests reflecting the difference between crystallized and fluid intelligence was a significant predictor for schizophrenia in adulthood.

Further evidence for the predictive power of an attention measure comes from the Israeli High-Risk Study (Mirsky, Ingraham, & Kugelmass, 1995; Mirsky, Kugelmass, Ingraham, Frenkel, & Nathan, 1995), which recruited 50 HR cases with parents with schizophrenia and 50 controls, who were investigated at ages 11, 17, 26 and again at 32. At the most recent assessment 13 subjects had developed a schizophrenia spectrum disorder and differed significantly from those who developed affective disorders ($n = 25$) or no psychiatric disorders ($n = 98$) in a letter cancellation task at age 11 but not at age 17.

The Copenhagen High-Risk Study could follow up a sample of 311 participants including 207 offspring of mothers with schizophrenia from childhood to the mean age of 39 (Sorensen, Mortensen, Parnas, & Mednick, 2006). All subjects were tested by the WISC (including 12 subtests) at age 15. Subjects developing a schizophrenia-spectrum disorder as adults ($n = 84$) differed significantly from both healthy subjects ($n = 127$) and those with other psychiatric diagnoses ($n = 81$) on the Digit Symbol Coding subtest (effect sizes $d = 0.41$ and 0.30, respectively) but not on full-scale IQ and all other 11 subtests. However, a cognitive functioning score defined by the total WISC did not contribute to the prediction of schizophrenia within a multivariate prediction model revealing the interaction of genetic risk status and rearing environment as significant predictors (Carter, Schulsinger, Parnas, Cannon, & Mednick, 2002).

In sum, there is evidence from genetic HR studies, that followed up the offspring of parents with schizophrenia through the period of maximum risk, for the predictive validity of attention (CPT, letter cancellation), Digit Symbol Coding, verbal memory (AVLT), verbal working memory (Digit Span) and maybe intellectual decline. These predictive deficits are again similar to those identified in clinical HR samples and may indicate a genetically mediated vulnerability observable as stable traits from childhood onward.

References

Addington, J., Penn, D., Woods, S. W., Addington, D., & Perkins, D. (2008). Facial affect recognition in individuals at clinical high risk for psychosis. *British Journal of Psychiatry, 192*, 67–68.

Brewer, W. J., Francey, S. M., Wood, S. J., Jackson, H. J., Pantelis, C., Phillips, L. J., et al. (2005). Memory impairments identified in people at ultra-high risk for psychosis who later develop first-episode psychosis. *American Journal of Psychiatry, 162*, 71–78.

Brewer, W. J., Wood, S. J., McGorry, P. D., Francey, S. M., Phillips, L. J., Yung, A. R., et al. (2003). Impairment of olfactory identification ability in individuals at ultra-high risk for psychosis who later develop schizophrenia. *American Journal of Psychiatry, 160*, 1790–1794.

Byrne, M., Clafferty, B. A., Cosway, R., Grant, E., Hodges, A., Whalley, H. C., et al. (2003). Neuropsychology, genetic liability and psychotic symptoms in those at high risk of schizophrenia. *Journal of Abnormal Psychology, 112*, 38–48.

Cannon, T. D., Bearden, C. E., & Hollister, J. M. (2000). Childhood cognitive functioning in schizophrenia patients and their unaffected siblings: A prospective cohort study. *Schizophrenia Bulletin, 26*, 379–393.

Carter, J. W., Schulsinger, F., Parnas, J., Cannon, T., & Mednick, S. A. (2002). A multivariate prediction model of schizophrenia. *Schizophrenia Bulletin, 28*, 649–682.

Chung, Y. S., Kang, D. H., Shin, N. Y., Yoo, S. Y., & Kwon, J. S. (2008). Deficit of theory of mind in individuals at ultra-high-risk for schizophrenia. *Schizophrenia Research, 99*, 111–118.

Cornblatt, B. A. (1996). *Continuous Performance Test—Identical Pairs Version computer software.* New York, NY: Author.

Cornblatt, B., & Obuchowski, M. (1997). Update of high-risk research: 1987–1997. *International Review of Psychiatry, 9*, 437–447.

Cornblatt, B., Obuchowski, M., Roberts, S., Pollack, S., & Erlenmeyer-Kimling, L. (1999). Cognitive and behavioral precursors of schizophrenia. *Developmental Psychopathology, 11*, 487–508.

Cosway, R., Byrne, M., Clafferty, R., Hodges, A., Grant, E., Morris, J., et al. (2002). Sustained attention in young people at high risk for schizophrenia. *Psychological Medicine, 32*, 277–286.

David, A. S., Malmberg, A., Brandt, L., Allebeck, P., & Lewis, G. (1997). IQ and risk for schizophrenia: A population-based cohort study. *Psychological Medicine, 27*, 1311–1323.

Davidson, M., Reichenberg, A., Rabinowitz, J., Weiser, M., Kaplan, Z., & Mark, M. (1999). Behavioral and intellectual markers for schizophrenia in apparently healthy male adolescents. *American Journal of Psychiatry, 156*, 1328–1335.

Dickinson, D., Ramsey, E. M., & Gold, J. M. (2007). Overlooking the obvious. A meta-analytic comparison of digit symbol coding tasks and other cognitive measures in schizophrenia. *Archives of General Psychiatry, 64*, 532–542.

Eastvold, A. D., Heaton, R. K., & Cadenhead, K. S. (2007). Neurocognitive deficits in the (putative) prodrome and first episode of psychosis. *Schizophrenia Research, 93*, 266–277.

Erlenmeyer-Kimling, L., Rock, D., Roberts, S. A., Janal, M., Kestenbaum, C., Cornblatt, B., et al. (2000). Attention, memory and motor skills as childhood predictors of schizophrenia-related psychoses: The New York High-Risk Project. *American Journal of Psychiatry, 157*, 1416–1422.

92   *Pukrop and Ruhrmann*

Francey, S. M., Jackson, H. J., Phillips, L. J., Wood, S. J., Yung, A. R., & McGorry, P. D. (2005). Sustained attention in young people at high risk of psychosis does not predict transition to psychosis. *Schizophrenia Research, 79,* 127–136.

Frommann, I., Pukrop, R., Brinkmeyer, J., Bechdolf, A., Ruhrmann, S., Berning, J., et al. (2010). Neuropsychological profiles in different at-risk states of psychosis: Executive control impairment in the early—and additional memory dysfunction in the late—prodromal state. *Schizophrenia Bulletin* [epub ahead of print].

Gschwandtner, U., Pflüger, M., Aston, J., Borgwardt, S., Drewe, M., Stieglitz, R.-D., et al. (2006). Fine motor function and neuropsychological deficits in individuals at risk for schizophrenia. *European Archives of Psychiatry and Clinical Neuroscience, 256,* 201–206.

Hawkins, K. A., Addington, J., Keefe, R. S. E., Christensen, B., Perkins, D. O., Zipursky, R., et al. (2004). Neuropsychological status of subjects at high risk for a first episode of psychosis. *Schizophrenia Research, 67,* 115–122.

Hawkins, K. A., Keefe, R. S. E., Christensen, B. K., Addington, J., Woods, S. W., Callahan, J., et al. (2008). Neuropsychological course in the prodrome and first episode of psychosis: Findings from the PRIME North America Double Blind Treatment Study. *Schizophrenia Research, 105,* 1–9.

Hoffman, R. E., Woods, S. W., Hawkins, K. A., Pittman, B., Tohen, M., Preda, A., et al. (2007). Extracting spurious messages from noise and risk of schizophrenia-spectrum disorders in a prodromal population. *British Journal of Psychiatry, 191,* 355–356.

Johnstone, E. C., Ebmeier, K. P., Miller, P., Owens, D. G. C., & Lawrie, S. M. (2005). Predicting schizophrenia: Findings from the Edinburgh High-Risk Study. *British Journal of Psychiatry, 186,* 18–25.

Jones, P., & Rodgers, B. (1994). Child developmental risk factors for adult schizophrenia in the British 1946 birth cohort. *Lancet, 344,* 1398–1402.

Keefe, R. S. E., Perkins, D. O., Gu, H., Zipursky, R. B., Christensen, B. K., & Liebermann, J. A. (2006). A longitudinal study of neurocognitive function in individuals at-risk for psychosis. *Schizophrenia Research, 88,* 26–35.

Keri, S., & Benedek, G. (2007). Visual contrast sensitivity alterations in inferred magnocellular pathways anomalous perceptual experiences in people at high-risk for psychosis. *Visual Neuroscience, 24,* 183–189.

Keshavan, M. S., Diwadkar, V. A., Montrose, D. M., Rajarethinam, R., & Sweeney, J. A. (2005). Premorbid indicators and risk for schizophrenia: A selective review and update. *Schizophrenia Research, 79,* 45–57.

Klosterkötter, J., Hellmich, M., Steinmeyer, E. M., & Schultze-Lutter, F. (2001). Diagnosing schizophrenia in the initial prodromal phase. *Archives of General Psychiatry, 58,* 158–164.

Koethe, D., Kranaster, L., Hoyer, C., Gross, S., Neatby, M. A., Schultze-Lutter, F., et al. (2009). Binocular depth inversion as a paradigm of reduced visual information processing in prodromal state, anti-psychotic naïve and treated schizophrenia. *European Archives of Psychiatry and Clinical Neuroscience, 259,* 195–202.

Kremen, W. S., Buka, S. L., Seidman, L. J., Goldstein, J. M., Koren, D., & Tsuang, M. T. (1998). IQ decline during childhood and adult psychotic symptoms in a community sample: A 19-year longitudinal study. *American Journal of Psychiatry, 155,* 672–677.

Lencz, T., Smith, C. W., McLaughlin, D., Auther, A., Nakayama, E., Hovey, L., et al. (2006). Generalized and specific neurocognitive deficits in prodromal schizophrenia. *Biological Psychiatry, 59,* 863–871.

Marjoram, D., Miller, P., McIntosh, A. M., Cunningham Owens, D. G., Johnstone, E. C., & Lawrie, S. (2006). A neuropsychological investigation into "Theory of Mind" and enhanced risk of schizophrenia. *Psychiatry Research, 144*, 29–37.

Mirsky, A. F., Ingraham, L. J., & Kugelmass, S. (1995). Neuropsychological assessment of attention and its pathology in the Israeli cohort. *Schizophrenia Bulletin, 21*, 193–204.

Mirsky, A. F., Kugelmass, S., Ingraham, L. J., Frenkel, E., & Nathan, M. (1995). Overview and summary: Twenty-five-year follow-up of high-risk children. *Schizophrenia Bulletin, 21*, 227–239.

Myles-Worsley, M., Ord, L. M., Ngiralmau, H., Weaver, S., Blailes, F., & Faraone, S. V. (2007). The Palau Early Psychosis Study: Neurocognitive functioning in high-risk adolescents. *Schizophrenia Research, 89*, 299–307.

Niemi, L. T., Suvisaari, J. M., Tuulio-Henriksson, A., & Lönnqvist, J. K. (2003). Childhood developmental abnormalities in schizophrenia: Evidence from high-risk studies. *Schizophrenia Research, 60*, 239–258.

Niendam, T. A., Bearden, C. E., Johnson, J. K., McKinley, M., Loewy, R., O'Brien, M., et al. (2006). Neurocognitive performance and functional disability in the psychosis prodrome. *Schizophrenia Research, 84*, 100–111.

Niendam, T. A., Bearden, C. E., Rosso, I. M., Sanchez, L. E., Hadley, T., Nuechterlein, K. H., et al. (2003). A prospective study of childhood neurocognitive functioning in schizophrenic patients and their siblings. *American Journal of Psychiatry, 160*, 2060–2062.

Niendam, T. A., Bearden, C. E., Zinberg, J., Johnson, J. K., O'Brian, M., & Cannon, T. D. (2007). The course of neurocognition and social functioning in individuals at ultra high risk for psychosis. *Schizophrenia Bulletin, 33*, 772–781.

O'Connor, M., Harris, J. M., McIntosh, A. M., Owens, D. G. C., Lawrie, E. C., & Johnstone, E. C. (2009). Specific cognitive deficits in a group at genetic high risk of schizophrenia. *Psychological Medicine, 39*, 1649–1655.

Ott, S. L., Spinelli, S., Rock, D., Roberts, S., Amminger, G. P., & Erlenmeyer-Kimling, L. (1998). The New York High-Risk Project: Social and general intelligence in children at risk for schizophrenia. *Schizophrenia Research, 31*, 1–11.

Owens-Cunningham, D. G., & Johnstone, E. C. (2006). Precursors and prodromata of schizophrenia: Findings from the Edinburgh High Risk Study and their literature context. *Psychological Medicine, 36*, 1501–1514.

Özgürdal, S., Littmann, E., Hauser, M., von Reventlow, H., Gudlowski, Y., Witthaus, H., et al. (2009). Neurocognitive performances in participants of at-risk mental state for schizophrenia and in first-episode patients. *Journal of Clinical and Experimental Neuropsychology, 31*, 392–401.

Parnas, J., Vianin, P., Saebye, D., Jansson, L., Volmer-Larsen, A., & Bovet, P. (2001). Visual binding abilities in the initial and advanced stages of schizophrenia. *Acta Psychiatrica Scandinavica, 103*, 171–180.

Pflüger, M. O., Gschwandtner, U., Stieglitz, R.-D., & Riecher-Rössler, A. (2007). Neuropsychological deficits in individuals with an at risk mental state for psychosis— Working memory as a potential trait marker. *Schizophrenia Research, 97*, 14–24.

Pinkham, A. E., Penn, D. L., Perkins, D. O., Graham, K. A., & Seigel, M. (2007). Emotion perception and social skill over the course of psychosis: A comparison of individuals "at-risk" for psychosis and individuals with early and chronic schizophrenia spectrum illness. *Cognitive Neuropsychiatry, 12*, 198–212.

Pukrop, R., Ruhrmann, S., Schultze-Lutter, F., Bechdolf, A., Brockhaus-Dumke, A., & Klosterkötter, J. (2007). Neurocognitive indicators for a conversion to psychosis:

Comparison of patients in a potentially initial prodromal state who did or did not convert to a psychosis. *Schizophrenia Research, 92*, 116–125.

Pukrop, R., Schultze-Lutter, F., Ruhrmann, S., Brockhaus-Dumke, A., Tendolkar, I., Bechdolf, A., et al. (2006). Neurocognitive functioning in subjects at risk for a first episode of psychosis compared with first and multiple episode schizophrenia. *Journal of Clinical and Experimental Neuropsychology, 28*, 1388–1407.

Reichenberg, A., Weiser, M., Rapp, M. A., Rabinowitz, J., Caspi, A., Schmeidler, J., et al. (2005). Elaboration on premorbid intellectual performance in schizophrenia. Premorbid intellectual decline and risk for schizophrenia. *Archives of General Psychiatry, 62*, 1297–1304.

Riecher-Rössler, A., Pflüger, M., Aston, J., Borgwardt, S., Brewer, W. J., Gschwandtner, U., et al. (2009). Efficacy of using cognitive status in predicting psychosis: A 7-year follow-up. *Biological Psychiatry, 66*(11), 1023–1030.

Seidman, L. J., Buka, S. L., Goldstein, J. M., & Tsuang, M. T. (2006). Intellectual decline in schizophrenia: Evidence from a prospective birth cohort 28 year follow-up study. *Journal of Clinical and Experimental Neuropsychology, 28*, 225–242.

Seidman, L. J., Giuliano, A. J., Meyer, E. C., Addington, J., Cadenhead, K. S., Cannon, T. D., et al. (2010). Neuropsychology of the prodrome to psychosis in the NAPLS consortium: Relationship to family history and conversion to psychosis. *Archives of General Psychiatry, 67*(6), 578–588.

Silverstein, S., Uhlhaas, P. J., Essex, B., Halpin, S., Schall, U., & Carr, V. (2006). Perceptual organization in first episode schizophrenia and ultra-high-risk states. *Schizophrenia Research, 83*, 41–52.

Simon, A. E., Cattapan-Ludewig, K., Zmilacher, S., Arbach, D., Gruber, K., Dvorsky, D. N., et al. (2007). Cognitive functioning in the schizophrenia prodrome. *Schizophrenia Bulletin, 33*, 761–771.

Smith, C. W., Park, S., & Cornblatt, B. (2006). Spatial working memory deficits in adolescents at clinical high risk for schizophrenia. *Schizophrenia Research, 81*, 211–215.

Sorensen, H. J., Mortensen, E. L., Parnas, J., & Mednick, S. A. (2006). Premorbid neurocognitive functioning in schizophrenia spectrum disorder. *Schizophrenia Bulletin, 32*, 578–583.

Trotman, H., McMillan, A., & Walker, E. (2006). Cognitive function and symptoms in adolescents with schizotypal personality disorder. *Schizophrenia Bulletin, 32*, 489–497.

Walder, D. J., Mittal, V., Trotman, H. D., McMillan, A. L., & Walker, E. F. (2008). Neurocognition and conversion to psychosis in adolescents at high-risk. *Schizophrenia Research, 101*, 161–168.

Whyte, M. C., Brett, C., Harrison, L. K., Byrne, M., Miller, P., Lawrie, S. M., et al. (2006). Neuropsychological performance over time in people at high risk of developing schizophrenia and controls. *Biological Psychiatry, 59*, 730–739.

Wolf, L. E., Cornblatt, B. A., Roberts, S. A., Shapiro, B. M., & Erlenmeyer-Kimling, L. (2002). Wisconsin Card Sorting deficits in the offspring of schizophrenics in the New York High-Risk Project. *Schizophrenia Research, 57*, 173–182.

Wood, S. J., Pantelis, C., Proffitt, T., Phillips, L. J., Stuart, G. W., Buchanan, J. A., et al. (2003). Spatial working memory ability is a marker of risk-for-psychosis. *Psychological Medicine, 33*, 1239–1247.

Yung, A. R., Phillips, L. J., Yuen, H. P., & McGorry, P. D. (2004). Risk factors for psychosis in an ultra high-risk group: Psychopathology and clinical features. *Schizophrenia Research, 67*, 131–142.

7 Grey matters: Mapping the transition to psychosis

Stefan Borgwardt, Paolo Fusar-Poli,
Anita Riecher-Rössler and Philip McGuire

Introduction

Despite a large body of neuroimaging studies in schizophrenia showing multiple subtle brain abnormalities in this disease, we do not know the exact time course of their occurrence. Meta-analytic reviews on studies so far primarily conducted on samples of chronic schizophrenic patients indicate that, compared to healthy controls, these patients show reduced brain size, enlarged lateral and third ventricles, reduced frontal lobe volume, reduced volumes of temporo-limbic structures and of corpus callosum, and increased volume of basal ganglia (Vita, De Peri, Silenzi, & Dieci, 2006).

Neuroimaging studies from first-episode schizophrenia subjects find small reductions in brain volumes at initial presentation (Steen, Mull, McClure, Hamer, & Lieberman, 2006), and volume loss over time in those patients who have a deteriorating clinical course (Ho et al., 2003). In this situation it seems fundamental for the understanding of the pathogenesis of these brain changes to establish the timing when they occur, in particular to find out whether they are already present prior to the occurrence of a first psychotic episode. It is also unclear what biological processes underlie the transition from an at-risk mental state to psychosis.

In this chapter, we will examine cross-sectional and longitudinal structural neuroimaging studies that aimed to distinguish high-risk subjects who later developed psychosis from those who did not. We have focused on studies using voxel-based morphometry (VBM) and thus assessing grey matter volumes by surveying the whole brain (Ashburner & Friston, 2000). We have included two summary tables of cross-sectional (Table 7.1) and longitudinal (Table 7.2) structural neuroimaging studies of subjects with an at-risk mental state (ARMS).

Grey matter volume abnormalities in the prodromal stage of psychosis: Findings from cross-sectional studies

Neuroimaging studies clearly indicate that schizophrenia is associated with neuroanatomical abnormalities, with the most replicated findings being ventricular enlargement and reductions in frontal and medial temporal lobe grey matter volume (Shenton, Dickey, Frumin, & McCarley, 2001; Wright et al., 2000).

However, the extent to which these are related to a vulnerability to schizophrenia, as opposed to the disorder per se, is less certain. Thus, qualitatively similar abnormalities are also evident in the first-degree relatives and co-twins of patients with schizophrenia (Baaré et al., 2001; Hulshoff Pol et al., 2004; Keshavan et al., 1997; Lawrie et al., 1999; Sharma et al., 1998; Staal et al., 2000; Suddath, Christison, Torrey, Casanova, & Weinberger, 1990). Twin studies suggest that these structural abnormalities (Baaré et al., 2001; van Haren et al., 2004), as well as others in dorsolateral prefrontal, and superior temporal cortex, the hippocampus and white matter are at least partially genetically determined (Borgwardt et al., 2010; Cannon et al., 2002; Hulshoff Pol et al., 2004).

It is not clear as yet at what stage of the disorder these brain abnormalities occur. Neurodevelopmental models of schizophrenia propose that brain abnormalities are present before the onset of psychosis, but there is also evidence that at least some of MRI abnormalities progress over the course of the disorder (Pantelis et al., 2005). MRI studies of non-psychotic subjects who are at high risk of psychosis indicate that regional volumetric abnormalities comparable to those seen in schizophrenia are evident in those who are vulnerable to psychosis.

Using a prospective design, the Edinburgh High-Risk Study identified reductions in the grey matter volume bilaterally in the anterior cingulate and in the left parahippocampal gyrus in the relatives of patients with schizophrenia (Job et al., 2003). From the same group, Lawrie et al. (1999) found that the relatives of patients with schizophrenia had reduced left medial temporal volume, and decreased global white and grey matter volumes were found in the non-psychotic co-twins of patients with schizophrenia (Lawrie et al., 1999). In the same group of subjects with a high genetic risk of developing schizophrenia, Job et al. reported no significant differences between high-risk subjects with or without later transition (Lawrie, McIntosh, Hall, Owens, & Johnstone, 2008).

Relatively little is known about the nature of the abnormalities in the "at-risk mental state" (see Table 7.1 for summary). Using a region-of-interest (ROI) approach, Phillips et al. (2002) reported that hippocampal volume in ARMS individuals was smaller than that in controls but not than in patients with first-episode psychosis. However, the prodromal group, those who later developed psychosis, had a larger left hippocampal volume than those who did not. More recently, using a voxel-based approach in subjects from the same centre in Melbourne, Pantelis et al. (2003) found that subjects with "prodromal" symptoms who later became psychotic had smaller inferior frontal and cingulate gyrus volumes than those who did not. In another longitudinal study, using an ROI approach, Velakoulis et al. (2006) reported that patients at high risk of psychosis had normal baseline hippocampal and amygdala grey matter volumes whether or not they subsequently developed psychosis.

In a cross-sectional study from Basel, MRI data from an ARMS sample ($n = 35$), independent of subsequent clinical outcome, were compared with healthy controls and first-episode patients. Compared with healthy controls, both first-episode patients and ARMS subjects showed significantly less grey matter volume in the posterior part of the left superior temporal gyrus and the adjacent

Table 7.1 Grey matter volumes in the At-Risk Mental State (ARMS): Findings from cross-sectional studies

Study	N	MRI method	MRI findings	
			ARMS vs. controls	Converters vs. non-converters
Phillips et al. (2002)	60 ARMS (20 ARMS-T vs. 40 ARMS-NT); 139 controls	ROI analysis of hippocampal and whole brain volume	Smaller left and right hippocampi in ARMS compared to controls	Larger left hippocampus in converters compared to non-converters
Pantelis et al. (2003)	75 ARMS (23 ARMS-T vs. 52 ARMS-NT)	VBM analysis	[No control group]	Converters had smaller grey matter volume in the right medial temporal, lateral temporal, and inferior frontal cortex, and in the cingulate bilaterally
Garner et al. (2005)	31 ARMS-T vs. 63 ARMS-NT	ROI analysis of pituitary volume	[No control group]	Converters had a significantly larger (12%) pituitary volume
Velakoulis et al. (2006)	135 ARMS (39 ARMS-T vs. 96 ARMS-NT); 87 controls	ROI analysis of hippocampal, amygdala, whole brain and intracranial volumes	No differences	No differences
Borgwardt, McGuire et al. (2007); Borgwardt, Riecher-Rössler et al. (2007)	35 ARMS (23 ARMS-T, 12 ARMS-NT), 25 FE, 22 controls	VBM analysis	Reduced grey matter volume in the posterior cingulate gyrus and precuneus	Subjects who later developed psychosis had less grey matter than subjects who did not in the right insula, inferior frontal and superior temporal gyrus

Notes: ARMS-T = subjects with an ARMS who made transition to psychosis; ARMS-NT = subjects with an ARMS who did not make transition to psychosis; FE = patients with first-episode psychosis; ROI = Region of Interest; VBM = Voxel-based morphometry.

part of the left insula, and in a second region involving the posterior cingulate gyrus and precuneus (Borgwardt et al., 2008; Borgwardt, Riecher-Rössler et al., 2007). However, the ARMS group was heterogeneous, including both patients who later developed psychosis and those who did not. Within the ARMS group, those subjects who developed psychosis (ARMS-T; $n = 12$) had less grey matter than subjects who did not (ARMS-NT; $n = 23$) in the right insula, inferior frontal and superior frontal gyrus (Borgwardt, Riecher-Rössler et al., 2007). These volumetric differences within the ARMS group were associated with the subsequent development of psychosis and could be related to a process that underlies a progression from a high-risk state towards a psychotic illness.

The subgroup of these ARMS subjects who subsequently became psychotic, relative to healthy controls, were found to have regional grey matter reductions in the posterior cingulate gyrus, precuneus, and paracentral lobule bilaterally, which extended into the left superior parietal lobule before transition to psychosis (Borgwardt, McGuire et al., 2007), but more grey matter volume in some areas of the left parietal/posterior temporal region. This was consistent with previous reports of relatively increased hippocampal volume (Phillips et al., 2002) in subjects with an ARMS who later develop psychosis. Borgwardt, McGuire et al. discussed the possibility that these differences might be related to an active pathological process that underlies the transition to psychosis. These results suggested that the at-risk mental state was associated with reductions in grey matter volume in areas that are also reduced in schizophrenia, suggesting that these abnormalities not only occur with transition to psychosis, but are a correlate of an increased vulnerability to psychosis.

Grey matter changes during the transition to psychosis: Findings from longitudinal studies

Relatively little is known about the nature of the brain abnormalities in this high-risk group close to the actual process of transition to psychosis (Wood et al., 2008; see Table 7.2 for a summary). The transition from prodromal phase into frank psychosis (Job, Whalley, Johnstone, & Lawrie, 2005; Pantelis et al., 2003) and the first two years of the first episode (Farrow, Whitford, Williams, Gomes, & Harris, 2005) has been associated with frontal and temporal decreases in grey matter. Using a similar voxel-based approach in subjects with an ARMS, Pantelis et al. (2003) found that subjects with "prodromal" symptoms who developed psychosis showed a longitudinal reduction in grey matter volume in the left parahippocampal, fusiform, orbitofrontal and cerebellar cortices, and the cingulate gyri. In this first longitudinal MRI study in ARMS, it was found that the subset who developed psychosis showed a longitudinal reduction in grey matter volume in the left parahippocampal, fusiform, orbitofrontal and cerebellar cortices, and the cingulate gyri. In another longitudinal study with largely the same subjects (Sun et al., 2008), greater brain contraction was found in the right prefrontal region in people with transition to psychosis compared with ARMS subjects who did not develop psychosis. Another VBM study in patients at genetic risk of psychosis reported that the onset of psychosis in these individuals was associated with reduced grey matter in the temporal lobes, the right frontal lobe and right parietal lobe (Job et al., 2005). These findings are consistent with prospective studies in patients with established schizophrenia, which indicate that longitudinal reductions in regional

Table 7.2 Grey matter volumes in the At-Risk Mental State (ARMS): Findings from longitudinal studies

Centre	Study group	Follow-up period	MRI method	MRI findings: Progressive changes
Edinburgh High-Risk Study[4]	Lawrie et al. (2002)			
	19 genetic high-risk subjects with sub-threshold psychotic symptoms (12 at first scan)	2 years	ROI[1] analyses	Reductions in temporal lobes (relative change: 2.3–2.5%), caudate (0.7–1.1%), and prefrontal cortex (0.3–0.4%) bilaterally
	Job et al. (2005)			
	(a) 18 genetic high-risk subjects with sub-threshold psychotic symptoms	2 years	VBM analysis of GM[3] density	(a) Reductions in the right cerebellum and amygdala as well as in the left fusiform gyrus, uncus, superior and inferior temporal gyrus, and in the parahippocampal gyrus bilaterally
	(b) 8 genetic high-risk subjects who have developed schizophrenia			(b) Reductions in the left inferior temporal gyrus, left uncus and the right cerebellum
Ultra high-risk (UHR) Studies from Melbourne[4]	Pantelis et al. (2003)			
	(a) 10 ARMS converters	1 year	VBM[2] analysis of GM[3] volume	(a) Converters had grey matter volume reductions in the left parahippocampal, fusiform, orbitofrontal and cerebellar cortices, and the cingulate gyri
	(b) 11 ARMS non-converters			(b) In non-converters, GM reductions were restricted to the cerebellum

(continued)

Table 7.2 Continued.

Centre	Study group	Follow-up period	MRI method	MRI findings: Progressive changes
	Sun et al. (2008)			
	12 ARMS converters vs. 23 ARMS non-converters	1 year	Cortical surface motion analysis	Compared to non-converters, converters had greater brain surface contraction in the right prefrontal region, and with a nonsignificant trend in the left prefrontal region and bilateral occipital poles
Basel FEPSY study	Borgwardt et al. (2008)			
	20 ARMS: 10 converters and 10 non-converters	3–4 years	VBM[2] analysis of GM[3] volume	In subjects who developed psychosis there were longitudinal volume reductions in the orbitofrontal, superior frontal, inferior temporal, medial and superior parietal cortex, and in the cerebellum. There were no longitudinal changes in subjects who did not develop psychosis

Notes: [1]ROI = Region of Interest; [2]VBM = Voxel-based morphometry; [3]GM = Grey matter; [4]Samples from the same centre are largely overlapping.

grey matter volume also occur in chronic patients (Cahn et al., 2002; Ho et al., 2003; Kasai et al., 2003; Kubicki et al., 2002; Mathalon, Sullivan, Lim, & Pfefferbaum, 2001; Sporn et al., 2003).

In another longitudinal MRI study (Borgwardt et al., 2008), ARMS subjects were scanned when they first presented with "prodromal" symptoms and were then followed clinically for three years. Those who developed psychosis during this period were scanned again after its onset. The other subjects were scanned at the end of the 3-year follow-up period. On the basis of previous longitudinal MRI studies of the ARMS and of other groups at high risk of psychosis (i.e., genetic risk), Borgwardt et al. tested the hypothesis that transition to psychosis would be associated with longitudinal reductions in grey matter volume in the frontal, cingulate and temporal cortex. In this longitudinal VBM study regional grey matter volumes were analysed in 10 subjects with an ARMS before and after transition to psychosis (converters) and in 10 comparable control ARMS subjects without transition to psychosis (non-converters). The main findings of this study were a decrease of cortical volumes in converters in the orbitofrontal cortex that included the right orbital and left rectal gyrus as well as in the right inferior temporal, superior frontal, and superior parietal lobule, the left precuneus, and the right hemisphere of the cerebellum. These findings suggest that at least some of the cortical grey matter abnormalities known in schizophrenia patients occur during the acute process of transition to psychosis.

A recent meta-analysis (Smieskova et al., 2010) of structural MRI studies of individuals at high risk of psychosis showed small to medium effect sizes of decreased prefrontal, cingulate, insular and cerebellar grey matter volume in subjects with later transition to psychosis (HR-T) compared to those without transition (HR-NT). This meta-analysis also revealed relatively larger whole brain volumes in HR-T compared to HR-NT subjects (mean Cohen's d 0.36; 95% CI 0.27–0.46). Despite methodological differences between studies, structural abnormalities in prefrontal, anterior cingulate, medial temporal and cerebellar cortex might be predictive for development of psychosis within HR subjects.

Overall, the few longitudinal studies of grey matter volume changes in subjects with an ARMS confirm previous reports on emerging psychosis and suggests that there may be subtle alterations in brain structure associated with vulnerability to psychosis, but other brain structural changes found in schizophrenia may emerge as psychosis develops.

Conclusions

People with an at-risk mental state show qualitatively similar volumetric abnormalities to patients with schizophrenia, although they are generally less severe. There is also evidence that some of these MRI abnormalities are specifically linked to the later onset of psychosis, as opposed to an increased vulnerability to psychosis. However, the studies which produced these findings involved relatively small samples, and larger studies are needed to clarify which abnormalities are illness specific.

References

Ashburner, J., & Friston, K. J. (2000). Voxel-based morphometry—The methods. *NeuroImage*, *11*, 805–821.

Baaré, W. F., van Oel, C. J., Hulshoff Pol, H. E., Schnack, H. G., Durston, S., Sitskoorn, M. M., et al. (2001). Volumes of brain structures in twins discordant for schizophrenia. *Archives of General Psychiatry*, *58*, 33–40.

Borgwardt, S. J., McGuire, P. K., Aston, J., Berger, G., Dazzan, P., Gschwandtner, U., et al. (2007). Structural brain abnormalities in individuals with an at-risk mental state who later develop psychosis. *British Journal of Psychiatry*, *51*(Suppl.), s69–s75.

Borgwardt, S. J., McGuire, P. K., Aston, J., Gschwandtner, U., Pfluger, M. O., Stieglitz, R. D., et al. (2008). Reductions in frontal, temporal and parietal volume associated with the onset of psychosis. *Schizophrenia Research*, *106*(2–3), 108–114.

Borgwardt, S. J., Picchioni, M. M., Ettinger, U., Toulopoulou, T., Murray, R., & McGuire, P. K. (2010). Regional gray matter volume in monozygotic twins concordant and discordant for schizophrenia. *Biological Psychiatry, 67*(10), 956–964.

Borgwardt, S. J., Riecher-Rössler, A., Dazzan, P., Chitnis, X., Aston, J., Drewe, M., et al. (2007). Regional gray matter volume abnormalities in the at risk mental state. *Biological Psychiatry, 61,* 1148–1156.

Cahn, W., Hulshoff Pol, H. E., Lems, E. B., van Haren, N. E., Schnack, H. G., van der Linden, J. A., et al. (2002). Brain volume changes in first-episode schizophrenia: A 1-year follow-up study. *Archives of General Psychiatry, 59,* 1002–1010.

Cannon, T. D., Thompson, P. M., van Erp, T. G., Toga, A. W., Poutanen, V. P., Huttunen, M., et al. (2002). Cortex mapping reveals regionally specific patterns of genetic and disease-specific gray-matter deficits in twins discordant for schizophrenia. *Proceedings of the National Academy of Sciences of the United States of America, 99,* 3228–3233.

Farrow, T. F., Whitford, T. J., Williams, L. M., Gomes, L., & Harris, A. W. (2005). Diagnosis-related regional gray matter loss over two years in first episode schizophrenia and bipolar disorder. *Biological Psychiatry, 58,* 713–723.

Garner, B., Pariante, C. M., Wood, S. J., Velakoulis, D., Phillips, L., Soulsby, B., et al. (2005). Pituitary volume predicts future transition to psychosis in individuals at ultra-high risk of developing psychosis. *Biological Psychiatry, 58*(5), 417–423.

Ho, B. C., Andreasen, N. C., Nopoulos, P., Arndt, S., Magnotta, V., & Flaum, M. (2003). Progressive structural brain abnormalities and their relationship to clinical outcome: A longitudinal magnetic resonance imaging study early in schizophrenia. *Archives of General Psychiatry, 60,* 585–594.

Hulshoff Pol, H. E., Brans, R. G., van Haren, N. E., Schnack, H. G., Langen, M., Baaré, W. F., et al. (2004). Gray and white matter volume abnormalities in monozygotic and same-gender dizygotic twins discordant for schizophrenia. *Biological Psychiatry, 55,* 126–130.

Job, D. E., Whalley, H. C., Johnstone, E. C., & Lawrie, S. M. (2005). Grey matter changes over time in high risk subjects developing schizophrenia. *NeuroImage, 25,* 1023–1030.

Job, D. E., Whalley, H. C., McConnell, S., Glabus, M., Johnstone, E. C., & Lawrie, S. M. (2003). Voxel-based morphometry of grey matter densities in subjects at high risk of schizophrenia. *Schizophrenia Research, 64,* 1–13.

Kasai, K., Shenton, M. E., Salisbury, D. F., Hirayasu, Y., Lee, C. U., Ciszewski, A. A., et al. (2003). Progressive decrease of left superior temporal gyrus gray matter volume in patients with first-episode schizophrenia. *American Journal of Psychiatry, 160,* 156–164.

Keshavan, M. S., Montrose, D. M., Pierri, J. N., Dick, E. L., Rosenberg, D., Talagala, L., et al. (1997). Magnetic resonance imaging and spectroscopy in offspring at risk for schizophrenia: Preliminary studies. *Progress in Neuropsychopharmacology and Biological Psychiatry, 21,* 1285–1295.

Kubicki, M., Shenton, M. E., Salisbury, D. F., Hirayasu, Y., Kasai, K., Kikinis, R., et al. (2002). Voxel-based morphometric analysis of gray matter in first episode schizophrenia. *NeuroImage, 17,* 1711–1719.

Lawrie, S. M., McIntosh, A. M., Hall, J., Owens, D. G., & Johnstone, E. C. (2008). Brain structure and function changes during the development of schizophrenia: The evidence from studies of subjects at increased genetic risk. *Schizophrenia Bulletin, 34,* 330–340.

Lawrie, S. M., Whalley, H., Kestelman, J. N., Abukmeil, S. S., Byrne, M., Hodges, A., et al. (1999). Magnetic resonance imaging of brain in people at high risk of developing schizophrenia. *Lancet, 353,* 30–33.

Lawrie, S. M., Whalley, H. C., Abukmeil, S. S., Kestelman, J. N., Miller, P., Best, J. J., et al. (2002). Temporal lobe volume changes in people at high risk of schizophrenia with psychotic symptoms. *British Journal of Psychiatry, 181*, 138–143.

Mathalon, D. H., Sullivan, E. V., Lim, K. O., & Pfefferbaum, A. (2001). Progressive brain volume changes and the clinical course of schizophrenia in men: A longitudinal magnetic resonance imaging study. *Archives of General Psychiatry, 58*, 148–157.

Pantelis, C., Velakoulis, D., McGorry, P. D., Wood, S. J., Suckling, J., Phillips, L. J., et al. (2003). Neuroanatomical abnormalities before and after onset of psychosis: A cross-sectional and longitudinal MRI comparison. *Lancet, 361*, 281–288.

Pantelis, C., Yucel, M., Wood, S. J., Velakoulis, D., Sun, D., Berger, G., et al. (2005). Structural brain imaging evidence for multiple pathological processes at different stages of brain development in schizophrenia. *Schizophrenia Bulletin, 31*, 672–696.

Phillips, L. J., Velakoulis, D., Pantelis, C., Wood, S., Yuen, H. P., Yung, A. R., et al. (2002). Non-reduction in hippocampal volume is associated with higher risk of psychosis. *Schizophrenia Research, 58*, 145–158.

Sharma, T., Lancaster, E., Lee, D., Lewis, S., Sigmundsson, T., Takei, N., et al. (1998). Brain changes in schizophrenia. Volumetric MRI study of families multiply affected with schizophrenia—The Maudsley Family Study 5. *British Journal of Psychiatry, 173*, 132–138.

Shenton, M. E., Dickey, C. C., Frumin, M., & McCarley, R. W. (2001). A review of MRI findings in schizophrenia. *Schizophrenia Research, 49*, 1–52.

Smieskova, R., Fusar-Poli, P., Allen, P., Bendfeldt, K., Stieglitz, R. D., Drewe, J., et al. (2010). Neuroimaging predictors of transition to psychosis—A systematic review and meta-analysis. *Neuroscience and Biobehavioral Reviews, 34*, 1207–1222.

Sporn, A. L., Greenstein, D. K., Gogtay, N., Jeffries, N. O., Lenane, M., Gochman, P., et al. (2003). Progressive brain volume loss during adolescence in childhood-onset schizophrenia. *American Journal of Psychiatry, 160*, 2181–2189.

Staal, W. G., Hulshoff Pol, H. E., Schnack, H. G., Hoogendoorn, M. L., Jellema, K., & Kahn, R. S. (2000). Structural brain abnormalities in patients with schizophrenia and their healthy siblings. *American Journal of Psychiatry, 157*, 416–421.

Steen, R. G., Mull, C., McClure, R., Hamer, R. M., & Lieberman, J. A. (2006). Brain volume in first-episode schizophrenia: Systematic review and meta-analysis of magnetic resonance imaging studies. *British Journal of Psychiatry, 188*, 510–518.

Suddath, R. L., Christison, G. W., Torrey, E. F., Casanova, M. F., & Weinberger, D. R. (1990). Anatomical abnormalities in the brains of monozygotic twins discordant for schizophrenia. *New England Journal of Medicine, 322*, 789–794.

Sun, D., Phillips, L., Velakoulis, D., Yung, A., McGorry, P. D., Wood, S. J., et al. (2008). Progressive brain structural changes mapped as psychosis develops in "at risk" individuals. *Schizophrenia Research, 108*(1–3), 85–92.

van Haren, N. E., Picchioni, M. M., McDonald, C., Marshall, N., Davis, N., Ribchester, T., et al. (2004). A controlled study of brain structure in monozygotic twins concordant and discordant for schizophrenia. *Biological Psychiatry, 56*, 454–461.

Velakoulis, D., Wood, S. J., Wong, M. T., McGorry, P. D., Yung, A., Phillips, L., et al. (2006). Hippocampal and amygdala volumes according to psychosis stage and diagnosis: A magnetic resonance imaging study of chronic schizophrenia, first-episode psychosis, and ultra-high-risk individuals. *Archives of General Psychiatry, 63*, 139–149.

Vita, A., De Peri, L., Silenzi, C., & Dieci, M. (2006). Brain morphology in first-episode schizophrenia: A meta-analysis of quantitative magnetic resonance imaging studies. *Schizophrenia Research, 82*(1), 75–88.

Wood, S. J., Pantelis, C., Velakoulis, D., Yucel, M., Fornito, A., & McGorry, P. D. (2008). Progressive changes in the development toward schizophrenia: Studies in subjects at increased symptomatic risk. *Schizophrenia Bulletin, 34*, 322–329.

Wright, I. C., Rabe-Hesketh, S., Woodruff, P. W., David, A. S., Murray, R. M., & Bullmore, E. T. (2000). Meta-analysis of regional brain volumes in schizophrenia. *American Journal of Psychiatry, 157*, 16–25.

8 Functional MRI in prodromal psychosis

Paolo Fusar-Poli, Marta Agosti and Stefan Borgwardt

In this chapter, we will consider the role of functional magnetic resonance imaging (fMRI) in the prodromal phases of psychosis. Functional MRI has rapidly developed into a powerful tool in psychiatry as it provides an unprecedented opportunity for the "in vivo" investigation of neurophysiological function of the human brain. We will first outline the basic principles of fMRI and will highlight their use in psychosis. Then we will discuss the specific potentials of fMRI in the study of the pre-psychotic phases. Such applications include investigation of the neurofunctional correlates of an enhanced risk to psychosis, identification of neurobiological markers of psychosis transition and assessment of antipsychotic effects on brain function during prodromal psychosis. In a separate section we will further discuss the use of fMRI to study the correlation between brain function and longitudinal psychopathological outcomes in subjects at high risk for psychosis. Then we will illustrate recent developments of fMRI methods, which allow the investigation of brain connectivity during prodromal psychosis. Finally, we will debate the integration of fMRI data across different neuroimaging modalities and will address the methodological limitations of fMRI in prodromal psychosis.

Principles of fMRI

An fMRI study involves the collection of images, which show signal changes that reflect neural activity. Its superior temporal and spatial resolution, compared to positron emission tomography (PET) and single photon emission tomography (SPET), has established fMRI as the major tool for the study of regional activity in relation to neuropsychology in mental disorders. Functional MRI generally involves the acquisition of a large series of images in each subject and to compensate for subject head movement it is usual to realign the images to one of the images in the series. In most studies the statistical analysis is conducted after the images from each subject in a group are transformed into a standard stereotactic space, such as that described by Talairach and Tournoux. This is designed to facilitate comparison of the same region in images from brains from different subjects that may have different size and shapes. Following this spatial normalization, statistical analysis may involve a number of methods, most of which result in some index at each voxel of how the brain has responded to the experimental manipulation of interest. In the final step of the analysis, voxels where there is a significant difference in signal are displayed, producing a statistical map of activation of the brain (Brett, Johnsrude, & Owen, 2002).

fMRI in established psychosis

Functional MRI measuring regional cerebral blood flow has demonstrated that neural activity during a variety of cognitive tasks is abnormal in several brain areas in schizophrenia. These brain areas include the prefrontal, cingulate and temporal cortex, the hippocampus, the striatum, the thalamus and the cerebellum (McGuire, Howes, Stone, & Fusar-Poli, 2008). These abnormalities are small in magnitude and are not evident in all patients within a given sample, making it difficult to use them as a diagnostic aid in an individual patient. A further complicating factor is that positive symptoms, disorganized speech and negative symptoms are present to varying degrees in different patients with schizophrenia and are associated with distinct patterns of regional cortical activity (McGuire et al., 2008). At one stage it was hoped that "hypofrontality", a reduction in task-related activation in the prefrontal cortex, might be pathognomonic for schizophrenia. However, subsequent research revealed that this was an inconsistent finding, varying with the cognitive task being studied, how well patients performed the task and with the symptom profile at the time of scanning.

Neurofunctional correlates of an enhanced risk to psychosis

Investigation of subjects at the beginning of psychotic illness allows researchers to minimize confounders such as neurodegenerative progress of disease, institutionalization and long-term treatment with antipsychotics. To explore liability to psychosis current research paradigms employed subjects at "high risk" for the disease. The genetic high-risk approach usually involves studying the non-psychotic first-degree relatives of patients (Lawrie, Hall, McIntosh, Cunningham-Owens, & Johnstone, 2008). The clinical high-risk strategy focuses on individuals who are considered to be at an increased risk for psychotic disorders based primarily on the presence of clinical features such as attenuated psychotic symptoms (Broome et al., 2005). Although these strategies allow researchers to identify individuals at high risk to develop psychosis (ranging from 9% to 54%; Olsen & Rosenbaum, 2006), these symptoms overlap with psychotic experiences in healthy individuals who are not at risk and do not seek clinical help. Consequently there is an urgent need of reliable neurofunctional markers linked to the pathophysiological mechanisms underlying the pre-psychotic phases to improve the validity and specificity of an early diagnosis. A number of fMRI studies of high-risk population are available in the current literature. Overall these studies indicate that some functional neuroimaging abnormalities in schizophrenia are evident before the onset of the disorder. These alterations are qualitatively similar to the changes seen in established schizophrenia but less marked (Broome et al., 2009). For example, our group has recently addressed the neurofunctional correlates of working memory in subjects at enhanced clinical risk for psychosis by employing a traditional *n*-back task (see Plate 8.1, situated between pp. 116 and 117). Subjects at high risk for psychosis showed reduced prefrontal and parietal activation relative to controls during the mnemonic paradigm (Plate 8.1). The fMRI data revealed a relatively reduced blood-oxygen-level-dependent response in the dorsolateral and medial prefrontal cortex of subjects at high risk for psychosis (Fusar-Poli, Howes et al., 2010). Because the differential activation observed was evident in the context of comparable response accuracy and the analysis was restricted to images associated with correct responses, it is unlikely to be related to group differences in task performance and may instead reflect a true difference at the neurophysiological level. Abnormalities in prefrontal activation during cognitive tasks have previously been described in the prodromal phases of psychosis (see Fusar-Poli, Broome et al., 2007, for a meta-analysis) and have consistently been reported in the early phases of schizophrenia. Furthermore, alterations in prefrontal regions appear to be more marked in the subgroup of subjects who later develop psychosis, suggesting that prefrontal abnormalities may be particularly related to the later onset of psychosis (see below). In another study fMRI was used to investigate cortical function in subjects at enhanced clinical risk for psychosis and in matched controls while they were performing a false memory task (Allen et al., 2009). During an encoding phase, subjects read lists of words aloud. Following a delay, they were presented with target words, semantically related lure words and novel words and were required to indicate if each had been presented before. Behaviourally, the subjects at clinical risk for psychosis made more false-alarm responses for novel words than controls and had lower discrimination accuracy for target words. During encoding, high-risk subjects showed less activation than healthy controls in the left middle frontal gyrus, the bilateral medial frontal gyri and the left parahippocampal gyrus (Allen et al., 2009). These neurofunctional differences were associated with diminished recognition performance and may reflect the greatly increased risk of psychosis associated with the prodromal phases of psychosis.

Overall, the fMRI studies addressing the neurofunctional correlates of vulnerability to psychosis raise the possibility that neuroimaging could be used to detect pathophysiological changes associated with the disorder before the onset of frank illness. This is of particular clinical interest because only a proportion of people with prodromal symptoms go on to develop schizophrenia (see below) and neuroimaging might facilitate the targeting of novel preventive treatments to this subgroup.

Neurofunctional mapping of psychosis transition

Overall functional imaging studies indicate that the neurofunctional abnormalities during cognitive tasks are qualitatively similar but less severe in high-risk subjects compared to first-episode patients (Fusar-Poli, Perez et al., 2007). However, the onset and the time course of such alterations are mostly unknown. Indeed, it is critical to the understanding of the pathogenesis of these brain changes to clarify their onset and the dynamic neurobiological processes underlying the transition from a high-risk state to full-blown psychosis. To address this point some fMRI studies have compared high-risk subjects with (HR-T) and without (HR-NT) later transition to psychosis. We have summarized fMRI longitudinal studies addressing psychosis transition in a recent meta-analysis, which confirmed abnormalities in the prefrontal cortex (Smieskova et al., 2010). Specifically, decreased activation in anterior cingulate cortex and increased activation in left parietal lobe were described in genetic HR-T relative to controls in a prospective fMRI cross-sectional study (Whalley et al., 2006), Compared to HR-NT, HR-T subjects showed smaller increases in activation with increasing task difficulty in the right lingual gyrus (Whalley et al., 2006). Another fMRI "Theory of Mind" imaging study, which requires the ability to understand a joke, investigated prefrontal cortex activation associated with memory and executive functioning tasks. Compared to HR-NT, HR-T showed less neural activation in the middle frontal gyrus right (Marjoram et al., 2006). The localization of fMRI abnormalities between HR-T and HR-NT corresponds to the region-specific neuroanatomical abnormalities revealed by structural neuroimaging studies. These neurofunctional abnormalities could delineate a pathological process in the affected brain regions as well as a compensatory process to volumetric region-specific reductions in grey or white matter.

Neurophysiological correlates of antipsychotic treatments in early psychosis

Functional MRI can be used to examine the influence of antipsychotic treatment on regional brain activity and on activation during cognitive tasks and thus indicate their neurocognitive effects in the early phases of psychosis. Subjects at risk for psychosis are antipsychotic-naive or are administered short-term treatments with low-dosage antipsychotics. Although it is widely held that acute treatment does not affect brain function, fMRI studies have documented modulation of the neural substrates of cognitive deficits by short-term atypical antipsychotic treatment (Snitz et al., 2005). Similarly, we observed in a fMRI study that low-dosage antipsychotic treatment can modulate brain activity during different neurocognitive tasks (Fusar-Poli, Broome et al., 2007). These fMRI findings are consistent with evidence that substantial blockade of the dopamine system by antipsychotic medications happens within the first hours of treatment (Kapur et al., 2005). For example, the effects of risperidone on cerebral metabolism were detectable within 2 h of administration of a single dose, both in healthy subjects (Lane, Ngan, Yatham, Ruth, & Liddle, 2004) and in patients with first-episode psychosis (Ngan, Lane, Ruth, & Liddle, 2002). Structural MRI studies have confirmed the fMRI findings indicating that short-term treatment with atypical antipsychotics may affect regional grey matter volume (Smieskova et al., 2009). At a behavioural level, recent research has shown that antipsychotic action can be discerned shortly after the first dose. A meta-analysis, which included data from 7450 patients in 42 double-blind active/drug or placebo/controlled trials, showed a significant change in psychotic symptoms within the first week of treatment. They also showed that the greatest improvement in psychotic symptoms was observed in the first week than in any week thereafter (Agid, Kapur, Arenovich, & Zipursky, 2003).

Brain connectivity in the pre-psychotic phases

An alternative approach to identifying functional abnormalities in particular brain regions has been to look for abnormalities in the integration of function between brain regions, such as the prefrontal and temporal cortex. In a recent study we have investigated frontotemporal connectivity in subjects at enhanced clinical risk for psychosis. Superior temporal gyrus (STG) dysfunction is a robust finding in functional neuroimaging studies of schizophrenia and is thought to be related to a disruption of frontotemporal functional connectivity but the stage of the disorder at which these functional alterations occur is unclear. We addressed this issue by using dynamic causal modelling and fMRI to study subjects in the prodromal and first-episode phases of schizophrenia during a working memory task (*n*-back; Crossley et al., 2009). We found that the STG was differentially engaged across the three groups. There was deactivation of this region during the task in controls, whereas subjects with a first episode of psychosis showed activation and the response in subjects at high risk was intermediate relative to the two other groups (Crossley et al., 2009). There were corresponding differences in the effective connectivity between the STG and the middle frontal gyrus across the three groups, with a negative coupling between these areas in controls, a positive coupling in the first-episode group and an intermediate value in the high-risk group. We concluded that a failure to deactivate the superior temporal lobe during tasks that engage prefrontal cortex is evident at the onset of schizophrenia and may reflect a disruption of frontotemporal connectivity (Crossley et al., 2009). Qualitatively similar alterations are evident in people with prodromal symptoms of the disorder. However, although there appear to be abnormalities in functional connectivity in schizophrenia, a single pattern of dysconnectivity that characterizes its pathophysiology has yet to be identified.

fMRI and longitudinal outcomes in subjects at high risk for psychosis

Although people with prodromal signs of psychosis show neurofunctional alterations underlying executive processes when they first present to clinical services, the longitudinal course of these abnormalities and how they relate to subsequent clinical and functional outcome is relatively unclear. To address this point we employed fMRI during verbal fluency in a cohort of subjects at clinical risk for psychosis and in healthy controls. Images were acquired at clinical presentation and again after one year. Levels of psychopathology and global functioning were assessed at the same time points using a number of psychometric instruments. At baseline subjects at risk for psychosis showed greater activation in the left inferior frontal gyrus than controls (Fusar-Poli, Broome et al., 2009). After one year the neural response in the left inferior frontal gyrus normalized and was similar to that in controls (see Plate 8.2, situated between pp. 116 and 117). Between presentation and follow-up, the severity of perceptual disorder and thought disorder and of general psychopathology decreased and the level of global functioning improved. However, the most striking result was that the psychopathological and neurofunctional changes were related (Fusar-Poli, Broome et al., 2009). In fact, the normalization of the abnormal prefrontal response during executive functioning was positively correlated with the improvement in severity of hallucination-like experiences. Interestingly, in the subjects who became psychotic, the normalization of prefrontal hyperactivation that was a feature of the rest of the group was not evident (Plate 8.2), suggesting that the onset of psychosis may be associated with the persistence of the original perturbation in prefrontal function.

These studies provide evidence that in prodromal psychosis brain changes concur with symptomatic improvement. In addition they emphasize the importance of early interventions in the treatment of schizophrenia, suggesting that the observed neurophysiological abnormalities are something that could perhaps be modulated by active interventions before the psychosis onset. Although longitudinal randomized controlled fMRI trials in the prodromal population are extremely complex, they will clarify the respective contribution of disease progression and clinical interventions in the prodromal phases preceding the illness onset.

Integration of fMRI across modalities

Recent advancements in imaging techniques allow researchers to combine different functional imaging modalities. Multimodal neuroimaging during the prodromal phases of psychosis is nowadays possible and has the potential to delineate the causal relationship between key pathophysiological processes in the evolution of psychosis. For example our group has recently conducted fMRI–PET (Fusar-Poli, Howes et al., 2009, 2010) and fMRI–MRS (magnetic resonance spectroscopy; Valli et al., 2011) studies in subjects with prodromal signs of psychosis. The former studies aimed at investigating the relationship between dopamine function and cortical activation in people experiencing prodromal symptoms of psychosis. Abnormal cortical function during cognitive tasks and elevated striatal dopaminergic transmission (Howes et al., 2007; see also Chapter 10 by Howes in this volume, pp. 127–146) are two of the most robust pathophysiological features of schizophrenia. Both alterations in prefrontal activation (Fusar-Poli, Perez et al., 2007) during working memory/executive processes and elevated subcortical dopamine (Howes et al., 2009) are also evident in individuals with an enhanced risk for psychosis. However, the exact relationship between them in the development of the disorder remains to be established. To address this issue we studied medication-naive subjects with prodromal signs for psychosis, measuring prefrontal activation during a verbal fluency task with fMRI and measuring dopamine synthesis capacity in the striatum with ^{18}F-labelled fluorodopa PET (Fusar-Poli, Howes et al., 2009; see Plate 8.3, situated between pp. 116 and 117). In line with the fMRI findings described in this chapter, subjects at enhanced risk for psychosis showed increased neural activation in the prefrontal cortex as compared to healthy controls. Similarly, striatal dopamine function was greater in the high-risk group than in controls. We then found that altered prefrontal activation in subjects at enhanced risk for psychosis was related to elevated striatal dopamine function (Plate 8.3). In a following PET–fMRI study on working memory we uncovered a positive correlation between frontal activation and fluorodopa uptake in the associative striatum in controls but a negative correlation in the high-risk group (see Plate 8.4, situated between pp. 116 and 117; Fusar-Poli, Howes et al., 2010). The key findings from these studies taken altogether is that in individuals at very high risk of schizophrenia, altered prefrontal activation during a task of executive/working memory function was directly related to striatal hyperdopaminergia. This provided in vivo evidence of a link between dopamine dysfunction and the perturbed prefrontal function, which may underlie the deficits in cognitive processing evident in people with prodromal symptoms of psychosis and predate the first episode of frank psychosis.

In another multimodal study using a combination of fMRI and proton MRS, we showed that in people with prodromal signs of psychosis, cortical and subcortical activation during a verbal fluency task is related to thalamic glutamate levels (Fusar-Poli et al., 2011; see Plate 8.5, situated between pp. 116 and 117). Both medial temporal cortical dysfunction and perturbed glutamatergic neurotransmission were regarded as fundamental pathophysiological features of psychosis but their relationship in humans was not clear. Such findings suggests that treatment of people with prodromal signs using glutamatergic drugs has the potential to impact on the subsequent development of psychosis.

Limits of fMRI in prodromal psychosis

Despite the above potentials of fMRI in prodromal psychosis, no reliable neurofunctional marker has been consistently described to date and the lack of methodological consistency across different imaging studies limits the application of these techniques in clinical psychiatry. Heterogeneity in neuroimaging studies of early phases psychosis originates from multiple methodological differences across studies: in the inclusion criteria for, and the clinical characteristics of, at-risk samples (Fusar-Poli, Borgwardt, & Valmaggia, 2008); the use of different cognitive tasks and designs; and the use of different forms of image acquisition and analysis (Fusar-Poli, Allen, & McGuire, 2008). Moreover, because these groups are difficult to recruit, sample sizes in the studies to date have been relatively small.

The inclusion criteria employed to define the high-risk groups are problematic. The term "high risk" can encompass different groups at increased risk for psychosis including: (a) genetic high-risk subjects, (a1) relatives of patients affected with psychosis, (a2) co-twins of patients with psychosis; and (a3) clinical high-risk subjects. Although the risk for psychosis in genetic/clinical high-risk samples is significantly higher than in the general population, it is not the same across these different groups: monozygotic twins have a 40–50% concordance rate for the illness over lifetime (Tsuang, Stone, & Faraone, 2002); first-degree relatives of schizophrenia patients have approximately a tenfold increased risk for later illness compared to non-relatives over lifetime (Chang et al., 2002); while in clinical high-risk cohorts the probability of developing psychosis ranges from 25% within three years (Bonn Scale for the Assessment of Basic Symptoms, BSABS; Velthorst et al., 2009), up to 35% within 2.5 years (Structured Interview for Prodromal Syndromes, SIPS; Cannon et al., 2008), 35% after two years (Basel Screening Instrument for Psychosis, BSIP; Riecher-Rössler et al., 2007) and 41% within two years (at-risk mental state, ARMS; Yung et al., 2003, 2007), depending on the different inclusion criteria. Within each of these different high-risk groups there is further heterogeneity in that a subset will develop psychosis whereas others will not. High-risk subjects also vary with respect to the severity of the symptoms they experience. In fact, observed fMRI alterations could reflect the ongoing psychopathology and not necessarily represent the neurofunctional trait of the psychotic spectrum, addressing the relevance of specific correlation analysis between brain activity and symptoms. For instance, Whalley et al. subdivided familial at-risk subjects with and without symptoms and reported significant differences in brain activity between these groups relative to controls (Whalley et al., 2004).

Although psychiatric imaging is a powerful instrument to detect subtle brain activation differences between subjects in the early stages of psychosis and healthy controls, the power to detect neuropsychological and behavioural differences has often been limited by small sample sizes (generally less than 15 subjects per group). This partly reflects the fact that recruiting subjects at enhanced risk for psychosis is often difficult and time consuming. These small sample sizes can leave studies underpowered to detect true positive activation and simultaneously enhance the risk of false positives, and are likely to contribute to inconsistencies in the results across studies. Functional MRI studies comparing high-risk subjects and healthy volunteers often report activation differences alongside differences in the ability of the groups to perform the task. It is thus difficult to determine whether any differences in activation are secondary to poor performance in the clinical group. Hence, interpretation of reduced brain activity in poorly performing high-risk subjects is not straightforward. The method of analysis and choice of parameters is another factor that is likely to affect the analysis sensitivity (Fusar-Poli, Bhattacharyya et al., 2010), although research in the area is limited. Thus, analytical approaches vary across studies with some using a whole brain approach and others studying preselected Regions of Interest (ROIs) mainly located in the prefrontal cortex. Consequently, the current imaging literature cannot exclude significant functional abnormalities on regions outside the set of the preselected ROIs and mainly features processes that involve the frontal cortex. Also, differences in scanning methodologies or brain templates employed to "normalize" individual anatomic differences may account for inconsistencies in neurofunctional findings.

Conclusions

Functional MRI studies of the prodromal phases of psychosis have the potential to identify core neurophysiological markers of an impending risk to psychosis, to clarify the dynamic neurofunctional changes underlying transition from a high-risk state to full psychotic episodes and to address significant correlations between brain function and prodromal psychopathology. Advanced functional imaging methods allow the investigation of functional connectivity between brain regions or the integration of fMRI with different functional imaging techniques. In particular the combination of fMRI with PET has the potential to clarify the relationship between dopamine alterations and prefrontal function in the pre-psychotic phases. Further developments of fMRI research in this field may result from the standardization of methods across centres and the use of multi-centre studies that permit the recruitment of larger samples.

References

Agid, O., Kapur, S., Arenovich, T., & Zipursky, R. (2003). Delayed onset hypothesis of antipsychotic action: A hypothesis tested and rejected. *Archives of General Psychiatry*, *60*, 1228–1235.

Allen, P., Seal, M. L., Valli, I., Fusar-Poli, P., Perlini, C., Day, F., et al. (2009). Altered prefrontal and hippocampal function during verbal encoding and recognition in people with prodromal symptoms of psychosis. *Schizophrenia Bulletin*, 37(4), 746–756. Epub 23 November.

Brett, M., Johnsrude, I. S., & Owen, A. M. (2002). The problem of functional localization in the human brain. *Nature Reviews Neuroscience*, *3*, 243–249.

Broome, M. R., Matthiasson, P., Fusar-Poli, P., Woolley, J. B., Johns, L. C., Tabraham, P., et al. (2009). Neural correlates of executive function and working memory in the "at-risk mental state". *British Journal of Psychiatry*, *194*, 25–33.

Broome, M. R., Woolley, J. B., Tabraham, P., Johns, L. C., Bramon, E., Murray, G. K., et al. (2005). What causes the onset of psychosis? *Schizophrenia Research*, *79*, 23–34.

Cannon, T. D., Cadenhead, K., Cornblatt, B., Woods, S. W., Addington, J., Walker, E., et al. (2008). Prediction of psychosis in youth at high clinical risk: A multisite longitudinal study in North America. *Archives of General Psychiatry*, *65*, 28–37.

Chang, C. J., Chen, W. J., Liu, S. K., Cheng, J. J., Yang, W. C., Chang, H. J., et al. (2002). Morbidity risk of psychiatric disorders among the first degree relatives of schizophrenia patients in Taiwan. *Schizophrenia Bulletin*, *28*, 379–392.

Crossley, N. A., Mechelli, A., Fusar-Poli, P., Broome, M. R., Matthiasson, P., Johns, L. C., et al. (2009). Superior temporal lobe dysfunction and frontotemporal dysconnectivity in subjects at risk of psychosis and in first-episode psychosis. *Human Brain Mapping*, *30*(12), 4129–4137.

Fusar-Poli, P., Allen, P., & McGuire, P. (2008). Neuroimaging studies of the early stages of psychosis: A critical review. *European Psychiatry*, *23*, 237–244.

Fusar-Poli, P., Bhattacharyya, S., Allen, P., Crippa, J. A., Borgwardt, S., Martin-Santos, R., et al. (2010). Effect of image analysis software on neurofunctional activation during processing of emotional human faces. *Journal of Clinical Neuroscience, 17,* 311–314.

Fusar-Poli, P., Borgwardt, S., & Valmaggia, L. (2008). Heterogeneity in the assessment of the at-risk mental state for psychosis. *Psychiatric Services, 59,* 813.

Fusar-Poli, P., Broome, M. R., Matthiasson, P., Williams, S. C., Brammer, M., & McGuire, P. K. (2007). Effects of acute antipsychotic treatment on brain activation in first episode psychosis: An fMRI study. *European Neuropsychopharmacology, 17,* 492–500.

Fusar-Poli, P., Broome, M. R., Matthiasson, P., Woolley, J. B., Mechelli, A., Johns, L. C., et al. (2009). Prefrontal function at presentation directly related to clinical outcome in people at ultra-high risk of psychosis. *Schizophrenia Bulletin, 37*(1), 189–198.

Fusar-Poli, P., Howes, O. D., Allen, P., Broome, M., Valli, I., Asselin, M. C., et al. (2009). Abnormal prefrontal activation directly related to pre-synaptic striatal dopamine dysfunction in people at clinical high risk for psychosis. *Molecular Psychiatry, 16*(1), 67–75.

Fusar-Poli, P., Howes, O. D., Allen, P., Broome, M., Valli, I., Asselin, M. C., et al. (2010). Abnormal frontostriatal interactions in people with prodromal signs of psychosis: A multimodal imaging study. *Archives of General Psychiatry, 67,* 683–691.

Fusar-Poli, P., Perez, J., Broome, M., Borgwardt, S., Placentino, A., Caverzasi, E., et al. (2007). Neurofunctional correlates of vulnerability to psychosis: A systematic review and meta-analysis. *Neuroscience and Biobehavioral Reviews, 31,* 465–484.

Fusar-Poli, P., Stone, J. M., Broome, M. R., Valli, I., Mechelli, A., McLean, M. A., et al. (2011). Thalamic glutamate levels as a predictor of cortical response during executive functioning in subjects at high risk for psychosis. *Archives of General Psychiatry* (Epub ahead of print 2 May).

Howes, O., Montgomery, A., Asselin, M. C., Murray, R. M., Valli, I., Tabraham, P., et al. (2009). Elevated striatal dopamine function linked to prodromal signs of schizophrenia. *Archives of General Psychiatry, 66,* 13–20.

Howes, O. D., Montgomery, A. J., Asselin, M., Murray, R., Grasby, P., & McGuire, P. (2007). Molecular imaging studies of the striatal dopaminergic system in psychosis and predictions for the prodromal phase of psychosis. *British Journal of Psychiatry, 51*(Suppl.), s13–s18.

Kapur, S., Arenovich, T., Agid, O., Zipursky, R., Lindborg, S. R., & Jones, B. (2005). Evidence for onset of antipsychotic effects within the first 24 hours of treatment. *American Journal of Psychiatry, 162,* 939–946.

Lane, C. J., Ngan, E. T., Yatham, L. N., Ruth, T. J., & Liddle, P. F. (2004). Immediate effects of risperidone on cerebral activity in healthy subjects: A comparison with subjects with first-episode schizophrenia. *Journal of Psychiatry and Neuroscience, 29,* 30–37.

Lawrie, S. M., Hall, J., McIntosh, A. M., Cunningham-Owens, D. G., & Johnstone, E. C. (2008). Neuroimaging and molecular genetics of schizophrenia: Pathophysiological advances and therapeutic potential. *British Journal of Pharmacology, 153*(Suppl. 1), S120–S124.

Marjoram, D., Job, D. E., Whalley, H. C., Gountouna, V. E., McIntosh, A. M., Simonotto, E., et al. (2006). A visual joke fMRI investigation into theory of mind and enhanced risk of schizophrenia. *NeuroImage, 31,* 1850–1858.

McGuire, P., Howes, O. D., Stone, J., & Fusar-Poli, P. (2008). Functional neuroimaging in schizophrenia: Diagnosis and drug discovery. *Trends in Pharmacological Sciences, 29,* 91–98.

Ngan, E. T., Lane, C. J., Ruth, T. J., & Liddle, P. F. (2002). Immediate and delayed effects of risperidone on cerebral metabolism in neuroleptic naive schizophrenic patients: Correlations with symptom change. *Journal of Neurology, Neurosurgery and Psychiatry, 72*, 106–110.

Olsen, K., & Rosenbaum, R. (2006). Prospective investigations of the prodromal state of schizophrenia: Review of studies. *Acta Psychiatrica Scandinavica, 113*, 247–272.

Riecher-Rössler, A., Gschwandtner, U., Aston, J., Borgwardt, S., Drewe, M., Fuhr, P., et al. (2007). The Basel early detection-of-psychosis (FEPSY) study—Design and preliminary results. *Acta Psychiatrica Scandinavica, 115*, 114–125.

Smieskova, R., Fusar-Poli, P., Allen, P., Bendfeldt, K., Stieglitz, R. D., Drewe, J., et al. (2009). The effects of antipsychotics on the brain: What have we learnt from structural imaging of schizophrenia?—A systematic review. *Current Pharmaceutical Design, 15*, 2535–2549.

Smieskova, R., Fusar-Poli, P., Allen, P., Bendfeldt, K., Stieglitz, R. D., Drewe, J., et al. (2010). Neuroimaging predictors of transition to psychosis—A systematic review and meta-analysis. *Neuroscience and Biobehavioural Reviews, 34*(8), 1207–1222.

Snitz, B. E., Macdonald, A., Cohen, J. D., Cho, R. Y., Becker, T., & Carter, C. S. (2005). Lateral and medial hypofrontality in first-episode schizophrenia: Functional activity in a medication-naive state and effects of short-term atypical antipsychotic treatment. *American Journal of Psychiatry, 162*, 2322–2329.

Tsuang, M. T., Stone, W. S., & Faraone, S. V. (2002). Understanding predisposition to schizophrenia: Toward intervention and prevention. *Canadian Journal of Psychiatry, 47*, 518–526.

Valli, I., Stone, J., Mechelli, A., Bhattacharyya, S., Raffin, M., Allen, P., et al. (2011). Altered medial temporal activation related to local glutamate levels in subjects with prodromal signs of psychosis. *Biological Psychiatry, 69*(1), 97–99.

Velthorst, E., Nieman, D. H., Becker, H. E., van de Fliert, R., Dingemans, P. M., Klaassen, R., et al. (2009). Baseline differences in clinical symptomatology between ultra high risk subjects with and without a transition to psychosis. *Schizophrenia Research, 109*, 60–65.

Whalley, H. C., Simonotto, E., Flett, S., Marshall, I., Ebmeier, K. P., Owens, D. G., et al. (2004). fMRI correlates of state and trait effects in subjects at genetically enhanced risk of schizophrenia. *Brain, 127*, 478–490.

Whalley, H. C., Simonotto, E., Moorhead, W., McIntosh, A., Marshall, I., Ebmeier, K. P., et al. (2006). Functional imaging as a predictor of schizophrenia. *Biological Psychiatry, 60*(5), 454–462.

Yung, A. R., Phillips, L. J., Yuen, H. P., Francey, S. M., McFarlane, C. A., Hallgren, M., et al. (2003). Psychosis prediction: 12-month follow-up of a high-risk ("prodromal") group. *Schizophrenia Research, 60*, 21–32.

Yung, A. R., Yuen, H. P., Berger, G., Francey, S., Hung, T. C., Nelson, B., et al. (2007). Declining transition rate in ultra high risk (prodromal) services: Dilution or reduction of risk? *Schizophrenia Bulletin, 33*, 673–681.

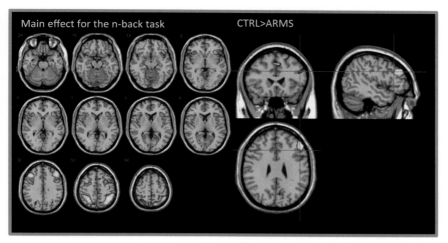

Plate 8.1 Neurofunctional correlates of enhanced risk to pychosis. Main effect for the *n*-back task (on the left) and reduced prefrontal and parietal activation in subjects with an at-risk mental state relative to controls (on the right) during the *n*-back task. The left side of the brain is shown on the left side of the figure.

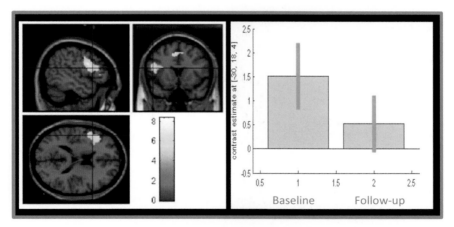

Plate 8.2 fMRI and longitudinal outcomes in subjects at high risk for psychosis. Longitudinal reduction in left inferior frontal activation during the verbal fluency task in the high-risk (ARMS) group (Baseline–Follow-up, left of the figure is left on the brain). Within the high-risk sample, the longitudinal change in cortical response was associated with changes in psychopathology. The greater the reduction in activation, the greater the improvement in perceptual symptoms, such as hallucinations.

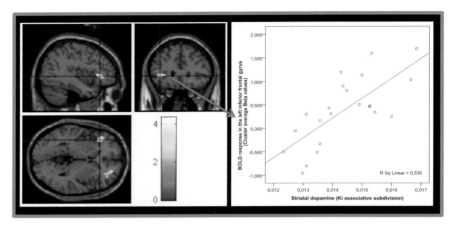

Plate 8.3 Integration of fMRI across modalities. (On the left) fMRI results: greater activation in the left inferior frontal gyrus (cross hairs) and right middle frontal gyrus in the high-risk (ARMS) group than controls during the verbal fluency task. (On the right) PET–fMRI results: correlation between left inferior frontal activation during verbal fluency and dopamine function in the associative subdivision of the striatum in the high-risk (ARMS) group.

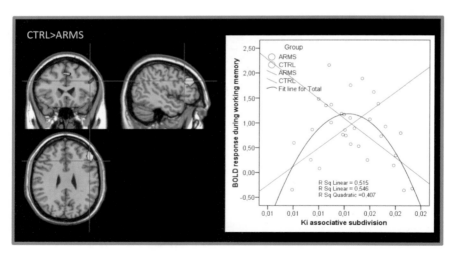

Plate 8.4 Integration of fMRI across modalities. Group differences in the relationship between prefrontal activation during the *n*-back task (on the left) and striatal dopamine function. There was a positive correlation between right middle frontal activation and ^{18}F-labelled fluorodopa uptake (Ki) in the associative striatum in controls (green) but a negative correlation in the high-risk (ARMS) group (blue). The left side of the brain is shown on the left side of the figure.

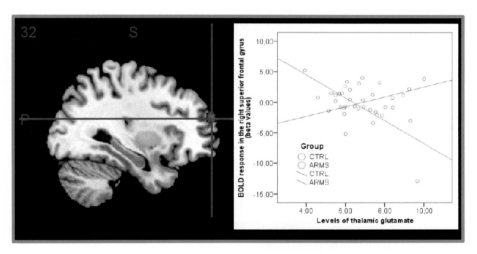

Plate 8.5 Integration of fMRI across modalities. Correlation between prefrontal functioning during verbal fluency and thalamic glutamate levels in subjects at enhanced clinical risk for psychosis. The plot is showing the right superior frontal region where high-risk (ARMS) subjects showed a negative correlation with thalamic glutamate levels and controls (CTRL) show a positive correlation.

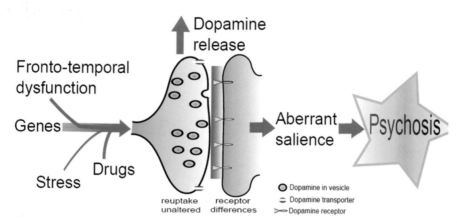

Plate 10.1 Illustrating the dopamine hypothesis: Version III—The final common pathway. Taken from Howes, O. D., & Kapur, S. (2009). The dopamine hypothesis of schizophrenia: Version III—The final common pathway. *Schizophrenia Bulletin*, *35*(3), 549–562. Copyright © 2009 Oxford University Press. Reproduced with kind permission.

9 Glutamate: Gateway to psychosis?

James M. Stone

Recent years have seen a resurgence of interest in the role of abnormal glutamatergic transmission in schizophrenia—as a factor in the pathoaetiology of the condition and as a potential target for novel treatments. In this chapter, I will attempt to summarize the key findings of the last 30 years and to highlight the possible role of abnormal glutamate transmission in prodrome, transition and first-episode schizophrenia.

The glutamate hypothesis of schizophrenia arose in the 1980s from converging findings—first, that patients with schizophrenia had reduced cerebrospinal fluid (CSF) glutamate (Kim, Kornhuber, Schmid-Burgk, & Holzmüller, 1980) and, second, that drugs such as phencyclidine (PCP) and ketamine, which induce effects markedly similar to both positive and negative symptoms of schizophrenia, act as high affinity antagonists for the N-methyl-D-aspartate receptor (NMDAR; Anis, Berry, Burton, & Lodge, 1983; Honey, Miljkovic, & MacDonald, 1985). Although several groups failed to replicate the original finding of reduced CSF glutamate, the unique quality of NMDAR antagonists to induce a much closer approximation to the full picture of psychosis in schizophrenia than drugs affecting the dopamine or serotonin systems (Vollenweider & Geyer, 2001), led to great interest in the possible role that abnormalities of glutamatergic transmission, particularly NMDAR-mediated dysfunction, might play in the idiopathic condition. This evidence has been further supported by the recent finding that most of the candidate genes for schizophrenia are associated with glutamatergic neurotransmission at the NMDAR containing synapse (Harrison & Weinberger, 2005).

NMDA receptors and glutamate

NMDARs are ubiquitous ion channel glutamate receptors present throughout the central nervous system. They play a variety of roles, with their primary function being the transmission of slow (calcium ion) current following co-activation by glutamate and glycine in the presence of membrane depolarization (Dingledine, Borges, Bowie, & Traynelis, 1999). The voltage block is achieved by a magnesium ion within the channel of the receptor at resting potential, with the block being removed only in the presence of multiple excitatory post-synaptic potentials

(EPSPs), arising usually from glutamate binding to post-synaptic α-amino-3-hydroxy-5-methyl-4-isoxazolepropionic acid (AMPA) or kainate receptors. Thus, NMDARs have been suggested to be biological "coincidence detectors" (Seeburg et al., 1995). In contrast, when expressed on γ-aminobutyric acid (GABA) interneurons, NMDARs have a role in fast synaptic transmission, contributing directly to EPSP formation and resulting in the modulation of GABA release (Grunze et al., 1996; Maccaferri & Dingledine, 2002).

Drugs such as ketamine, PCP and dizocilpine (MK-801) block NMDARs in a use-dependent manner (Anis et al., 1983; Honey et al., 1985; Huettner & Bean, 1988; MacDonald, Miljkovic, & Pennefather, 1987). This has been interpreted as blocking the channel through intrachannel binding, although recent evidence suggests that, as well as blocking open channels (reducing channel open time), ketamine, PCP and MK-801 may also bind to the closed channel, reducing the probability of channel opening through action at an allosteric site on the lipophilic surface of the receptor (Javitt & Zukin, 1989; MacDonald, Bartlett, Mody, Reynolds, & Salter, 1990; Orser, Pennefather, & MacDonald, 1997).

The effect of NMDAR blockade in rats was investigated by Olney and Farber (1995). They found that chronic treatment led to cortical brain lesions (Olney & Farber, 1995). These lesions could be prevented by treatment with AMPA receptor antagonists (Olney & Farber, 1995). They hypothesized that systemic NMDAR antagonist administration primarily affected GABAergic interneuron function and the resultant loss of inhibitory tone led to disinhibition of glutamatergic projections. Subsequent microdialysis studies in rats confirmed that NMDAR antagonists led to increased glutamate release in medial prefrontal cortex (Lorrain, Baccei, Bristow, Anderson, & Varney, 2003; Moghaddam, Adams, Verma, & Daly, 1997). Furthermore, direct injection cortical of NMDAR antagonists did not lead to local glutamate release, nor to any evidence of neuronal toxicity (Lorrain et al., 2003; Sharp, Tomitaka, Bernaudin, & Tomitaka, 2001), whereas injection into anterior thalamus showed the same pattern of injury to that of systemic administration (Sharp et al., 2001). One study in healthy human subjects using proton magnetic resonance spectroscopy (1H-MRS) has demonstrated an increase in glutamine levels (suggested to be as a marker of synaptic glutamate release) in anterior cingulate following ketamine administration (Rowland et al., 2005).

Brain volume loss in schizophrenia and prodromal psychosis

The toxic changes and neural loss occurring in animal NMDAR antagonist models are notable as brain volume reduction in schizophrenia is one of the most robust findings in the illness. Patients with chronic schizophrenia were shown to have increased lateral ventricle volume by CT imaging in the 1970s (Johnstone, Crow, Frith, Husband, & Kreel, 1976). Since then, many groups have replicated this finding by a variety of imaging methods (Shenton, Dickey, Frumin, & McCarley, 2001). Grey matter reductions relative to controls, affecting many regions of the brain, but in particular hippocampus, have been reported in patients with first-episode psychosis (Steen, Mull, McClure, Hamer, & Lieberman, 2006). With disease progression, the rate of grey matter loss in schizophrenia appears to slow, with the highest rates of grey matter loss early in the illness (van Haren et al., 2008).

Studies of individuals at high risk of developing psychosis have demonstrated that reductions in grey matter volume relative to controls are present before the onset of frank psychosis (Borgwardt et al., 2007; Job, Whalley, Johnstone, & Lawrie, 2005; Lawrie et al., 1999; Pantelis et al., 2003) and that with transition to psychosis, a further reduction in cortical grey matter volume occurs (Borgwardt et al., 2007; Pantelis et al., 2003; Takahashi et al., 2009). Other groups have shown that a longer duration of untreated psychosis is associated with greater grey matter reductions (Lappin et al., 2006; Takahashi et al., 2007), and worse outcome (Marshall et al., 2005). Similarly, it has been shown that cognitive deterioration occurs at its fastest rate in the years prior to the development of schizophrenia, up to and including the first psychotic episode (Bilder et al., 2006; Hoff, Svetina, Shields, Stewart, & DeLisi, 2005).

Proton magnetic resonance spectroscopy studies in schizophrenia examining N-acetyl aspartate (NAA), thought to be an index of neuronal integrity, closely mirror the changes in grey matter volume. These studies have generally found reductions in NAA in patients with chronic and first-episode schizophrenia, affecting frontal and temporal cortices (Steen, Hamer, & Lieberman, 2005). In subjects with an at-risk mental state (ARMS), who are at high clinical risk of schizophrenia, we found NAA reductions in the left thalamus compared to healthy controls, but no reductions in frontal or hippocampal NAA (Stone et al., 2009). This finding was replicated by another group in subjects at high genetic risk of psychosis (Yoo et al., 2009). Post-mortem studies have also found loss of thalamic volume (primarily from pyramidal projection neurons) in patients with schizophrenia (Clinton & Meador-Woodruff, 2004; Danos et al., 1998), and at genetic risk for the illness (McIntosh et al., 2004). Together these findings suggest that thalamic changes may contribute to vulnerability to schizophrenia. It is interesting to note that an earlier study found a correlation between duration of prodromal phase and thalamic NAA reductions (Theberge et al., 2004).

Thus, there is good evidence for reductions in brain volume in schizophrenia. Current evidence suggests that the majority of these losses occur before and during the transition to the first episode of psychosis, with relatively low reductions after the first episode. It has been suggested that these reductions might arise secondary to excess glutamate release through an excitotoxic process (Deutsch, Rosse, Schwartz, & Mastropaolo, 2001; Olney, Newcomer, & Farber, 1999). Thus, elevated cortical glutamate may be the final and key neurochemical event driving transition to schizophrenia, a "gateway to psychosis".

Glutamatergic abnormalities in schizophrenia: Relationship to transition

Evidence for glutamatergic abnormalities in schizophrenia has arisen from a number of different sources. In addition to the growing genetic support for a primary glutamatergic basis for the illness (Harrison & Weinberger, 2005), two groups have reported reduced NMDAR messenger ribonucleic acid (mRNA) in the left hippocampus of post-mortem brain (Gao et al., 2000; Law & Deakin, 2001), while an in vivo single photon emission tomography (SPET) study by Pilowsky and colleagues at the Institute of Psychiatry showed a relative reduction in left hippo-campal NMDAR binding in patients with schizophrenia who were not taking any antipsychotic medication (Pilowsky et al., 2006). This finding was partially normalized in patients on typical antipsychotics and clozapine (Pilowsky et al., 2006).

Other groups have examined brain glutamate levels using 1H-MRS. Theberge and colleagues reported elevated glutamine levels in the anterior cingulate and thalamus in patients with first-episode schizophrenia (Theberge et al., 2002), but in patients with chronic schizophrenia, they reported reduced glutamine levels in the anterior cingulate (Theberge et al., 2003). From these data, it can be suggested that glutamatergic change and, by extension, excitotoxicity, appears to be a feature of the early phase of psychosis. If glutamatergic changes do drive transition to psychosis, it might be expected that these changes may also be present in individuals prodromal for the illness.

Several groups have investigated brain glutamate abnormalities in individuals at high risk of psychosis. Adolescents at high genetic risk of schizophrenia (having relatives with schizophrenia) were reported to have increased glutamine/glutamate in the medial frontal cortex by Tibbo and colleagues (Tibbo, Hanstock, Valiakalayil, & Allen, 2004), and work in our laboratory has found increased glutamine in the anterior cingulate, but reduced glutamate in the left thalamus in subjects at risk of psychosis (Stone et al., 2009). Two groups (including our own) have investigated the relationship between brain glutamate levels and grey matter volume. We found that in ARMS subjects, lower thalamic glutamate levels were associated with reduced grey matter volume in the medial temporal cortex and insula (Stone et al., 2009), and in a longitudinal study of patients with first-episode schizophrenia, Theberge found that reductions in thalamic glutamine levels correlated with reductions in parietal and temporal grey matter (Theberge et al., 2007). Reductions in thalamic glutamate could lead to reduced thalamic GABAergic interneuron activity and, by extension, disinhibition of thalamocortical glutamate projection neurons. Thus, the reductions in temporal cortex grey matter volume could arise secondary to excess glutamate release. Alternatively, reductions in temporal cortex volume could be primary and lead to secondary reductions in thalamic glutamate levels through reductions in glutamatergic efferents from the temporal cortex. Future studies examining the longitudinal change in grey matter and glutamate levels in individuals with prodromal psychosis are required to clarify these points.

The evidence for glutamate excitotoxicity in schizophrenia: Post-mortem findings

The strongest post-mortem findings in schizophrenia point to a reduction in GABA interneuron density or function in the frontal cortex and hippocampus (Lewis, Hashimoto, & Volk, 2005; Reynolds, Abdul-Monim, Neill, & Zhang, 2004). In these brain regions, there are several types of GABAergic interneurons.

The interneurons that co-express parvalbumin as well as the GAD67 subtype of glutamic acid decarboxylase (chandelier cells) appear to be differentially affected, as specific reductions in parvalbumin-containing cells and in GAD67 levels have been reported in these regions (Lewis et al., 2005; Reynolds et al., 2004). These changes, particularly impairment of GABAergic interneuron function, would be expected to lead to loss of control over burst-firing and disinhibition of glutamatergic projection neurons. The resultant potential excitotoxic damage from glutamate to GABAergic interneurons might lead to further disinhibition of the network, with the positive feedback loop eventually burning itself out through toxicity to the pyramidal projection neurons themselves (Stone, Morrison, & Pilowsky, 2007).

Mechanisms underlying parvalbumin and GAD67 deficits

A recent review suggested several mechanisms that might underlie the GAD67 deficit and, by extension, the GABAergic interneuron dysfunction in schizophrenia (Akbarian & Huang, 2006). These include impairments in glutamatergic transmission via NMDAR, early developmental impairments in brain connectivity, reductions in brain-derived neurotrophic factor (BDNF) and its receptor TrkB and reduced reelin levels.

Glutamatergic deficits

In animal studies, deprivation of visual sensory input, as well as NMDAR antagonists such as ketamine and PCP have been shown to lead to reductions in brain parvalbumin and GAD67 levels (Akbarian & Huang, 2006; Cochran et al., 2003; Keilhoff, Becker, Grecksch, Wolf, & Bernstein, 2004). Thus, an underlying impairment in glutamatergic transmission, perhaps arising as a result of genetic risk factors could potentially drive the neurochemical and anatomical changes seen in post-mortem studies of patients with psychosis.

BDNF

Brain-derived neurotrophic factor is involved in neural plasticity, with a particular role in the regulation of inhibitory interneurons (Akbarian & Huang, 2006). Reductions in BDNF levels have been shown in the frontal cortex and hippocampus of patients with schizophrenia, associated with reductions in GAD67 in the same regions, suggesting that GABA interneuron dysfunction might be driven by impairments in BDNF stimulation. Animal models support this hypothesis, with changes in BDNF and TrkB expression being associated with changes in GAD and GABA levels (Akbarian & Huang, 2006).

Reelin

Reelin is a molecule involved in brain development and neuron positioning. Brain levels are reduced in patients with schizophrenia, probably arising as a result of methylation of the gene-promoter region of the reelin gene, rather than from a polymorphism of the gene. Methylation of gene promoters occurs in life and affects gene expression, but methylation states of genes can be inherited. This environmental control of gene expression, which has been termed epigenetics, is of particular interest in the case of reelin, given the gene–environment interaction hypothesized to underlie schizophrenia. Reelin is associated with changes in GABAergic interneuron function, with reeler (reelin deficient) mice showing reduced neuropil and dendritic spine density, as well as GAD67 reductions. Reelin appears to be upstream of changes in GAD67 expression as GAD67-deficient mice do not show any changes in reelin or in dendritic spine density (Akbarian & Huang, 2006). Thus, in-life methylation of the reelin promoter region might be one factor in the development of abnormal GABA-glutamate transmission underlying the development of psychosis.

Glutamate dopamine interactions

There are several theories as to the relationship between excess subcortical dopaminergic transmission and abnormalities in GABA–glutamate transmission in schizophrenia. Most of these suggest that GABA or glutamatergic changes are primary and that increases in striatal dopamine neuron activity arise as a result of these changes (Laruelle, Kegeles, & Abi-Dargham, 2003; Lisman et al., 2008; Stone et al., 2007). A recently developed animal model of schizophrenia has demonstrated that abnormalities of the hippocampus leading to increased glutamatergic projections result in increased striatal dopamine cell activity (Lisman et al., 2008). Similarly, in healthy volunteers, ketamine administration leads to increased dopamine release following amphetamine (Kegeles et al., 2000).

Time course of glutamatergic abnormalities in schizophrenia

Evidence from 1H-MRS studies suggest that increases in glutamate transmission might occur only in the very early stages of schizophrenia (Stone et al., 2009; Theberge et al., 2002; Tibbo et al., 2004) and that, with disease progression, glutamate levels may normalize or even reduce below control levels (Tayoshi et al., 2009; Theberge et al., 2003, 2007), perhaps as a result of excitotoxicity leading to a potentially irreversible "deficit" state reminiscent of Emil Kraepelin's original description of "dementia praecox" (Deutsch et al., 2001; Stone et al., 2007). As a result, treatments targeting the GABA or glutamate system, would be most likely to be of greatest use if given early in the illness, with the aim of preventing transition to psychosis, or progression from the first episode (Stone et al., 2007; Stone & Pilowsky, 2007).

Conclusions

Together, these results suggest that glutamatergic changes are central to the development of psychosis and that the changes in brain volume associated with schizophrenia may arise as a result of an excitotoxic process from excess cortical glutamate. It is likely that, in the near future, drugs specifically targeting this system with the aim of reducing or preventing progression of the illness will be developed.

References

Akbarian, S., & Huang, H. S. (2006). Molecular and cellular mechanisms of altered GAD1/GAD67 expression in schizophrenia and related disorders. *Brain Research Reviews*, *52*(2), 293–304.

Anis, N. A., Berry, S. C., Burton, N. R., & Lodge, D. (1983). The dissociative anaesthetics, ketamine and phencyclidine, selectively reduce excitation of central mammalian neurones by N-methyl-aspartate. *British Journal of Pharmacology*, *79*(2), 565–575.

Bilder, R. M., Reiter, G., Bates, J., Lencz, T., Szeszko, P., Goldman, R. S., et al. (2006). Cognitive development in schizophrenia: Follow-back from the first episode. *Journal of Clinical Neuropsychology*, *28*(2), 270–282.

Borgwardt, S. J., Riecher-Rössler, A., Dazzan, P., Chitnis, X., Aston, J., Drewe, M., et al. (2007). Regional gray matter volume abnormalities in the at risk mental state. *Biological Psychiatry*, *61*(10), 1148–1156.

Clinton, S. M., & Meador-Woodruff, J. H. (2004). Thalamic dysfunction in schizophrenia: Neurochemical, neuropathological and in vivo imaging abnormalities. *Schizophrenia Research*, *69*(2–3), 237–253.

Cochran, S. M., Kennedy, M., McKerchar, C. E., Steward, L. J., Pratt, J. A., & Morris, B. J. (2003). Induction of metabolic hypofunction and neurochemical deficits after chronic intermittent exposure to phencyclidine: Differential modulation by antipsychotic drugs. *Neuropsychopharmacology*, *28*(2), 265–275.

Danos, P., Baumann, B., Bernstein, H. G., Franz, M., Stauch, R., Northoff, G., et al. (1998). Schizophrenia and anteroventral thalamic nucleus: Selective decrease of parvalbumin-immunoreactive thalamocortical projection neurons. *Psychiatry Research*, *82*(1), 1–10.

Deutsch, S. I., Rosse, R. B., Schwartz, B. L., & Mastropaolo, J. (2001). A revised excitotoxic hypothesis of schizophrenia: Therapeutic implications. *Clinical Neuropharmacology*, *24*(1), 43–49.

Dingledine, R., Borges, K., Bowie, D., & Traynelis, S. F. (1999). The glutamate receptor ion channels. *Pharmacological Reviews*, *51*(1), 7–61.

Gao, X. M., Sakai, K., Roberts, R. C., Conley, R. R., Dean, B., & Tamminga, C. A. (2000). Ionotropic glutamate receptors and expression of N-methyl-D-aspartate receptor subunits in subregions of human hippocampus: Effects of schizophrenia. *American Journal of Psychiatry*, *157*(7), 1141–1149.

Grunze, H. C., Rainnie, D. G., Hasselmo, M. E., Barkai, E., Hearn, E. F., McCarley, R. W., et al. (1996). NMDA-dependent modulation of CA1 local circuit inhibition. *Journal of Neuroscience*, *16*(6), 2034–2043.

Harrison, P. J., & Weinberger, D. R. (2005). Schizophrenia genes, gene expression and neuropathology: On the matter of their convergence. *Molecular Psychiatry*, *10*(1), 40–68.

Hoff, A. L., Svetina, C., Shields, G., Stewart, J., & DeLisi, L. E. (2005). Ten year longitudinal study of neuropsychological functioning subsequent to a first episode of schizophrenia. *Schizophrenia Research*, *78*(1), 27–34.

Honey, C. R., Miljkovic, Z., & MacDonald, J. F. (1985). Ketamine and phencyclidine cause a voltage-dependent block of responses to L-aspartic acid. *Neuroscience Letters*, *61* (1–2), 135–139.

Huettner, J. E., & Bean, B. P. (1988). Block of N-methyl-D-aspartate-activated current by the anticonvulsant MK-801: Selective binding to open channels. *Proceedings of the National Academy of Sciences of the United States of America*, *85*(4), 1307–1311.

Javitt, D. C., & Zukin, S. R. (1989). Biexponential kinetics of [3H]MK-801 binding: Evidence for access to closed and open N-methyl-D-aspartate receptor channels. *Molecular Pharmacology*, *35*(4), 387–393.

Job, D. E., Whalley, H. C., Johnstone, E. C., & Lawrie, S. M. (2005). Grey matter changes over time in high risk subjects developing schizophrenia. *NeuroImage*, *25*(4), 1023– 1030.

Johnstone, E. C., Crow, T. J., Frith, C. D., Husband, J., & Kreel, J. (1976). Cerebral ventricular size and cognitive impairment in chronic schizophrenia. *Lancet*, *2*(7992), 924–926.

Kegeles, L. S., Abi-Dargham, A., Zea-Ponce, Y., Rodenhiser-Hill, J., Mann, J. J., Van Heertum, R. L., et al. (2000). Modulation of amphetamine-induced striatal dopamine release by ketamine in humans: Implications for schizophrenia. *Biological Psychiatry*, *48*, 627–640.

Keilhoff, G., Becker, A., Grecksch, G., Wolf, G., & Bernstein, H. G. (2004). Repeated application of ketamine to rats induces changes in the hippocampal expression of parvalbumin, neuronal nitric oxide synthase and cFOS similar to those found in human schizophrenia. *Neuroscience*, *126*(3), 591–598.

Kim, J. S., Kornhuber, H. H., Schmid-Burgk, W., & Holzmüller, B. (1980). Low cerebrospinal fluid glutamate in schizophrenic patients and a new hypothesis on schizophrenia. *Neuroscience Letters*, *20*(3), 379–382.

Lappin, J. M., Morgan, K., Morgan, C., Hutchison, G., Chitnis, X., Suckling, J., et al. (2006). Gray matter abnormalities associated with duration of untreated psychosis. *Schizophrenia Research*, *83*(2–3), 145–153.

Laruelle, M., Kegeles, L. S., & Abi-Dargham, A. (2003). Glutamate, dopamine and schizophrenia: From pathophysiology to treatment. *Annals of the New York Academy of Sciences*, *1003*, 138–158.

Law, A. J., & Deakin, J. F. (2001). Asymmetrical reductions of hippocampal NMDAR1 glutamate receptor mRNA in the psychoses. *Neuroreport*, *12*(13), 2971–2974.

Lawrie, S. M., Whalley, H., Kestelman, J. N., Abukmeil, S. S., Byrne, M., Hodges, A., et al. (1999). Magnetic resonance imaging of brain in people at high risk of developing schizophrenia. *Lancet*, *353*(9146), 30–33.

Lewis, D. A., Hashimoto, T., & Volk, D. W. (2005). Cortical inhibitory neurons and schizophrenia. *Nature Reviews Neuroscience*, *6*(4), 312–324.

Lisman, J. E., Coyle, J. T., Green, R. W., Javitt, D. C., Benes, F. M., Heckers, S., et al. (2008). Circuit-based framework for understanding neurotransmitter and risk gene interactions in schizophrenia. *Trends in Neurosciences*, *31*(5), 234–242.

Lorrain, D. S., Baccei, C. S., Bristow, L. J., Anderson, J. J., & Varney, M. A. (2003). Effects of ketamine and N-methyl-D-aspartate on glutamate and dopamine release in the rat prefrontal cortex: Modulation by a group II selective metabotropic glutamate receptor agonist LY379268. *Neuroscience*, *117*(3), 697–706.

Maccaferri, G., & Dingledine, R. (2002). Control of feedforward dendritic inhibition by NMDA receptor-dependent spike timing in hippocampal interneurons. *Journal of Neuroscience*, *22*(13), 5462–5472.

MacDonald, J. F., Bartlett, M. C., Mody, I., Reynolds, J. N., & Salter, M. W. (1990). The PCP site of the NMDA receptor complex. *Advances in Experimental Medicine and Biology, 268*, 27–34.

MacDonald, J. F., Miljkovic, Z., & Pennefather, P. (1987). Use-dependent block of excitatory amino acid currents in cultured neurons by ketamine. *Journal of Neurophysiology, 58*(2), 251–266.

Marshall, M., Lewis, S., Lockwood, A., Drake, R., Jones, P., & Croudace, T. (2005). Association between duration of untreated psychosis and outcome in cohorts of first-episode patients: A systematic review. *Archives of General Psychiatry, 62*(9), 975–983.

McIntosh, A. M., Job, D. E., Moorhead, T. W., Harrison, L. K., Forrester, K., Lawrie, S. M., et al. (2004). Voxel-based morphometry of patients with schizophrenia or bipolar disorder and their unaffected relatives. *Biological Psychiatry, 56*(8), 544–552.

Moghaddam, B., Adams, B., Verma, A., & Daly, D. (1997). Activation of glutamatergic neurotransmission by ketamine: A novel step in the pathway from NMDA receptor blockade to dopaminergic and cognitive disruptions associated with the prefrontal cortex. *Journal of Neuroscience, 17*(8), 2921–2927.

Olney, J. W., & Farber, N. B. (1995). Glutamate receptor dysfunction and schizophrenia. *Archives of General Psychiatry, 52*(12), 998–1007.

Olney, J. W., Newcomer, J. W., & Farber, N. B. (1999). NMDA receptor hypofunction model of schizophrenia. *Journal of Psychiatric Research, 33*(6), 523–533.

Orser, B. A., Pennefather, P. S., & MacDonald, J. F. (1997). Multiple mechanisms of ketamine blockade of N-methyl-D-aspartate receptors. *Anesthesiology, 86*(4), 903–917.

Pantelis, C., Velakoulis, D., McGorry, P. D., Wood, S. J., Suckling, J., Phillips, L. J., et al. (2003). Neuroanatomical abnormalities before and after onset of psychosis: A cross-sectional and longitudinal MRI comparison. *Lancet, 361*(9354), 281–288.

Pilowsky, L. S., Bressan, R. A., Stone, J. M., Erlandsson, K., Mulligan, R. S., Krystal, J. H., et al. (2006). First in vivo evidence of an NMDA receptor deficit in medication-free schizophrenic patients. *Molecular Psychiatry, 11*(2), 118–119.

Reynolds, G. P., Abdul-Monim, Z., Neill, J. C., & Zhang, Z. J. (2004). Calcium binding protein markers of GABA deficits in schizophrenia—Post-mortem studies and animal models. *Neurotoxicity Research, 6*(1), 57–61.

Rowland, L. M., Bustillo, J. R., Mullins, P. G., Jung, R. E., Lenroot, R., Landgraf, E., et al. (2005). Effects of ketamine on anterior cingulate glutamate metabolism in healthy humans: A 4-T proton MRS study. *American Journal of Psychiatry, 162*(2), 394–396.

Seeburg, P. H., Burnashev, N., Kohr, G., Kuner, T., Sprengel, R., & Monyer, H. (1995). The NMDA receptor channel: Molecular design of a coincidence detector. *Recent Progress in Hormone Research, 50*, 19–34.

Sharp, F. R., Tomitaka, M., Bernaudin, M., & Tomitaka, S. (2001). Psychosis: Pathological activation of limbic thalamocortical circuits by psychomimetics and schizophrenia? *Trends in Neurosciences, 24*(6), 330–334.

Shenton, M. E., Dickey, C. C., Frumin, M., & McCarley, R. W. (2001). A review of MRI findings in schizophrenia. *Schizophrenia Research, 49*(1–2), 1–52.

Steen, R. G., Hamer, R. M., & Lieberman, J. A. (2005). Measurement of brain metabolites by 1H magnetic resonance spectroscopy in patients with schizophrenia: A systematic review and meta-analysis. *Neuropsychopharmacology, 30*(11), 1949–1962.

Steen, R. G., Mull, C., McClure, R., Hamer, R. M., & Lieberman, J. A. (2006). Brain volume in first-episode schizophrenia: Systematic review and meta-analysis of magnetic resonance imaging studies. *British Journal of Psychiatry, 188*, 510–518.

126   *Stone*

Stone, J. M., Day, F., Tsagaraki, H., Valli, I., McLean, M. A., Lythgoe, D. J., et al. (2009). Glutamate dysfunction in people with prodromal symptoms of psychosis: Relationship to gray matter volume. *Biological Psychiatry*, *66*(6), 533–539.

Stone, J. M., Morrison, P. D., & Pilowsky, L. S. (2007). Glutamate and dopamine dysregulation in schizophrenia—A synthesis and selective review. *Journal of Psychopharmacology*, *21*(4), 440–452.

Stone, J. M., & Pilowsky, L. S. (2007). Novel targets for drugs in schizophrenia. *CNS & Neurological Disorders – Drug Targets*, *6*(4), 265–272.

Takahashi, T., Suzuki, M., Tanino, R., Zhou, S. Y., Hagino, H., Niu, L., et al. (2007). Volume reduction of the left planum temporal gray matter associated with long duration of untreated psychosis in schizophrenia: A preliminary report. *Psychiatry Research*, *154*(3), 209–219.

Takahashi, T., Wood, S. J., Yung, A. R., Soulsby, B., McGorry, P. D., Suzuki, M., et al. (2009). Progressive gray matter reduction of the superior temporal gyrus during transition to psychosis. *Archives of General Psychiatry*, *66*(4), 366–376.

Tayoshi, S., Sumitani, S., Taniguchi, K., Shibuya-Tayoshi, S., Numata, S., Iga, J., et al. (2009). Metabolite changes and gender differences in schizophrenia using 3-Tesla proton magnetic resonance spectroscopy (1H-MRS). *Schizophrenia Research*, *108*(1–3), 69–77.

Theberge, J., Al-Semaan, Y., Drost, D. J., Malla, A. K., Neufeld, R. W., Bartha, R., et al. (2004). Duration of untreated psychosis vs. N-acetylaspartate and choline in first episode schizophrenia: A 1H magnetic resonance spectroscopy study at 4.0 Tesla. *Psychiatry Research*, *131*(2), 107–114.

Theberge, J., Al-Semaan, Y., Williamson, P. C., Menon, R. S., Neufeld, R. W., Rajakumar, N., et al. (2003). Glutamate and glutamine in the anterior cingulate and thalamus of medicated patients with chronic schizophrenia and healthy comparison subjects measured with 4.0-T proton MRS. *American Journal of Psychiatry*, *160*(12), 2231–2233.

Theberge, J., Bartha, R., Drost, D. J., Menon, R. S., Malla, A., Takhar, J., et al. (2002). Glutamate and glutamine measured with 4.0-T proton MRS in never-treated patients with schizophrenia and healthy volunteers. *American Journal of Psychiatry*, *159*(11), 1944–1946.

Theberge, J., Williamson, K. E., Aoyama, N., Drost, D. J., Manchanda, R., Malla, A. K., et al. (2007). Longitudinal grey-matter and glutamatergic losses in first-episode schizophrenia. *British Journal of Psychiatry*, *191*, 325–334.

Tibbo, P., Hanstock, C., Valiakalayil, A., & Allen, P. (2004). 3-T proton MRS investigation of glutamate and glutamine in adolescents at high genetic risk for schizophrenia. *American Journal of Psychiatry*, *161*(6), 1116–1118.

van Haren, N. E., Pol, H. E., Schnack, H. G., Cahn, W., Brans, R., Carati, I., et al. (2008). Progressive brain volume loss in schizophrenia over the course of the illness: Evidence of maturational abnormalities in early adulthood. *Biological Psychiatry*, *63*(1), 106–113.

Vollenweider, F. X., & Geyer, M. A. (2001). A systems model of altered consciousness: Integrating natural and drug-induced psychoses. *Brain Research Bulletin*, *56*(5), 495–507.

Yoo, S. Y., Yeon, S., Choi, C. H., Kang, D. H., Lee, J. M., Shin, N. Y., et al. (2009). Proton magnetic resonance spectroscopy in subjects with high genetic risk of schizophrenia: Investigation of anterior cingulate, dorsolateral prefrontal cortex and thalamus. *Schizophrenia Research*, *111*(1–3), 86–93.

10 Does dopamine start the psychotic "fire"?

Oliver Howes

Introduction

The hypothesis that dopaminergic mechanisms are central to schizophrenia has been one of the most enduring ideas about the illness. Despite a relatively inauspicious start—dopamine was initially thought to be a precursor molecule of little functional significance—the idea has evolved and accommodated new evidence to provide an increasingly sophisticated account of the involvement of dopamine in schizophrenia. The following chapter summarizes the evolution of the dopamine hypothesis, describing its evolution through the initial expositions, characterized as Version I, to Version II, which has been the guiding framework for many years, before describing the new evidence, which has formed the basis of a revised hypothesis—Version III. Version II was articulated in 1991 (Davis, Kahn, Ko, & Davidson, 1991). At this time molecular imaging research into the dopaminergic system in psychosis had only recently started and consequently does not feature greatly in the hypothesis. As a result Version II has three main limitations: (i) the anatomical location and nature of the dopaminergic dysfunction is poorly defined; (ii) it does not account for how known risk factors for psychosis might lead to dopaminergic function; and (iii) it provides no framework to link dopaminergic function to symptoms. Since 1991 a substantial body of molecular imaging evidence concerning dopaminergic function in psychosis has accrued, which has refined understanding of the anatomical location and nature of the dopaminergic dysfunction. This is reviewed and synthesized to provide an overview of the current state of knowledge of the in vivo dopaminergic system in psychosis. In this period understanding of how risk factors for schizophrenia may lead to dopaminergic dysfunction has also evolved and the relevant findings are reviewed in the following section. Finally, the link between dopaminergic dysfunction and the symptoms of the illness is discussed.

The dopamine hypothesis of schizophrenia: Version I

The first versions of the dopamine hypothesis of schizophrenia—characterized here as Version I—emerged from the seminal work of Arvid Carlsson and colleagues, who identified that chlorpromazine and haloperidol increased the

Table 10.1 Summarizing the features of Versions I and II of the dopamine hypothesis

	Nature of neurochemical dysfunction	*Anatomical localization*	*Symptom domains covered*	*Mechanism linking to symptoms*	*Accounts for risk factors?*
Version I	Focus on post-synaptic receptors	Not specified	Not specified	Not specified	No
Version II	Low frontal dopamine levels	Regional specificity: frontal cortical abnormalities lead to excess subcortical dopamine	Psychosis, negative symptoms and cognitive impairment	No explicit mechanism proposed	No

metabolism of dopamine when administered to animals (Carlsson & Lindqvist, 1963). Further evidence came from studies of amphetamine, which increases synaptic monoamine levels and can induce psychotic symptoms (see Lieberman, Kane, & Alvir, 1987, for a review). The dopamine hypothesis was finally crystallized in the 1970s with the finding that the clinical potency of antipsychotic drugs was directly correlated with their affinity for dopamine receptors (Creese, Burt, & Snyder, 1976; Seeman & Lee, 1975; Seeman, Lee, Chau-Wong, & Wong, 1976). The focus of the hypothesis was on dopamine receptors and blockade of these receptors to treat the psychosis (e.g., Matthysse, 1973; Snyder 1976). While Version I accounted for the data available then, it had a number of limitations (summarized in Table 10.1). There was no explanation of how the neurochemical abnormality translated into the different symptoms seen in the clinic (e.g., positive vs. negative symptoms). Furthermore, there was no localization of the abnormality within the living brain and little consideration of how it might relate to known risk factors for schizophrenia.

The dopamine hypothesis of schizophrenia: Version II

In 1991 Davis and colleagues published what they called "a modified dopamine hypothesis of schizophrenia" (Davis et al., 1991). The main advance was the addition of regional specificity into the hypothesis and a move away from D2 receptors to dopamine levels. Several lines of evidence formed the basis of this shift. In particular, clozapine had been found to have superior efficacy for patients who were refractory to other antipsychotic drugs despite having rather low affinity and occupancy at D2 receptors. Furthermore, the early positron emission tomography (PET) studies of D2/3 receptors in drug-naive patients showed conflicting results.

These findings were incompatible with the simple D2 excess proposed in Version I. Furthermore, dopamine metabolite levels in serum or spinal fluid were found to be reduced in some patients with schizophrenia but still correlated with symptom severity. Davis and colleagues drew on emerging evidence that dopamine receptors show different brain distributions—characterized as D1 predominantly cortical and D2 predominantly subcortical—to suggest that dopamine abnormalities could vary by brain region. PET studies showing hypofrontality, which was directly correlated with low cerebrospinal fluid (CSF) dopamine metabolite levels, provided support for this regional link. They argued that the relationship between hypofrontality and low spinal fluid dopamine metabolite levels indicated low frontal dopamine levels. Version II proposed that schizophrenia was characterized by regionally selective frontal hypodopaminergia and subcortical hyperdopaminergia. Animal studies provided direct evidence of a link between hypo- and hyperdopaminergia: lesions of dopamine neurons in the prefrontal cortex result in increased levels of dopamine in the striatum (Pycock, Kerwin, & Carter, 1980) and dopamine agonists applied to prefrontal areas have the opposite effects (Scatton, Worms, Lloyd, & Bartholini, 1982). Furthermore, negative symptoms of schizophrenia were hypothesized to result from frontal hypodopaminergia, based on the similarities between negative symptoms and frontal-lobe syndromes. Positive symptoms were hypothesized to result from subcortical hyperdopaminergia, based on the findings that higher dopamine metabolite levels are related to greater positive symptoms and response to antipsychotic drug treatment.

Limitations of Version II

While a substantial advance, Version II had a number of limitations (summarized in Table 10.1). In particular, because Version II predated most of the molecular imaging studies of dopaminergic function in schizophrenia, it did not describe the aetiological origins of the dopaminergic abnormality and, beyond specifying "hyperdopaminergia" or "hypodopaminergia", it did not pinpoint which element of dopaminergic transmission was abnormal. Furthermore, there was no framework describing how subcortical hyperdopaminergia translates into delusions, or how frontal hypodopaminergia results into blunted affect, for example. Neither was there a mechanism to account for how known risk factors for schizophrenia, such as a family history of the illness or obstetric complications, might lead to the neurochemical dysfunction. Furthermore, it has subsequently become clear that the cortical abnormalities are more complicated than just hypofrontality (Davidson & Heinrichs, 2003) and little clear evidence of frontal hypodopaminergia has emerged (see below).

Evidence since Version II: The molecular imaging findings

At the time Version II of the dopamine hypothesis was elaborated there had been only a few molecular imaging studies of dopaminergic function in schizophrenia. Since then a considerable body of molecular imaging evidence has amassed on the nature of the dopaminergic abnormalities in schizophrenia. The following section focuses on the in vivo molecular imaging findings in schizophrenia and describes a revision of the dopamine hypothesis that draws on this evidence as well as recent animal and other findings.

Dopamine synthesis and availability: Striatum

Although it is not possible to measure dopamine levels directly in humans, techniques have been developed that provide in vivo indices of dopamine synthesis, release and putative synaptic dopamine levels. Pre-synaptic striatal dopaminergic function can be measured using radiolabelled L-dopa, which is converted to dopamine and trapped in striatal dopamine nerve terminals ready for release. This provides an index of the synthesis and storage of dopamine in the pre-synaptic terminals of striatal dopaminergic neurons (see Moore, Whone, McGowan, & Brooks, 2003, for a review). Eight out of ten studies in patients with schizophrenia using this technique have reported elevated pre-synaptic striatal dopamine synthesis capacity in schizophrenia (Hietala et al., 1995, 1999; Howes et al., 2009; Lindstrom et al., 1999; McGowan, Lawrence, Sales, Quested, & Grasby, 2004; Meyer-Lindenberg et al., 2002; Reith et al., 1994), with effect sizes in these studies ranging from 0.63–1.89 (see Table 10.2, adapted from Howes et al., 2007). The other two studies, both in chronic patients, reported either a small but not significant elevation (Dao-Castellana et al., 1997) or a reduction in levels (Elkashef et al., 2000). All the studies that investigated patients who were acutely psychotic at the time of PET scanning found elevated pre-synaptic striatal dopamine availability (Hietala et al., 1995, 1999; Howes et al., 2009; Lindstrom et al., 1999), with effect sizes from 0.63–1.25 (Howes et al., 2007). This, then, is the single most widely replicated brain dopaminergic abnormality in schizophrenia and the evidence indicates that the effect size is moderate to large.

The next step in dopamine transmission is the release of dopamine. Striatal synaptic dopamine release can be assessed, following a challenge that releases dopamine from the neuron, using PET and single photon emission computerized tomography (SPECT). The released dopamine competes with the radioligand and leads to a reduction in radiotracer binding and is considered to be an indirect index of released dopamine (Laruelle, 2000; Laruelle et al., 1997). All the studies using this approach have found evidence of roughly doubled radiotracer displacement

Table 10.2 Summary of the PET studies of the pre-synaptic striatal dopamine synthesis capacity

Authors	Radio tracer	p	Effect size
Reith et al. (1994)	[18F] DOPA	< .05	0.91
Hietala et al. (1995)	[18F] DOPA	< .05	1.54
Dao-Castellana et al. (1997)	[18F] DOPA	ns	0.3
Hietala et al. (1999)	[18F] DOPA	< .05	1.09
Lindstrom et al. (1999)	[11C] DOPA	< .05	0.77
Elkashef et al. (2000)	[18F] DOPA	< .05	−0.65
Meyer-Lindenberg et al. (2002)	[18F] DOPA	< .02	1.96
McGowan et al. (2004)	[18F] DOPA	.001	1.6
Howes et al. (2009)	[18F] DOPA	.02	1.29
Nozaki et al. (2009)	[11C] DOPA	< .05	0.67

Note: Adapted from the review by Howes et al. (2007).

in patients with schizophrenia compared with controls—an elevation that is again equivalent to a moderate to large effect size (Abi-Dargham et al., 1998; Breier et al., 1997; Kestler, Walker, & Vega, 2001; Laruelle & Abi-Dargham, 1999; Laruelle et al., 1996). Finally, if dopamine synthesis is increased and is more sensitive to release in the face of challenges, one would expect heightened levels of endogenous synaptic dopamine when patients are psychotic. Evidence in line with this comes from a SPECT study using a dopamine depletion technique, which found that baseline occupancy of D2 receptors by dopamine is also increased in schizophrenia (Abi-Dargham et al., 2000). This has recently been replicated and extended to show that baseline occupancy of D2 receptors and the induced release of dopamine are strongly positively correlated in schizophrenia, but not in healthy controls (Abi-Dargham, Giessen, Slifstein, Kegeles, & Laruelle, 2009).

Dopamine synthesis and availability: Cortex

Although the density of dopaminergic projections to cortical areas is sparser than to the striatum, it is possible to measure cortical dopamine synthesis capacity in man using PET and get a reliable signal (Moore et al., 2003). Cortical dopamine synthesis capacity in schizophrenia has been evaluated using [18F]-DOPA and [11C]-DOPA PET (McGowan et al., 2004; Meyer-Lindenberg et al., 2002; Nozaki et al., 2009). McGowan et al. examined anterior cingulate and medial prefrontal regions in patients with chronic schizophrenia who were taking antipsychotic medication. They found no evidence of alterations in the patient group compared with the control group, although they estimated that they only had power to detect a 30% or greater difference. Nozaki et al. have subsequently examined the prefrontal cortex, as well as temporal and hippocampal cortex and thalamus and found no evidence for differences between patients and controls. Meyer-Lindenberg et al. used a voxel-based approach to examine cortical dopamine synthesis capacity and found no difference between a group of patients with schizophrenia and controls (Meyer-Lindenberg et al., 2002). These studies therefore indicate that cortical dopamine synthesis capacity is not significantly altered in schizophrenia, although, as McGowan et al. highlight, these studies are underpowered to detect differences less than 30% between groups, indicating that a small reduction in cortical dopamine availability cannot be excluded. However, it is apparent from reviewing the data in the studies that there is no indication of even a trend for a difference between groups—indeed values are almost exactly the same in all cortical areas. This suggests that there is unlikely to be a difference and if there is it is likely to be small, which suggests it would not be clinically meaningful even if detectable.

Dopamine receptors in untreated schizophrenia

PET and SPECT studies have used various radiotracers to image dopamine D2/3 receptors in schizophrenia. As Davis et al. (1991) noted, the findings of the initial studies were inconsistent, with some reporting increased D2/3 receptor binding in schizophrenia (Crawley et al., 1986; Gjedde & Wong, 1987; Wong et al., 1986) and others no difference from controls (Farde et al., 1990; Martinot et al., 1990). There have now been at least 19 studies investigating striatal D2/3 receptors in patients with schizophrenia and three meta-analyses (Kestler et al., 2001; Laruelle, 1998; Zakzanis & Hansen, 1998). These meta-analyses conclude that there is at most a modest (10–20%) elevation in striatal D2/3 receptor density in schizophrenia independent of the effects of antipsychotic drugs. This appears to be specific to D2/3 receptors—striatal D1 receptor densities are unaltered (Karlsson, Farde, Halldin, & Sedvall, 2002; Kestler et al., 2001; Laruelle, 1998; Okubo et al., 1997)—and this elevation may be regionally specific because these increases are not seen in the extra-striatal regions. If anything, there is a decrease in D2/D3 receptors in extra-striatal areas such as the thalamus and anterior cingulate (Buchsbaum et al., 2006; Suhara et al., 2002; Takahashi, Higuchi, & Suhara, 2006; Talvik et al., 2006). The D2 receptor exists in two states and it remains to be determined whether the balance between these two states is altered in schizophrenia (Seeman et al., 2006). Also, since the current tracers bind to a mix of D2 and D3 receptors, it is difficult to be precise about whether changes are in the D3 or the D2 subtype of the receptors—though preliminary data with a recently developed tracer, 11C-PHNO, show that there is no abnormality in high-states or in D3 receptors in schizophrenia (Graf-Guerrero et al., 2009).

Dopaminergic transmission in the prefrontal cortex is mainly mediated by D1 receptors and it has been proposed that D1 dysfunction underlies cognitive impairment and negative symptom in schizophrenia (see Goldman-Rakic, Castner, Svensson, Siever, & Williams, 2004; Tamminga, 2006, for reviews). There have been three studies to index D1 receptor levels in vivo (Abi-Dargham et al., 2002; Karlsson et al., 2002; Okubo et al., 1997). However, the radiotracers used may also bind to serotonin receptors (Ekelund et al., 2007), which complicates interpretation of the findings. Currently it is most parsimonious to conclude that further studies are required with more selective radiotracers.

The role of dopamine receptors in treatment response

Although all currently licensed antipsychotic drugs block D2 receptors, they also act at a number of other brain receptors, including other dopamine receptors and those for serotonin, histamine and acetylcholine. Given this rich pharmacology it was far from clear which receptor mediated the clinical response to antipsychotic treatment. The in vitro studies linking the affinity of antipsychotic drugs for D2 receptors to their clinical potency in the 1970s (Creese, Burt, & Snyder, 1976; Seeman, Lee, Chau-Wong, & Wong, 1976) indicated that there is a relationship between the blockade of dopamine receptors and the resolution of symptoms. However, these studies could not determine whether the drugs crossed the blood–brain barrier or acted on brain dopamine receptors in vivo. A MEDLINE search (using the following search terms: PET, SPECT, dopamine, receptor and antipsychotic over the period 1965–2008) indicates that over 120 neurochemical imaging studies have investigated the in vivo effects of antipsychotic treatments on dopamine receptors in schizophrenia (see, for example, Frankle & Laruelle,

2002, for a review). There is now a considerable body of evidence from studies using either SPECT (e.g., Brucke et al., 1991, 1992; Klemm et al., 1996; Pilowsky et al., 1993; Volk et al., 1994) or PET (e.g., Baron et al., 1989; Farde, Wiesel, Jansson et al., 1988; Goyer et al., 1996; Kapur et al., 1996; Nordstrom, Farde, & Halldin, 1992; Nordstrom et al., 1993; Wolkin, Brodie et al., 1989) demonstrating that all antipsychotic drugs cross the blood–brain barrier and block striatal D2/3 receptors in vivo at clinically effective doses. These data support the in vitro findings, although this does not establish the link between D2 occupancy and clinical response (see below).

The relationship between dopaminergic blockade and clinical response

Interestingly, the initial PET and SPECT studies found no relationship between occupancy and clinical response (Frankle & Laruelle, 2002). However, it has subsequently transpired that this was the first clue to a curious property of the relationship between antipsychotic drug occupancy of D2 receptors and clinical response—it appears to be non-linear. The early studies generally used moderate to high antipsychotic drug doses, which resulted in levels of D2 occupancy greater than 65% (e.g., Farde, Wiesel, Halldin, & Sedvall, 1988). Studies since then have used low doses as well and indicate that there is little clinical response seen when occupancy is less than 50%, with clinical response increasing from this point (Nordstrom et al., 1993). This suggests that a therapeutic threshold of D2 occupancy is required for clinical response to antipsychotic drugs. A subsequent double-blind study of patients experiencing their first episode of schizophrenic psychosis tested this idea (Kapur, Zipursky, Jones, Remington, & Houle, 2000). Their D2 receptor occupancy was determined with [11C]-raclopride PET imaging following two weeks of antipsychotic treatment and clinical response assessed in the patients. The results confirmed that clinical efficacy requires a threshold of occupancy of D2 receptors. D2 occupancy of 65% was found to best separate responders from non-responders: at 65% receptor occupancy, 80% of responders were above the threshold while 67% of the non-responders lay below the threshold. Receptor occupancy much above 65% was associated with a much higher risk of side-effects and little further clinical improvement. This is an important finding—in the past if there was little or no initial response the clinical practice was to keep increasing the antipsychotic dose under the misguided belief that this would increase the chance of a subsequent response. However, the PET findings indicate that in general high doses offer no therapeutic advantages and only increase the risk of adverse events.

Another therapeutic insight to come out of PET and SPECT imaging studies is the high level of individual variation in D2 occupancy (e.g., 38–87%), despite patients receiving identical doses of the same antipsychotic. This variation may partly underlie the large differences in individual response to standard doses of antipsychotic and explain why it can be so difficult to predict the dose of antipsychotic to use. A further critical insight arising from the functional ligand studies is the evidence that some patients show little or no response despite having

D2 occupancy well above the threshold (Wolkin, Barouche et al., 1989). D2 occupancy that is greater than the threshold is thus necessary for antipsychotic treatment response.

It follows from the discussion of the functional imaging evidence above that D2 occupancy is central to antipsychotic treatment response. However, a major criticism of the dopamine hypothesis in the past was that dopaminergic blockade did not result in a rapid resolution of symptoms. This criticism rested on the dogma that antipsychotic drugs took a number of weeks to effect a clinical response, although antipsychotic drugs produced high levels of D2 occupancy within days of treatment commencing. Recent evidence, discussed in the section below, indicates that this criticism is not valid.

The relationship between D2 occupancy and time to response

The dogma in most textbooks of psychiatry states that patients take weeks to show any response to antipsychotic treatment. However, PET imaging studies have brought this received wisdom into question by showing that adequate striatal D2 occupancy by antipsychotic drugs occurs within hours of starting treatment (Nordstrom, Farde, & Halldin, 1992). These findings are not compatible with the dogma, at least not in a straightforward way. It is possible that treatment response requires a chain of secondary events following on from the D2 blockade, such as a depolarization blockade, that might take weeks to happen. However, new clinical findings suggest, instead, that the dogma appears to be wrong. Rather, clinical improvement does occur within the first two weeks of starting regular antipsychotic treatment (Agid, Kapur, Arenovich, & Zipursky, 2003). In fact, the evidence is that the largest improvement occurs over the *first two weeks* (Agid et al., 2003). Furthermore, higher D2 occupancy by the drug forty-eight hours after starting antipsychotic treatment is directly associated with greater clinical response two weeks later (Catafau et al., 2006). Taken together these findings provide further evidence that excess dopaminergic transmission underlies the symptoms of schizophrenia.

Specificity of striatal dopaminergic abnormalities to schizophrenia

Striatal dopaminergic function is not elevated in non-psychotic patients with other psychiatric or neurological conditions including mania (without psychotic symptoms), Tourette's syndrome and depression (Ernst, Zametkin, Matochik, Pascualvaca, & Cohen, 1997; Martinot et al., 2001; Parsey et al., 2001; Reith et al., 1994; Turjanski et al., 1994; Yatham et al., 2002). Ernst et al. (1999) report no significant difference in striatal FDOPA uptake between children or adults with attention deficit hyperactivity disorder (ADHD) and controls, although there may be differences in other brain regions (Ernst, Zametkin, Matochik, Jons, & Cohen, 1998). The findings in these studies indicate that elevated pre-synaptic striatal dopamine synthesis capacity is not a non-specific indicator of stress or psychiatric/

neurological morbidity. However, elevated pre-synaptic striatal dopamine synthesis capacity has been reported in patients with psychosis secondary to temporal lobe epilepsy (Reith et al., 1994), suggesting that elevated striatal dopaminergic function may underlie the development of psychosis in other psychotic disorders as well as schizophrenia. As patients with psychotic mania or depression have yet to be investigated using these PET techniques it remains to be determined if these findings are specific to schizophrenia or are present in psychotic disorders more generally.

Linking dopaminergic dysfunction to symptoms

It is apparent from the molecular imaging studies reviewed above that the initial idea that abnormalities in D2 receptor densities underlie schizophrenia hasn't been supported by the subsequent PET and SPECT evidence. Rather the data show that schizophrenia is characterized by elevated dopamine pre-synaptic availability and synaptic release in the striatum.

There is fairly robust evidence linking schizophrenic symptoms, particularly psychotic symptoms, to striatal synaptic dopamine availability. First, the degree of striatal dopamine release following amphetamine administration is positively correlated with the worsening of symptoms overall and particularly psychotic symptoms (Breier et al., 1997). Furthermore, it also correlates with the change in psychotic symptoms following treatment, see Figure 10.1 (Abi-Dargham et al., 1998; Laruelle et al., 1996; Laruelle, Abi-Dargham, Gil, Kegeles, & Innis, 1999).

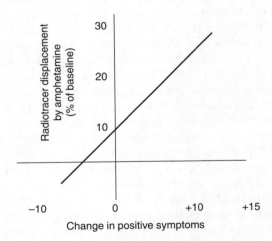

Figure 10.1 Striatal dopamine release correlates with the change in psychotic symptoms. Figure reprinted from Laruelle, M., Abi-Dargham, A., Gil, R., Kegeles, L., & Innis, R. (1999). Increased dopamine transmission in schizophrenia: Relationship to illness phases. *Biological Psychiatry, 46*(1), 56–72. Copyright © 1999, with permission from the Society of Biological Psychiatry (published by Elsevier).

In addition, the dopaminergic dysfunction is related to illness phase: striatal dopamine release is much greater during relapse than in remission (Laruelle et al., 1999), suggesting that it underlies the development of new and acute symptoms. A similar pattern of results is seen in the studies using radiolabelled DOPA. Among those that report the relationship with symptoms, the studies of chronic stable patients showed no relationship with symptoms (Dao-Castellana et al., 1997; McGowan et al., 2004), while the study of acutely unwell patients showed a positive relationship between paranoid positive symptom severity and striatal dopamine availability, albeit only at a trend level (Hietala et al., 1999). Finally, greater striatal dopamine synaptic availability is directly associated with better subsequent response to treatment (Abi-Dargham et al., 2000; Laruelle et al., 1999).

Dopamine dysregulation prior to the onset of psychosis

While the data reviewed in the section above suggest a link between dopamine dysregulation and psychosis, all the studies were conducted in people who had already developed psychosis. It is therefore possible that rather than causing psychosis, the dopamine dysregulation is secondary—occurring as a consequence of some other factor. To determine whether this is the case or not it is necessary to study people in the phase just preceding the development of psychosis. Schizophrenia is generally preceded by a prodromal phase of 1–5 years and recent research has characterized this to enable prospective research into the pathoaetiology of the illness. People meeting operationalized criteria for an at-risk mental state (ARMS) have prodromal signs of schizophrenia and an ultra high risk of developing a psychotic illness, predominantly schizophrenia, within 1–2 years (Cannon et al., 2008; Yung et al., 2003, 2006). Dopamine function has recently been studied in subjects with prodromal signs of schizophrenia, all of whom had attenuated psychotic symptoms. Pre-synaptic striatal dopamine synthesis capacity was elevated in people who were at high risk of schizophrenia but did not have the disorder, to a degree approaching that in patients with established schizophrenia. Furthermore, striatal dopamine levels were directly correlated with the severity of prodromal symptoms in the ARMS subjects (see Figure 10.2).

The findings remained robust after adjustment for putative factors that might influence the PET measurements. These data suggest that increased subcortical dopamine activity is already present before the full expression of schizophrenia, consistent with the putative role of dopamine in the pathophysiology of psychosis (Kapur, Mizrahi, & Li, 2005; Laruelle & Abi-Dargham, 1999). However, as not all ARMS subjects go on to develop psychosis and dopamine dysfunction may also occur in the relatives of patients with schizophrenia (Huttunen et al., 2007), elevated dopamine activity may also be a correlate of an increased vulnerability to psychosis. Follow-up of ARMS subjects is therefore needed to determine whether elevated striatal dopamine activity leads to psychosis or is a correlate of vulnerability.

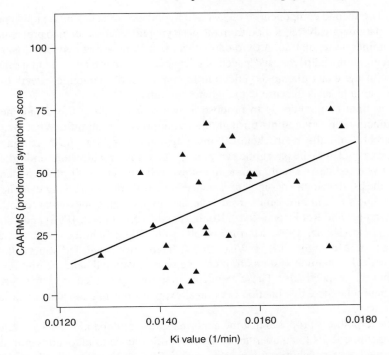

Figure 10.2 Showing the relationship between striatal dopaminergic function and prodromal symptoms. The positive relationship between total Comprehensive
Assessment of At-Risk Mental States (CAARMS) score (higher score
indicates greater severity of prodromal symptoms) and Ki value (influx
rate constant) ($r = .48$, $p = .02$). Figure reprinted from Howes, O. D.,
Montgomery, A. J., Asselin, M. C., Murray, R. M., Valli, I., Tabraham, P.,
et al. (2009). Elevated striatal dopamine function linked to prodromal signs
of schizophrenia. *Archives of General Psychiatry*, *66*(1), 13–20. Copyright
© 2009 American Medical Association. All rights reserved.

The revised dopamine hypothesis of schizophrenia

A revised version of the dopamine hypothesis, Version III—the final common
pathway, has recently been proposed (see Plate 10.1, situated between pp. 116 and
117) based on the new information from the molecular imaging studies, but also
drawing on animal, genetic and other findings that show how risk factors for
schizophrenia may act on the dopaminergic system (Howes & Kapur, 2009).
Version III proposes that dopamine dysregulation is the final common pathway to
psychosis in schizophrenia. The first component of this hypothesis is that multiple,
interacting "hits" interact and lead to dopamine dysregulation. This is analogous
to diabetes mellitus, for example, where hyperglycaemia is the final
pathophysiology that results in the clinical symptoms, but different paths lead to
hyperglycaemia (insulin insensitivity in the case of type II diabetes, or insulin
insufficiency in the case of type I diabetes) with an array of risk factors underlying

this. The second component of the revised hypothesis is a shift in the localization of dopaminergic dysregulation from the postsynaptic receptor level to pre-synaptic dopaminergic regulation. A third component is making a link between dopamine dysregulation and psychosis/"psychosis proneness" rather than schizophrenia per se, with the exact diagnosis reflecting the nature and interacting effects of the upstream hits, as is the case with diabetes mellitus.

The final component is to propose a mechanism linking the dopaminergic dysfunction and symptoms through altered appraisal of stimuli. What was not apparent from the neurochemical imaging data was how the dopaminergic abnormality led to the psychotic symptoms—this was a major shortcoming of the first two versions of the dopamine hypothesis. Since Version II of the dopamine hypothesis, developments in neuroscience have provided increasing evidence of dopamine's role in motivational salience. The experiments and syntheses of data by Berridge and Robinson (1998), Robbins and Everitt (1982, 1996) and Schultz and others (Heinz, 1999; Martin-Soelch et al., 2001; Schultz, 2002; Schultz, Dayan, & Montague, 1997; Wise, 2004) have implicated a distinct role for subcortical dopamine systems in incentive or motivational salience and reward prediction respectively. These conceptualizations provided a framework to link neurochemical dysfunction to clinical expression using concepts of salience and reward.

The hypothesis proposes that the abnormal firing of dopamine neurons/release of dopamine leads to an aberrant assignment of salience to innocuous stimuli. It is argued that psychotic symptoms, especially delusions and hallucinations, emerge over time as the individual's own explanation of the experience of aberrant salience. Psychosis is, therefore, aberrant salience driven by dopamine and filtered through the individual's existing cognitive and sociocultural schemas—thus allowing the same chemical (dopamine) to have different clinical manifestations in different cultures and individuals (Kapur, 2003; Kapur et al., 2005).

Implications of the dopamine hypothesis of schizophrenia: Version III

The revised hypothesis has a number of major clinical and research implications. It indicates that current antipsychotic drugs are acting down stream of the main neurochemical abnormality. As a result they may paradoxically worsen the primary abnormality by blocking feedback mechanisms. Findings in healthy volunteers indicate that acute antipsychotic treatment does, indeed, elevate dopamine synthesis (Vernaleken et al., 2006). This may explain the rapid relapse some patients experience on stopping their medication. It may also explain why some patients experience more severe relapses after discontinuing treatment. However, it is not clear if chronic treatment in patients has the same effects on pre-synaptic dopamine as the acute treatment in healthy volunteers.

Another implication is that future drug development should logically move from further attempts to emulate the existing pharmacology of licensed antipsychotic drugs to focus on the modulation of pre-synaptic striatal dopamine function. The dopaminergic neurons in the striatum originate in the midbrain—particularly in the substantia nigra and to a lesser extent in the ventral tegmentum (VTA; Haber, Fudge, & McFarland, 2000; Joel & Weiner, 2000). A further implication of the revised dopamine hypothesis is that the function and regulation of the dopamine cell bodies in the midbrain is dysregulated in psychosis. Supporting this, post-mortem studies of patients with schizophrenia have found increased dopaminergic markers in the substantia nigra (Mueller, Haroutunian, Davis, & Meador-Woodruff, 2004; Toru et al., 1988). However, it remains to be established if dopamine levels are increased in vivo in the nigra of patients with schizophrenia.

Limitations and future directions

Current evidence has particular limitations and there are a number of outstanding questions. One limitation is a relative paucity of data on specificity: while there is a substantial and consistent body of evidence linking pre-synaptic dopaminergic abnormalities to schizophrenia and now to the development of the illness, there is relatively little evidence on dopaminergic function in other psychiatric disorders. However, there have been studies of pre-synaptic dopaminergic function in depression and mania without psychosis (e.g., Bragulat et al., 2007; Martinot et al., 2001; Yatham et al., 2002). These studies have found no evidence of elevation and even indications that dopaminergic function may be reduced in depression. Nevertheless, further studies would be useful to confirm the specificity to psychosis and to determine whether striatal dopaminergic elevation is specific to schizophrenia, or seen in other psychoses. A more significant area for future research is the observation that there is an overlap in dopaminergic function between people with schizophrenia and healthy controls, although this may be partially due to the image analytic methods used (Bose et al., 2008). One explanation for the overlap could be that dopaminergic elevation is a feature of some but not all subtypes of schizophrenia (such as paranoid vs. catatonic), or stages of illness (such as chronic vs. acute/early course). Furthermore, the molecular imaging indices do not provide information on all aspects of dopaminergic function and aspects of dopaminergic function that, at present, cannot be directly measured, such as the balance of phasic to tonic dopaminergic firing, may be particularly important to the nature of dysfunction in schizophrenia (Grace, 1991). A further focus for future research is that the mechanisms linking environmental and genetic risk factors for schizophrenia and dopaminergic dysfunction need to be further evaluated. Although potential mechanisms are indicated in Version III of the dopamine hypothesis, detailed descriptions of pathways are missing and the hypothesis is agnostic about how different routes interact. Also, the proposed link between dopaminergic dysfunction and the development of psychotic symptoms requires further direct evaluation. While it provides a compelling explanation of the development of some symptoms, particularly delusions, it is less clear how it explains others, such as negative symptoms. Finally, there is a lack of in vivo data on whether aspects of pre-synaptic dopaminergic function underlie the marked variability in treatment response seen in schizophrenia.

Conclusions

In summary, substantial new evidence of dopamine's role in the pathophysiology of psychosis has accrued since Version II of the dopamine hypothesis. Animal studies provide evidence to link known risk factors for schizophrenia to striatal dopaminergic dysfunction. But perhaps most critically, the large body of molecular imaging studies since 1991 has provided in vivo evidence that has refined understanding of the nature of the dopaminergic dysfunction in psychosis. These studies provide direct evidence that: (i) pre-synaptic dopaminergic function is elevated in patients with psychosis and in high-risk patients with prodromal signs of the illness; (ii) measures of striatal synaptic dopamine availability and release correlate with symptoms, particularly the dimension of psychosis; (iii) blockade of this heightened dopaminergic function with antipsychotic drugs leads to a resolution of symptoms for most patients; and (iv) molecular imaging and animal studies indicate that risk factors for psychosis may converge to alter the dopaminergic system in man. The recently proposed dopamine hypothesis: Version III provides a framework for integrating this and understanding the development of psychosis in schizophrenia. However, Version III is far from a complete model of schizophrenia and further work is required to test it. Critically, it provides relatively little detail about the role of other neurotransmitter systems. It is highly likely that, as further evidence becomes available, Version III will be superseded by a Version IV. Nevertheless, given the body of evidence implicating dopaminergic dysfunction in the pathophysiology of schizophrenia, it is likely that dopamine will remain central to future neurochemical explanations of schizophrenia. Furthermore, modulating the control of pre-synaptic dopaminergic function is a potentially exciting avenue for the development of novel treatment strategies. In conclusion, a growing body of evidence points to dopaminergic dysfunction as the "fire" underlying psychotic symptoms (the "smoke signal" seen in the clinic) and that multiple pathways fuel this "fire".

References

Abi-Dargham, A., Giessen, E. V., Slifstein, M., Kegeles, L. S., & Laruelle, M. (2009). Baseline and amphetamine-stimulated dopamine activity are related in drug-naive schizophrenic subjects. *Biological Psychiatry*, *65*(12), 1091–1093.

Abi-Dargham, A., Gil, R., Krystal, J., Baldwin, R. M., Seibyl, J. P., Bowers, M., et al. (1998). Increased striatal dopamine transmission in schizophrenia: Confirmation in a second cohort. *American Journal of Psychiatry*, *155*(6), 761–767.

Abi-Dargham, A., Mawlawi, O., Lombardo, I., Gil, R., Martinez, D., Huang, Y., et al. (2002). Prefrontal dopamine D1 receptors and working memory in schizophrenia. *Journal of Neuroscience*, *22*(9), 3708–3719.

Abi-Dargham, A., Rodenhiser, J., Printz, D., Zea-Ponce, Y., Gil, R., Kegeles, L. S., et al. (2000). Increased baseline occupancy of D2 receptors by dopamine in schizophrenia.

Proceedings of the National Academy of Sciences of the United States of America, *97*(14), 8104–8109.

Agid, O., Kapur, S., Arenovich, T., & Zipursky, R. B. (2003). Delayed-onset hypothesis of antipsychotic action: A hypothesis tested and rejected. *Archives of General Psychiatry*, *60*(12), 1228–1235.

Baron, J. C., Martinot, J. L., Cambon, H., Boulenger, J. P., Poirier, M. F., Caillard, V., et al. (1989). Striatal dopamine receptor occupancy during and following withdrawal from neuroleptic treatment: Correlative evaluation by positron emission tomography and plasma prolactin levels. *Psychopharmacology (Berlin)*, *99*(4), 463–472.

Berridge, K. C., & Robinson, T. E. (1998). What is the role of dopamine in reward: Hedonic impact, reward learning, or incentive salience? *Brain Research Reviews*, *28*(3), 309–369.

Bose, S. K., Turkheimer, F. E., Howes, O. D., Mehta, M. A., Cunliffe, R., Stokes, P. R., et al. (2008). Classification of schizophrenic patients and healthy controls using [18F] fluorodopa PET imaging. *Schizophrenia Research*, *106*(2–3), 148–155.

Bragulat, V., Paillere-Martinot, M. L., Artiges, E., Frouin, V., Poline, J. B., & Martinot, J. L. (2007). Dopaminergic function in depressed patients with affective flattening or with impulsivity: [18F]fluoro-L-dopa positron emission tomography study with voxel-based analysis. *Psychiatry Research*, *154*(2), 115–124.

Breier, A., Su, T. P., Saunders, R., Carson, R. E., Kolachana, B. S., de Bartolomeis, A., et al. (1997). Schizophrenia is associated with elevated amphetamine-induced synaptic dopamine concentrations: Evidence from a novel positron emission tomography method. *Proceedings of the National Academy of Sciences of the United States of America*, *94*(6), 2569–2574.

Brucke, T., Podreka, I., Angelberger, P., Wenger, S., Topitz, A., Kufferle, B., et al. (1991). Dopamine D2 receptor imaging with SPECT: Studies in different neuropsychiatric disorders. *Journal of Cerebral Blood Flow & Metabolism*, *11*(2), 220–228.

Brucke, T., Roth, J., Podreka, I., Strobl, R., Wenger, S., & Asenbaum, S. (1992). Striatal dopamine D2-receptor blockade by typical and atypical neuroleptics. *Lancet*, *339*(8791), 497.

Buchsbaum, M. S., Christian, B. T., Lehrer, D. S., Narayanan, T. K., Shi, B., Mantil, J., et al. (2006). D2/D3 dopamine receptor binding with [F-18]fallypride in thalamus and cortex of patients with schizophrenia. *Schizophrenia Research*, *85*(1–3), 232–244.

Cannon, T. D., Cadenhead, K., Cornblatt, B., Woods, S. W., Addington, J., Walker, E., et al. (2008). Prediction of psychosis in youth at high clinical risk: A multisite longitudinal study in North America. *Archives of General Psychiatry*, *65*(1), 28–37.

Carlsson, A., & Lindqvist, M. (1963). Effect of chlorpromazine or haloperidol on the formation of 3-methoxytyramine and normetanephrine in mouse brain. *Acta Pharmacologica et Toxicologica (Copenhagen)*, *20*, 140–144.

Catafau, A. M., Corripio, I., Perez, V., Martin, J. C., Schotte, A., Carrio, I., et al. (2006). Dopamine D2 receptor occupancy by risperidone: Implications for the timing and magnitude of clinical response. *Psychiatry Research*, *148*(2–3), 175–183.

Crawley, J. C., Crow, T. J., Johnstone, E. C., Oldland, S. R., Owen, F., Owens, D. G., et al. (1986). Uptake of 77Br-spiperone in the striata of schizophrenic patients and controls. *Nuclear Medicine Communications*, *7*(8), 599–607.

Creese, I., Burt, D. R., & Snyder, S. H. (1976). Dopamine receptor binding predicts clinical and pharmacological potencies of antischizophrenic drugs. *Science*, *192*(4238), 481–483.

Dao-Castellana, M. H., Paillere-Martinot, M. L., Hantraye, P., Attar-Levy, D., Remy, P., Crouzel, C., et al. (1997). Presynaptic dopaminergic function in the striatum of schizophrenic patients. *Schizophrenia Research, 23*(2), 167–174.

Davidson, L. L., & Heinrichs, R. W. (2003). Quantification of frontal and temporal lobe brain-imaging findings in schizophrenia: A meta-analysis. *Psychiatry Research, 122*(2), 69–87.

Davis, K. L., Kahn, R. S., Ko, G., & Davidson, M. (1991). Dopamine in schizophrenia: A review and reconceptualization. *American Journal of Psychiatry, 148*(11), 1474–1486.

Ekelund, J., Slifstein, M., Narendran, R., Guillin, O., Belani, H., Guo, N. N., et al. (2007). In vivo DA D(1) receptor selectivity of NNC 112 and SCH 23390. *Molecular Imaging and Biology, 9*(3), 117–125.

Elkashef, A. M., Doudet, D., Bryant, T., Cohen, R. M., Li, S. H., & Wyatt, R. J. (2000). 6-(18)F-DOPA PET study in patients with schizophrenia. Positron emission tomography. *Psychiatry Research, 100*(1), 1–11.

Ernst, M., Zametkin, A. J., Matochik, J. A., Jons, P. H., & Cohen, R. M. (1998). DOPA decarboxylase activity in attention deficit hyperactivity disorder adults. A [fluorine-18] fluorodopa positron emission tomographic study. *Journal of Neuroscience, 18*(15), 5901–5907.

Ernst, M., Zametkin, A. J., Matochik, J. A., Pascualvaca, D., & Cohen, R. M. (1997). Low medial prefrontal dopaminergic activity in autistic children. *Lancet, 350*(9078), 638.

Ernst, M., Zametkin, A. J., Matochik, J. A., Pascualvaca, D., Jons, P. H., & Cohen, R. M. (1999). High midbrain [18F]DOPA accumulation in children with attention deficit hyperactivity disorder. *American Journal of Psychiatry, 156*(8), 1209–1215.

Farde, L., Wiesel, F. A., Halldin, C., & Sedvall, G. (1988). Central D2-dopamine receptor occupancy in schizophrenic patients treated with antipsychotic drugs. *Archives of General Psychiatry, 45*(1), 71–76.

Farde, L., Wiesel, F. A., Jansson, P., Uppfeldt, G., Wahlen, A., & Sedvall, G. (1988). An open label trial of raclopride in acute schizophrenia. Confirmation of D2-dopamine receptor occupancy by PET. *Psychopharmacology (Berlin), 94*(1), 1–7.

Farde, L., Wiesel, F. A., Stone-Elander, S., Halldin, C., Nordstrom, A. L., Hall, H., et al. (1990). D2 dopamine receptors in neuroleptic-naive schizophrenic patients. A positron emission tomography study with [11C]raclopride. *Archives of General Psychiatry, 47*(3), 213–219.

Frankle, W. G., & Laruelle, M. (2002). Neuroreceptor imaging in psychiatric disorders. *Annals of Nuclear Medicine, 16*(7), 437–446.

Gjedde, A., & Wong, D. F. (1987). Positron tomographic quantitation of neuroreceptors in human brain in vivo—With special reference to the D2 dopamine receptors in caudate nucleus. *Neurosurgical Review, 10*(1), 9–18.

Goldman-Rakic, P. S., Castner, S. A., Svensson, T. H., Siever, L. J., & Williams, G. V. (2004). Targeting the dopamine D1 receptor in schizophrenia: Insights for cognitive dysfunction. *Psychopharmacology (Berlin), 174*(1), 3–16.

Goyer, P. F., Berridge, M. S., Morris, E. D., Semple, W. E., Compton-Toth, B. A., Schulz, S. C., et al. (1996). PET measurement of neuroreceptor occupancy by typical and atypical neuroleptics. *Journal of Nuclear Medicine, 37*(7), 1122–1127.

Grace, A. A. (1991). Phasic versus tonic dopamine release and the modulation of dopamine system responsivity: A hypothesis for the etiology of schizophrenia. *Neuroscience, 41*(1), 1–24.

Graf-Guerrero, A., Romina, M., Agid, O., Marcon, H., Barsoum, P., Rusjan, P., et al. (2009). The dopamine D2 receptors in high-affinity state and D3 receptors in schizophrenia: A clinical [11C]-(+)-PHNO PET study. *Neuropsychopharmacology*, *34*(4), 1078–1086.

Haber, S. N., Fudge, J. L., & McFarland, N. R. (2000). Striatonigrostriatal pathways in primates form an ascending spiral from the shell to the dorsolateral striatum. *Journal of Neuroscience*, *20*(6), 2369–2382.

Heinz, A. (1999). Anhedonie—nosologieübergreifendes Korrelat einer Dysfunktion des dopaminergen Verstärkungssystems [Anhedonia—A general nosology surmounting correlate of a dysfunctional dopaminergic reward system?]. *Nervenarzt*, *70*(5), 391–398.

Hietala, J., Syvalahti, E., Vilkman, H., Vuorio, K., Rakkolainen, V., Bergman, J., et al. (1999). Depressive symptoms and presynaptic dopamine function in neuroleptic-naive schizophrenia. *Schizophrenia Research*, *35*(1), 41–50.

Hietala, J., Syvalahti, E., Vuorio, K., Rakkolainen, V., Bergman, J., Haaparanta, M., et al. (1995). Presynaptic dopamine function in striatum of neuroleptic-naive schizophrenic patients. *Lancet*, *346*(8983), 1130–1131.

Howes, O. D., & Kapur, S. (2009). The dopamine hypothesis of schizophrenia: Version III–The final common pathway. *Schizophrenia Bulletin*, *35*(3), 549–562.

Howes, O. D., Montgomery, A. J., Asselin, M. C., Murray, R. M., Grasby, P. M., & McGuire, P. K. (2007). Molecular imaging studies of the striatal dopaminergic system in psychosis and predictions for the prodromal phase of psychosis. *British Journal of Psychiatry*, *51*(Suppl.), s13–s18.

Howes, O. D., Montgomery, A. J., Asselin, M. C., Murray, R. M., Valli, I., Tabraham, P., et al. (2009). Elevated striatal dopamine function linked to prodromal signs of schizophrenia. *Archives of General Psychiatry*, *66*(1), 13–20.

Huttunen, J., Heinimaa, M., Svirskis, T., Nyman, M., Kajander, J., Forsback, S., et al. (2007). Striatal dopamine synthesis in first-degree relatives of patients with schizophrenia. *Biological Psychiatry*, *63*(1), 114–117.

Joel, D., & Weiner, I. (2000). The connections of the dopaminergic system with the striatum in rats and primates: An analysis with respect to the functional and compartmental organization of the striatum. *Neuroscience*, *96*(3), 451–474.

Kapur, S. (2003). Psychosis as a state of aberrant salience: A framework linking biology, phenomenology and pharmacology in schizophrenia. *American Journal of Psychiatry*, *160*(1), 13–23.

Kapur, S., Mizrahi, R., & Li, M. (2005). From dopamine to salience to psychosis—Linking biology, pharmacology and phenomenology of psychosis. *Schizophrenia Research*, *79*(1), 59–68.

Kapur, S., Zipursky, R., Jones, C., Remington, G., & Houle, S. (2000). Relationship between dopamine D(2) occupancy, clinical response and side effects: A double-blind PET study of first-episode schizophrenia. *American Journal of Psychiatry*, *157*(4), 514–520.

Kapur, S., Zipursky, R. B., Jones, C., Remington, G. J., Wilson, A. A., DaSilva, J., et al. (1996). The D2 receptor occupancy profile of loxapine determined using PET. *Neuropsychopharmacology*, *15*(6), 562–566.

Karlsson, P., Farde, L., Halldin, C., & Sedvall, G. (2002). PET study of D(1) dopamine receptor binding in neuroleptic-naive patients with schizophrenia. *American Journal of Psychiatry*, *159*(5), 761–767.

Kestler, L. P., Walker, E., & Vega, E. M. (2001). Dopamine receptors in the brains of schizophrenia patients: A meta-analysis of the findings. *Behavioural Pharmacology*, *12*(5), 355–371.

Klemm, E., Grunwald, F., Kasper, S., Menzel, C., Broich, K., Danos, P., et al. (1996). [123I]IBZM SPECT for imaging of striatal D2 dopamine receptors in 56 schizophrenic patients taking various neuroleptics. *American Journal of Psychiatry*, *153*(2), 183–190.

Laruelle, M. (1998). Imaging dopamine transmission in schizophrenia. A review and meta-analysis. *Quarterly Journal of Nuclear Medicine*, *42*(3), 211–221.

Laruelle, M. (2000). Imaging synaptic neurotransmission with in vivo binding competition techniques: A critical review. *Journal of Cerebral Blood Flow & Metabolism*, *20*(3), 423–451.

Laruelle, M., & Abi-Dargham, A. (1999). Dopamine as the wind of the psychotic fire: New evidence from brain imaging studies. *Journal of Psychopharmacology*, *13*(4), 358–371.

Laruelle, M., Abi-Dargham, A., Gil, R., Kegeles, L., & Innis, R. (1999). Increased dopamine transmission in schizophrenia: Relationship to illness phases. *Biological Psychiatry*, *46*(1), 56–72.

Laruelle, M., Abi-Dargham, A., van Dyck, C. H., Gil, R., D'Souza, C. D., Erdos, J., et al. (1996). Single photon emission computerized tomography imaging of amphetamine-induced dopamine release in drug-free schizophrenic subjects. *Proceedings of the National Academy of Sciences of the United States of America*, *93*(17), 9235–9240.

Laruelle, M., Iyer, R. N., al-Tikriti, M. S., Zea-Ponce, Y., Malison, R., Zoghbi, S. S., et al. (1997). Microdialysis and SPECT measurements of amphetamine-induced dopamine release in nonhuman primates. *Synapse*, *25*(1), 1–14.

Lieberman, J. A., Kane, J. M., & Alvir, J. (1987). Provocative tests with psychostimulant drugs in schizophrenia. *Psychopharmacology (Berlin)*, *91*(4), 415–433.

Lindstrom, L. H., Gefvert, O., Hagberg, G., Lundberg, T., Bergstrom, M., Hartvig, P., et al. (1999). Increased dopamine synthesis rate in medial prefrontal cortex and striatum in schizophrenia indicated by L-(beta-11C) DOPA and PET. *Biological Psychiatry*, *46*(5), 681–688.

Martin-Soelch, C., Leenders, K. L., Chevalley, A. F., Missimer, J., Kunig, G., Magyar, S., Mino, A., & Schultz, W. (2001). Reward mechanisms in the brain and their role in dependence: Evidence from neurophysiological and neuroimaging studies. *Brain Research Reviews*, *36*(2–3), 139–149.

Martinot, J. L., Peron-Magnan, P., Huret, J. D., Mazoyer, B., Baron, J. C., Boulenger, J. P., et al. (1990). Striatal D2 dopaminergic receptors assessed with positron emission tomography and [76Br]bromospiperone in untreated schizophrenic patients. *American Journal of Psychiatry*, *147*(1), 44–50.

Martinot, M., Bragulat, V., Artiges, E., Dolle, F., Hinnen, F., Jouvent, R., et al. (2001). Decreased presynaptic dopamine function in the left caudate of depressed patients with affective flattening and psychomotor retardation. *American Journal of Psychiatry*, *158*(2), 314–316.

Matthysse, S. (1973). Antipsychotic drug actions: A clue to the neuropathology of schizophrenia? *Federation Proceedings*, *32*(2), 200–205.

McGowan, S., Lawrence, A. D., Sales, T., Quested, D., & Grasby, P. (2004). Presynaptic dopaminergic dysfunction in schizophrenia: A positron emission tomographic [18F] fluorodopa study. *Archives of General Psychiatry*, *61*(2), 134–142.

Meyer-Lindenberg, A., Miletich, R. S., Kohn, P. D., Esposito, G., Carson, R. E., Quarantelli, M., et al. (2002). Reduced prefrontal activity predicts exaggerated striatal dopaminergic function in schizophrenia. *Nature Neuroscience*, *5*(3), 267–271.

Moore, R. Y., Whone, A. L., McGowan, S., & Brooks, D. J. (2003). Monoamine neuron innervation of the normal human brain: An 18F-DOPA PET study. *Brain Research*, *982*(2), 137–145.

Mueller, H. T., Haroutunian, V., Davis, K. L., & Meador-Woodruff, J. H. (2004). Expression of the ionotropic glutamate receptor subunits and NMDA receptor-associated intracellular proteins in the substantia nigra in schizophrenia. *Molecular Brain Research, 121*(1–2), 60–69.

Nordstrom, A. L., Farde, L., & Halldin, C. (1992). Time course of D2-dopamine receptor occupancy examined by PET after single oral doses of haloperidol. *Psychopharmacology (Berlin), 106*(4), 433–438.

Nordstrom, A. L., Farde, L., Wiesel, F. A., Forslund, K., Pauli, S., Halldin, C., et al. (1993). Central D2-dopamine receptor occupancy in relation to antipsychotic drug effects: A double-blind PET study of schizophrenic patients. *Biological Psychiatry, 33*(4), 227–235.

Nozaki, S., Kato, M., Takano, H., Ito, H., Takahashi, H., Arakawa, R., et al. (2009). Regional dopamine synthesis in patients with schizophrenia using L-[beta-(11)C]DOPA PET. *Schizophrenia Research, 108*(1–3), 78–84.

Okubo, Y., Suhara, T., Suzuki, K., Kobayashi, K., Inoue, O., Terasaki, O., et al. (1997). Decreased prefrontal dopamine D1 receptors in schizophrenia revealed by PET. *Nature, 385*(6617), 634–636.

Parsey, R. V., Oquendo, M. A., Zea-Ponce, Y., Rodenhiser, J., Kegeles, L. S., Pratap, M., et al. (2001). Dopamine D(2) receptor availability and amphetamine-induced dopamine release in unipolar depression. *Biological Psychiatry, 50*(5), 313–322.

Pilowsky, L. S., Costa, D. C., Ell, P. J., Murray, R. M., Verhoeff, N. P., & Kerwin, R. W. (1993). Antipsychotic medication, D2 dopamine receptor blockade and clinical response: A 123I IBZM SPET (single photon emission tomography) study. *Psychological Medicine, 23*(3), 791–797.

Pycock, C. J., Kerwin, R. W., & Carter, C. J. (1980). Effect of lesion of cortical dopamine terminals on subcortical dopamine receptors in rats. *Nature, 286*(5768), 74–76.

Reith, J., Benkelfat, C., Sherwin, A., Yasuhara, Y., Kuwabara, H. Andermann, F., et al. (1994). Elevated dopa decarboxylase activity in living brain of patients with psychosis. *Proceedings of the National Academy of Sciences of the United States of America, 91*(24), 11651–11654.

Robbins, T. W., & Everitt, B. J. (1982). Functional studies of the central catecholamines. *International Review of Neurobiology, 23*, 303–365.

Robbins, T. W., & Everitt, B. J. (1996). Neurobehavioural mechanisms of reward and motivation. *Current Opinion in Neurobiology, 6*(2), 228–236.

Scatton, B., Worms, P., Lloyd, K. G., & Bartholini, G. (1982). Cortical modulation of striatal function. *Brain Research, 232*(2), 331–343.

Schultz, W. (2002). Getting formal with dopamine and reward. *Neuron, 36*(2), 241–263.

Schultz, W., Dayan, P., & Montague, P. R. (1997). A neural substrate of prediction and reward. *Science, 275*(5306), 1593–1599.

Seeman, P., & Lee, T. (1975). Antipsychotic drugs: Direct correlation between clinical potency and presynaptic action on dopamine neurons. *Science, 188*(4194), 1217–1219.

Seeman, P., Lee, T., Chau-Wong, M., & Wong, K. (1976). Antipsychotic drug doses and neuroleptic/dopamine receptors. *Nature, 261*(5562), 717–719.

Seeman, P., Schwarz, J., Chen, J. F., Szechtman, H., Perreault, M., McKnight, G. S., et al. (2006). Psychosis pathways converge via D2 high dopamine receptors. *Synapse, 60*(4), 319–346.

Snyder, S. H. (1976). The dopamine hypothesis of schizophrenia: Focus on the dopamine receptor. *American Journal of Psychiatry, 133*(2), 197–202.

Suhara, T., Okubo, Y., Yasuno, F., Sudo, Y., Inoue, M., Ichimiya, T., et al. (2002). Decreased dopamine D2 receptor binding in the anterior cingulate cortex in schizophrenia. *Archives of General Psychiatry, 59*(1), 25–30.

Takahashi, H., Higuchi, M., & Suhara, T. (2006). The role of extrastriatal dopamine D2 receptors in schizophrenia. *Biological Psychiatry, 59*(10), 919–928.

Talvik, M., Nordstrom, A. L., Okubo, Y., Olsson, H., Borg, J., Halldin, C., et al. (2006). Dopamine D2 receptor binding in drug-naive patients with schizophrenia examined with raclopride-C11 and positron emission tomography. *Psychiatry Research, 148*(2–3), 165–173.

Tamminga, C. A. (2006). The neurobiology of cognition in schizophrenia. *Journal of Clinical Psychiatry, 67*(9), e11.

Toru, M., Watanabe, S., Shibuya, H., Nishikawa, T., Noda, K., Mitsushio, H., et al. (1988). Neurotransmitters, receptors and neuropeptides in post-mortem brains of chronic schizophrenic patients. *Acta Psychiatrica Scandinavica, 78*(2), 121–137.

Turjanski, N., Sawle, G. V., Playford, E. D., Weeks, R., Lammerstma, A. A., Lees, A. J., et al. (1994). PET studies of the presynaptic and postsynaptic dopaminergic system in Tourette's syndrome. *Journal of Neurology, Neurosurgery and Psychiatry, 57*(6), 688–692.

Vernaleken, I., Kumakura, Y., Cumming, P., Buchholz, H. G., Siessmeier, T., Stoeter, P., et al. (2006). Modulation of [18F]fluorodopa (FDOPA) kinetics in the brain of healthy volunteers after acute haloperidol challenge. *NeuroImage, 30*(4), 1332–1339.

Volk, S., Maul, F. D., Hor, G., Schreiner, M., Weppner, M., Holzmann, T., et al. (1994). Dopamine D2 receptor occupancy measured by single photon emission computed tomography with 123I-Iodobenzamide in chronic schizophrenia. *Psychiatry Research, 55*(2), 111–118.

Wise, R. A. (2004). Dopamine, learning and motivation. *Nature Reviews Neuroscience, 5*(6), 483–494.

Wolkin, A., Barouche, F., Wolf, A. P., Rotrosen, J., Fowler, J. S., Shiue, C. Y., et al. (1989). Dopamine blockade and clinical response: Evidence for two biological subgroups of schizophrenia. *American Journal of Psychiatry, 146*(7), 905–908.

Wolkin, A., Brodie, J. D., Barouche, F., Rotrosen, J., Wolf, A. P., Smith, M., et al. (1989). Dopamine receptor occupancy and plasma haloperidol levels. *Archives of General Psychiatry, 46*(5), 482–484.

Wong, D. F., Wagner, H. N., Jr., Tune, L. E., Dannals, R. F., Pearlson, G. D., Links, J. M., et al. (1986). Positron emission tomography reveals elevated D2 dopamine receptors in drug-naive schizophrenics. *Science, 234*(4783), 1558–1563.

Yatham, L. N., Liddle, P. F., Shiah, I. S., Lam, R. W., Ngan, E., Scarrow, G., et al. (2002). PET study of [(18)F]6-fluoro-L-dopa uptake in neuroleptic- and mood-stabilizer-naive first-episode nonpsychotic mania: Effects of treatment with divalproex sodium. *American Journal of Psychiatry, 159*(5), 768–774.

Yung, A. R., Phillips, L. J., Yuen, H. P., Francey, S. M., McFarlane, C. A., Hallgren, M., et al. (2003). Psychosis prediction: 12-month follow up of a high-risk ("prodromal") group. *Schizophrenia Research, 60*(1), 21–32.

Yung, A. R., Stanford, C., Cosgrave, E., Killackey, E., Phillips, L., Nelson, B., et al. (2006). Testing the ultra high risk (prodromal) criteria for the prediction of psychosis in a clinical sample of young people. *Schizophrenia Research, 84*(1), 57–66.

Zakzanis, K. K., & Hansen, K. T. (1998). Dopamine D2 densities and the schizophrenic brain. *Schizophrenia Research, 32*(3), 201–206.

11 Neurophysiological alterations in the pre-psychotic phases

Nicolas Crossley and Elvira Bramon

Introduction

Over the last 90 years neurophysiology has been used to study the activity of the brain in a non-invasive manner. Already by the 1920s Berger had tried to correlate the electrical currents he measured from the scalp with levels of consciousness. Due to the variability and rather chaotic nature of the electroencephalogram (EEG) trace, the development of a superimposition method by Dawson in the 1950s and the consequent birth of the evoked potentials field (Niedermayer, 2005) were enthusiastically received by neuroscientists. For the first time small and stable responses could be obtained from the EEG trace. In the case of psychiatry, the interest was mostly focused on the mid and long latency event-related potentials, which were produced by cortical activity while subjects were performing several cognitive tests. A huge number of studies have been published in the last 20 years, particularly looking at measures such as the P50, N100, P300 and mismatch negativity (MMN) in subjects with psychosis.

Historically there have been different approaches to investigating people who are at high risk of developing psychosis. These include studying healthy relatives, for example children of patients with psychotic disorders, or subjects who score high on measures of schizotypy or who fulfil criteria for schizotypal personality disorder. Although we will mention these approaches when relevant throughout this chapter, we will focus on the neurophysiological abnormalities present in people who are deemed to have an "at-risk mental state" (ARMS) and as such have a risk of making the transition to psychosis of around 20–30% within one year of assessment (Cannon et al., 2008; Yung et al., 2007).

P300

The P300 is a positive deflection elicited in oddball paradigms where a train of frequent stimuli are followed by a rare or deviant target and the subject is instructed to respond to the latter. It peaks 300 ms after a target event that has been attended by the subject and is elicited reliably in parietocentral electrodes in different task settings including various modalities of stimuli or types of response by the subjects. In terms of cognitive processes underlying this brain response, it is thought that attention, context updating and subsequent memory storage are involved (Polich, 2007). When the task includes a novelty oddball (an irrelevant new stimulus) as well as a target oddball, the resulting positive deflection is divided into a P3a, which is a slightly earlier deflection present in the novelty oddball, and a later P3b, present in both conditions. Regarding the neural generators of the P300, intracranial recordings of patients with epilepsy have suggested hippocampal (McCarthy, Wood, Williamson, & Spencer, 1989), parietal (Halgren et al., 1995) and frontal sources (Alain, Richer, Achim, & Saint Hilaire, 1989) and the existence of this distributed generator across the brain has been supported by studies in healthy controls using non-invasive techniques such as fMRI and source analysis of EEG (Bledowski et al., 2004).

There is substantial evidence showing a decrease in P300 amplitude in subjects with schizophrenia (Bramon, Rabe-Hesketh, Sham, Murray, & Frangou, 2004). A few studies have shown that reduced P300 amplitudes are already present in the early phase of psychosis (Hirayasu et al., 1998; Salisbury et al., 1998). There seems to be an important genetic component in this decrease, with studies looking at healthy relatives and co-twins of subjects with schizophrenia or psychotic bipolar disorder showing a decreased amplitude (Bramon et al., 2005; Hall, Rijsdijk, Kalidindi et al., 2007; Hall et al., 2009) and hence the P300 is a putative endophenotype for genetic studies in psychosis. It has been shown that P300 amplitudes correlate with superior temporal lobe sizes (McCarley et al., 2002), suggesting this area of the brain is abnormal when subjects present abnormal P300 waveforms.

Apart from amplitude, studies have looked at the P300 latency, a measure of the speed of neural transmission and cognitive processing. Latency of the P300 waveform is increased in subjects with schizophrenia (Bramon, Rabe-Hesketh et al., 2004). There also appears to be a genetic component in the increased latency, with twins and other relatives of subjects with schizophrenia and psychotic bipolar disorder also showing altered latencies (Bramon et al., 2005; Hall et al., 2009; Schulze et al., 2008). A recent preliminary study has shown that this P300 latency alteration is associated with variation in neuregulin 1, a candidate gene for schizophrenia, which supports the usefulness of EEG biomarkers in early detection of and genetic research on psychotic disorders (Bramon, Dempster et al., 2008).

Four studies to date have looked at the P300 response in subjects clinically at risk of psychosis (Bramon, Shaikh et al., 2008; Frommann et al., 2008; Özgürdal et al., 2008; van der Stelt, Lieberman, & Belger, 2005; see Table 11.1 for characteristics). All four of them used a similar paradigm with a target oddball, hence looking at the P3b only. They all showed a consistent decrease in the P300 amplitude in midline sagittal electrodes compared to healthy controls, but no differences in latency between the groups.

An interesting question that could be answered with this population is whether P300 alterations are stable markers of a vulnerability to psychosis (trait factor) as proposed by studies with relatives, mentioned above, or whether there is a progressive deterioration in the course of psychosis becoming a marker of disease progression (state factor). Although none of the four studies reported longitudinal changes in P300, they did compare different phases of psychosis cross-sectionally,

Table 11.1 P300 studies

Study	Modality	Number of subjects	Definition of putative prodrome	Other observations
van der Stelt et al. (2005)	EEG	10 high-risk subjects; 10 recent-onset schizophrenia patients; 14 chronic schizophrenia patients; 14 young controls; 14 elderly controls	SIPS[1]	Young controls were matched to high-risk and recent-onset group, elderly controls to chronic schizophrenia
Bramon, Shaikh et al. (2008)	EEG	35 high-risk subjects; 57 controls	CAARMS[2]	Transition rate of 21% within 24 months
Özgürdal et al. (2008)	EEG	54 high-risk subjects; 31 first-episode patients; 27 chronic schizophrenia patients; 54 controls	Two basic cognitive symptoms (Klosterkötter et al., 2001), or attenuated positive symptoms, or brief lasting intermittent psychotic symptoms (BLIPS) according to SIPS	15% of prodromal patients receiving antipsychotics, 52% of first episode and 85% of chronic schizophrenia
Frommann et al. (2008)	EEG	50 early prodromal subjects; 50 late prodromal patients; 40 controls	BSABS[3]	Early prodrome was characterized by presence of basic symptoms, first-degree relative with schizophrenia, or perinatal complications, plus functional decline
				Late prodrome was defined as the presence of BLIPS or attenuated positive psychotic symptoms

Notes: [1]Structured Interview for Prodromal Syndromes (Miller et al., 2002). [2]Comprehensive Assessment of the At-Risk Mental States (Yung et al., 2005). [3]Bonn Scale for the Assessment of Basic Symptoms (Gross et al., 1987).

which suggests the existence of a further reduction in amplitude in the early phase of the illness, at least from prodrome to full-blown psychosis. The study by Frommann et al. (2008) divided their prodromal subjects into early and late prodrome following the approach by the German Research Network on Schizophrenia (Häfner et al., 2004), where the early prodromal phase consists of cognitive changes preceding the onset of psychosis by several years, while the late phase consists of the emergence of the first positive symptoms. In this study, decreased P300 amplitudes were seen only in the late prodromal phase. Two studies also included a sample of first-episode patients and chronic schizophrenia (Özgürdal et al., 2008; van der Stelt et al., 2005). Özgürdal reported that the magnitude of the decrease in at-risk subjects was significantly less than in chronic schizophrenia, with first episodes being in between but this difference not reaching statistical significance, although this was not replicated by van der Stelt who did not find any differences among the groups. The idea of a decrease in the P300 amplitude in the early phase of psychosis is consistent with our estimation that the effect size of P300 amplitude deficits in subjects with an ARMS is 0.49 (Cohen's *d*), which is similar to the decrease observed in unaffected relatives of subjects with schizophrenia but smaller than the effect size reported in chronic schizophrenia of 0.85 (Bramon, Shaikh et al., 2008). Although a decline in P300 amplitude is seen with age, and in both studies that included a group with chronic schizophrenia these subjects were older than ARMS and controls, none of the studies found a correlation between age and P300 amplitude. Another possible explanation of these results is that people with ARMS are a heterogeneous group, consisting of subjects with trait-like predisposing factors to psychosis as well as "false positives" without them. In terms of group responses, possible reductions in the former group would be diluted by the latter subjects, getting a mean average lower than subjects with psychosis. Supporting this idea, Frommann reported that the subjects with an ARMS who do not have a family history of psychosis do not show reductions in their P300 amplitude compared to healthy controls. So far cohorts reported are not big enough to look at only those subjects who later made the transition to psychosis (e.g., the "true prodromals") and therefore bigger sample sizes and, ideally, longitudinal studies will be needed to settle the question about trait or state of the P300 amplitude decrease.

It has been proposed that there is a laterality effect in P300 abnormalities in schizophrenia, with a meta-analysis supporting a left-side alteration in subjects with chronic schizophrenia (Jeon & Polich, 2001). Two studies reported no laterality effects (Bramon, Shaikh et al., 2008; van der Stelt et al., 2005) and although a laterality effect was reported by Frommann et al. (2008) it was bordering statistical significance.

In summary, midline amplitudes of P300 in subjects with an ARMS are consistently decreased. There is also evidence pointing towards a further reduction in the transition to psychosis, although data showing lack of abnormalities in this waveform in at-risk subjects without a positive family history support the idea of a trait rather than a state factor. Unlike chronic schizophrenics, there is no evidence of laterality of the abnormality.

Sensory gating

The brain has to negotiate constantly with many stimuli that are of little importance to the organism. The automatic process by which the brain filters out repetitive stimuli deemed of no importance is called sensory gating. An example of sensory gating can be elicited by the pre-pulse inhibition paradigm in which a startling stimulus (in any modality) is immediately preceded by the same stimulus but attenuated, normally causing a decrease in the startling response compared to the unpaired one (Kumari, Soni, Mathew, & Sharma, 2000). Another electrophysiological marker of the sensory gating is the P50, a positive deflection seen 50 ms after subjects have been exposed to an auditory stimulus. In a typical two-click conditioning–testing paradigm, subjects are exposed to pairs of identical auditory clicks separated usually by 500 ms, in which the P50 response to the second stimulus is attenuated or "gated" compared to the first. Regarding its neural generators, source analysis of magnetoencephalography studies have shown that P50 is generated in the primary auditory cortex (Mäkelä, Hämäläinen, Hari, & McEvoy, 1994) and also in the frontal cortices (Weisser et al., 2001).

P50 attenuation is consistently abnormal in subjects with schizophrenia, showing less reduction in the waveform elicited by the second click (Bramon, Rabe-Hesketh et al., 2004). This abnormal response is also seen in healthy twins of schizophrenic patients (Hall, Rijsdijk, Picchioni et al., 2007), in patients with psychotic bipolar disorder as well as their unaffected relatives (Schulze et al., 2007) and in subjects with schizotypal personality disorder (Cadenhead, Light, Geyer, & Braff, 2000), making it a very interesting marker for vulnerability to psychosis.

Three trials have looked into the P50 response in subjects clinically at risk of psychosis. Table 11.2 shows the characteristics of the studies. Myles-Worsley, Ord, Blailes, Ngiralmau, and Freedman (2004) studied adolescents from an isolated area with a higher prevalence of schizophrenia and where cases cluster in large multigenerational families. Adolescents fulfilling criteria for an "ARMS" were compared to those with a strong genetic load for schizophrenia (one parent affected or at least two siblings) and healthy controls without family history. P50 ratios were consistently elevated compared to controls in both clinically and genetically at-risk groups. Interestingly, when they divided the genetically at-risk subjects into those with or without symptoms consistent with the prodrome period (clinically at risk) only those who were symptomatic were significantly different in their P50 responses from healthy controls, although dividing the groups decreased the power of the comparison and there was still a trend for an increase in P50 ratios in the genetically but not clinically at-risk group ($p = .086$ reported). The higher prevalence of psychosis in this isolated area raises the question about how generalizable these findings are to other populations. Cadenhead, Light, Shafer, and Braff (2005) failed to detect a difference between a group of subjects with at-risk mental states and healthy controls. Nevertheless, subjects clinically at risk who had a first-degree family history had abnormal responses. It should be

Table 11.2 Sensory gating studies

Study	Modality	Number of subjects	Definition of putative prodrome	Other observations
Myles-Worsley et al. (2004)	EEG	43 high-risk subjects; 44 genetically at risk subjects; 39 controls	CAARMS	Subjects were recruited from isolated community with high risk of psychosis aggregated in families
				Genetically high risk was defined as those with a parent or two siblings affected with schizophrenia
Cadenhead et al. (2005)	EEG	31 high-risk subjects; 21 controls	SIPS	32.3% of the high-risk subjects were taking atypical antipsychotics
Brockhaus-Dumke et al. (2008)	EEG	18 high-risk subjects; 21 prodromal patients; 46 first-episode psychosis patients; 20 chronic schizophrenia subjects; 46 controls	BSABS	Prodromal patients refers to those at risk who developed psychosis within 24 months; high risk to those who did not
				First-episode patients were drug-naive and chronic schizophrenic subjects were free of medication for 4 weeks

noted that one third of their subjects at risk were taking an atypical antipsychotic at the time of testing, which could potentially have improved their P50 performance (Hong et al., 2009). Brockhaus-Dumke et al. (2008) were able to analyse independently the baseline responses of those at risk who made the transition to psychosis (truly prodromal) to those who did not within the next 24 months. Significant differences were found in both groups compared to controls but these did not resist correction for multiple comparisons (albeit there was still a trend of $p < .1$ for the true prodromal subjects). Their sample of subjects clinically at risk included subjects who presented with basic symptoms (Klosterkötter, Hellmich, Steinmeyer, & Schultze-Lutter, 2001), which is different to the clinically defined criteria used by Myles-Worsley and Cadenhead, and it is unclear, therefore, how comparable the groups from these studies are. They also included a first-episode and chronic schizophrenia group, being able to cross-sectionally analyse different stages of the illness. They found a significant increase in the P50 ratio of chronic schizophrenic subjects, suggesting a progressive deterioration of sensory gating in psychosis.

Another mid-latency potential used to investigate sensory gating is the N100 waveform elicited by the auditory stimulus and its attenuation when paired to a previous stimulus. Although there are not as many studies as with P50, a few have found abnormal N100 attenuations in schizophrenic subjects (Rosburg, Boutros, & Ford, 2008). Brockhaus-Dumke et al. (2008) reported N100 results from their sensory gating tasks. Differences between N100 elicited for the first and second stimuli were smaller in truly prodromal, first-episode and chronic schizophrenia subjects compared to controls, although only the latter two groups' results remained significant after correction for multiple comparisons. Using the ratio between the two stimuli's amplitudes they found differences between chronic schizophrenic subjects and all the other groups, which did not resist correction for multiple comparisons.

In summary, there is some evidence of abnormalities in electrophysiological markers of sensory gating in the prodromal phase (with increased P50 or N100 ratios) although this is not consistent and appears to be dependent on genetic load at times. There appears to be a further deterioration in this process in the transition from early to chronic psychosis.

Mismatch negativity

Mismatch negativity (MMN) refers to the negative waveform with a frontocentral distribution that peaks 100 ms after infrequent auditory stimuli presented alongside a train of frequent stimuli that differ in pitch or duration. It is best visualized by subtracting the average waveform of the frequent stimuli from the infrequent stimuli. Subjects are requested to draw their attention to something else, usually by being asked to watch a film or read something. It is thought that the MMN reflects the operation of an automatic sensory memory, which is pre-attentive, drawing our attention to novelty automatically (Tiitinen, May, Reinikainen, & Näätänen, 1994). Subdural electroencephalographic recordings (Rosburg et al., 2005), source analysis of EEG (Park et al., 2002) and fMRI studies (Opitz, Rinne, Mecklinger, von Cramon, & Schröger, 2002) consistently report a superior temporal lobe generator for the waveform and to a lesser extent an inferior frontal one.

A meta-analysis looking at MMN in schizophrenia found a robust decrease in patients (Umbricht & Krljes, 2005). MMN correlates with levels of functioning in subjects with chronic schizophrenia (Light & Braff, 2005) and there appears to be a decrease in MMN with illness progression that correlates with changes in the superior temporal lobe (Salisbury, Kuroki, Kasai, Shenton, & McCarley, 2007). An abnormal MMN has also been described in schizotypal personality disorder

(Niznikiewicz et al., 2009), while studies looking at MMN in relatives have not found significant differences (Bramon, Croft et al., 2004). The fact that the MMN deficits seem to progress in the course of the disease and are present in schizotypal disorder but not necessarily in those with a strong genetic load for psychosis, makes it an interesting marker of psychosis (state marker). The question, therefore, is whether it is present already in the prodrome, becoming a marker of high risk of psychosis.

Two studies have looked into the MMN waveform in subjects clinically at risk of psychosis (Table 11.3). Brockhaus-Dumke et al. (2005) studied clinically high-risk subjects, defined by the presence of basic cognitive symptoms (see above), healthy controls and schizophrenic patients who had been off antipsychotic medication for four weeks, while they performed a passive oddball task controlling attention with a visual task, and recorded their EEG. They found a significant decrease in the amplitude of the MMN in subjects with schizophrenia, with the at-risk group showing an intermediate amplitude between them and healthy controls. When discussing these results, Brockhaus-Dumke et al. raised the possibility of a heterogeneous response in the at-risk group, which might dilute significant results when averaged across the whole group, proposing the need to do follow-up studies to determine those who made the transition to psychosis and analyse them separately. Shin et al. (2009) used magnetoencephalography (MEG) to record the MMN waveform, which they argued was a better method to detect this waveform, particularly considering that the proposed source, namely the Heschl gyrus, is perpendicular to the cortical surface and electrode cap and therefore "invisible" to the EEG but not to the MEG. They recruited subjects

Table 11.3 MMN studies

Study	Modality	Number of subjects	Definition of putative prodrome	Other observations
Brockhaus-Dumke et al. (2005)	EEG	43 high-risk patients; 31 sub-jects with schiz-ophrenia; 33 controls	BSABS	Patients with schizophrenia were medication free for 4 weeks in an in-patient setting
Shin et al. (2009)	MEG	16 high-risk patients; 18 controls	CAARMS	19% of the high-risk subjects were on low-dose atypical antipsychotics 12.5% rate of transition to psychosis within a year reported

clinically at risk as defined by the Comprehensive Assessment of At-Risk Mental States (CAARMS; Yung et al., 2005) and compared them to controls while performing a passive auditory oddball task while attention was controlled in a visual search task. They found a significantly reduced amplitude of the right MMN dipole and an increased latency in high-risk subjects. No correlations were found with scores of Global Assessment of Functioning (GAF), but they did report a negative correlation with CAARMS positive symptoms scales and left MMN dipole in high-risk subjects, which probably should be considered with caution since no multiple comparison correction was reported. In summary, there is some evidence supporting a decrease in MMN in the prodrome. It remains to be seen whether this is specific to subjects who later develop psychosis (true prodromals), which would be an invaluable prognostic tool in the suspected prodrome stage.

Conclusions

Alterations in electrophysiological markers are present in people at ultra high risk of psychosis. Most of the studies so far have focused on event-related potentials and so far little is known about other neurophysiological alterations in the prodrome, which are known to be present in chronic schizophrenia such as evoked oscillatory activity or long-range synchrony (Uhlhaas, Haenschel, Nikolić, & Singer, 2008). Waveforms such as P300 and P50 could work potentially as trait factors and both appear to show further changes in the course of psychotic illness. On the other hand, an interesting state factor has been studied such as the MMN. Certainly the very nature of this heterogeneous population makes looking at biological state or trait factors of psychosis difficult, since it would always be confounded by the large proportion of "false positives" (e.g., those at risk who do not make the transition to psychosis). Future studies with larger samples and a longitudinal design might be able to look specifically at those "true prodromals" to clarify this.

References

Alain, C., Richer, F., Achim, A., & Saint Hilaire, J. M. (1989). Human intracerebral potentials associated with target, novel and omitted auditory stimuli. *Brain Topography*, *1*(4), 237–245.
Bledowski, C., Prvulovic, D., Hoechstetter, K., Scherg, M., Wibral, M., Goebel, R., et al. (2004). Localizing P300 generators in visual target and distractor processing: A combined event-related potential and functional magnetic resonance imaging study. *Journal of Neuroscience*, *24*(42), 9353–9360.
Bramon, E., Croft, R. J., McDonald, C., Virdi, G. K., Gruzelier, J. G., Baldeweg, T., et al. (2004). Mismatch negativity in schizophrenia: A family study. *Schizophrenia Research*, *67*(1), 1–10.
Bramon, E., Dempster, E., Frangou, S., Shaikh, M., Walshe, M., Filbey, F. M., et al. (2008). Neuregulin-1 and the P300 waveform—a preliminary association study using a psychosis endophenotype. *Schizophrenia Research*, *103*(1–3), 178–185.

Bramon, E., McDonald, C., Croft, R. J., Landau, S., Filbey, F., Gruzelier, J. H., et al. (2005). Is the P300 wave an endophenotype for schizophrenia? A meta-analysis and a family study. *NeuroImage, 27*(4), 960–968.

Bramon, E., Rabe-Hesketh, S., Sham, P., Murray, R. M., & Frangou, S. (2004). Meta-analysis of the P300 and P50 waveforms in schizophrenia. *Schizophrenia Research, 70*(2–3), 315–329.

Bramon, E., Shaikh, M., Broome, M., Lappin, J., Bergé, D., Day, F., et al. (2008). Abnormal P300 in people with high risk of developing psychosis. *NeuroImage, 41*(2), 553–560.

Brockhaus-Dumke, A., Schultze-Lutter, F., Mueller, R., Tendolkar, I., Bechdolf, A., Pukrop, R., et al. (2008). Sensory gating in schizophrenia: P50 and N100 gating in antipsychotic-free subjects at risk, first-episode and chronic patients. *Biological Psychiatry, 64*(5), 376–384.

Brockhaus-Dumke, A., Tendolkar, I., Pukrop, R., Schultze-Lutter, F., Klosterkötter, J., & Ruhrmann, S. (2005). Impaired mismatch negativity generation in prodromal subjects and patients with schizophrenia. *Schizophrenia Research, 73*(2–3), 297–310.

Cadenhead, K. S., Light, G. A., Geyer, M. A., & Braff, D. L. (2000). Sensory gating deficits assessed by the P50 event-related potential in subjects with schizotypal personality disorder. *American Journal of Psychiatry, 157*(1), 55–59.

Cadenhead, K. S., Light, G. A., Shafer, K. M., & Braff, D. L. (2005). P50 suppression in individuals at risk for schizophrenia: The convergence of clinical, familial and vulnerability marker risk assessment. *Biological Psychiatry, 57*(12), 1504–1509.

Cannon, T. D., Cadenhead, K., Cornblatt, B., Woods, S. W., Addington, J., Walker, E., et al. (2008). Prediction of psychosis in youth at high clinical risk: A multisite longitudinal study in North America. *Archives of General Psychiatry, 65*(1), 28–37.

Frommann, I., Brinkmeyer, J., Ruhrmann, S., Hack, E., Brockhaus-Dumke, A., Bechdolf, A., et al. (2008). Auditory P300 in individuals clinically at risk for psychosis. *International Journal of Psychophysiology, 70*(3), 192–205.

Gross, G., Huber, G., Klosterkötter, J., & Linz, M. (1987). *Bonner Skala für die Beurteilung von Basissymptomen* [*BSABS: Bonn Scale for the Assessment of Basic Symptoms*. Berlin, Germany: Springer.

Häfner, H., Maurer, K., Ruhrmann, S., Bechdolf, A., Klosterkötter, J., Wagner, M., et al. (2004). Early detection and secondary prevention of psychosis: Facts and visions. *European Archives of Psychiatry and Clinical Neuroscience, 254*(2), 117–128.

Halgren, E., Baudena, P., Clarke, J. M., Heit, G., Liégeois, C., Chauvel, P., et al. (1995). Intracerebral potentials to rare target and distractor auditory and visual stimuli. I. Superior temporal plane and parietal lobe. *Electroencephalography and Clinical Neurophysiology, 94*(3), 191–220.

Hall, M. H., Rijsdijk, F., Kalidindi, S., Schulze, K., Kravariti, E., Kane, F., et al. (2007). Genetic overlap between bipolar illness and event-related potentials. *Psychological Medicine, 37*(5), 667–678.

Hall, M. H., Rijsdijk, F., Picchioni, M., Schulze, K., Ettinger, U., Toulopoulou, T., et al. (2007). Substantial shared genetic influences on schizophrenia and event-related potentials. *American Journal of Psychiatry, 164*(5), 804–812.

Hall, M. H., Schulze, K., Rijsdijk, F., Kalidindi, S., McDonald, C., Bramon, E., et al. (2009). Are auditory P300 and duration MMN heritable and putative endophenotypes of psychotic bipolar disorder? A Maudsley Bipolar Twin and Family Study. *Psychological Medicine, 39*(8), 1277–1287.

Hirayasu, Y., Asato, N., Ohta, H., Hokama, H., Arakaki, H., & Ogura, C. (1998). Abnormalities of auditory event-related potentials in schizophrenia prior to treatment. *Biological Psychiatry, 43*(4), 244–253.

Hong, X., Chan, R. C., Zhuang, X., Jiang, T., Wan, X., Wang, J., et al. (2009). Neuroleptic effects on P50 sensory gating in patients with first-episode never-medicated schizophrenia. *Schizophrenia Research, 108*(1–3), 151–157.

Jeon, Y. W., & Polich, J. (2001). P300 asymmetry in schizophrenia: A meta-analysis. *Psychiatry Research, 104*(1), 61–74.

Klosterkötter, J., Hellmich, M., Steinmeyer, E. M., & Schultze-Lutter, F. (2001). Diagnosing schizophrenia in the initial prodromal phase. *Archives of General Psychiatry, 58*(2), 158–164.

Kumari, V., Soni, W., Mathew, V. M., & Sharma, T. (2000). Prepulse inhibition of the startle response in men with schizophrenia: Effects of age of onset of illness, symptoms and medication. *Archives of General Psychiatry, 57*(6), 609–614.

Light, G. A., & Braff, D. L. (2005). Mismatch negativity deficits are associated with poor functioning in schizophrenia patients. *Archives of General Psychiatry, 62*(2), 127–136.

Mäkelä, J. P., Hämäläinen, M., Hari, R., & McEvoy, L. (1994). Whole-head mapping of middle-latency auditory evoked magnetic fields. *Electroencephalography and Clinical Neurophysiology, 92*(5), 414–421.

McCarley, R. W., Salisbury, D. F., Hirayasu, Y., Yurgelun-Todd, D. A., Tohen, M., Zarate. C., et al. (2002). Association between smaller left posterior superior temporal gyrus volume on magnetic resonance imaging and smaller left temporal P300 amplitude in first-episode schizophrenia. *Archives of General Psychiatry, 59*(4), 321–331.

McCarthy, G., Wood, C. C., Williamson, P. D., & Spencer, D. D. (1989). Task-dependent field potentials in human hippocampal formation. *Journal of Neuroscience, 9*(12), 4253–4268.

Miller, T. J., McGlashan, T. H., Rosen, J. L., Somjee, L., Markovich, P. J., Stein, K., et al. (2002). Prospective diagnosis of the initial prodrome for schizophrenia based on the Structured Interview for Prodromal Syndromes: Preliminary evidence of inter-rater reliability and predictive validity. *American Journal of Psychiatry, 159*(5), 863–865.

Myles-Worsley, M., Ord, L., Blailes, F., Ngiralmau, H., & Freedman, R. (2004). P50 sensory gating in adolescents from a pacific island isolate with elevated risk for schizophrenia. *Biological Psychiatry, 55*(7), 663–667.

Niedermayer, E. (2005). Historical aspects. In E. Niedermayer & F. Lopes da Silva (Eds.), *Electroencephalography: Basic principles, clinical applications and related fields* (5th ed., Ch. 1, pp. 1–16). Philadelphia, PA: Lippincott Williams & Wilkins.

Niznikiewicz, M. A., Spencer, K. M., Dickey, C., Voglmaier, M., Seidman, L. J., Shenton, M. E., et al. (2009). Abnormal pitch mismatch negativity in individuals with schizotypal personality disorder. *Schizophrenia Research, 110*(1–3), 188–193.

Opitz, B., Rinne, T., Mecklinger, A., von Cramon, D. Y., & Schröger, E. (2002). Differential contribution of frontal and temporal cortices to auditory change detection: fMRI and ERP results. *NeuroImage, 15*(1), 167–174.

Özgürdal, S., Gudlowski, Y., Witthaus, H., Kawohl, W., Uhl, I., Hauser, M., et al. (2008). Reduction of auditory event-related P300 amplitude in subjects with at-risk mental state for schizophrenia. *Schizophrenia Research, 105*(1–3), 272–278.

Park, H. J., Kwon, J. S., Youn, T., Pae, J. S., Kim, J. J., Kim, M. S., et al. (2002). Statistical parametric mapping of LORETA using high density EEG and individual MRI: Application to mismatch negativities in schizophrenia. *Human Brain Mapping, 17*(3), 168–178.

Polich, J. (2007). Updating P300: An integrative theory of P3a and P3b. *Clinical Neurophysiology, 118*(10), 2128–2148.

Rosburg, T., Boutros, N. N., & Ford, J. M. (2008). Reduced auditory evoked potential component N100 in schizophrenia—A critical review. *Psychiatry Research, 161*(3), 259–274.

Rosburg, T., Trautner, P., Dietl, T., Korzyukov, O. A., Boutros, N. N., Schaller, C., et al. (2005). Subdural recordings of the mismatch negativity (MMN) in patients with focal epilepsy. *Brain, 128*(Pt. 4), 819–828.

Salisbury, D. F., Kuroki, N., Kasai, K., Shenton, M. E., & McCarley, R. W. (2007). Progressive and interrelated functional and structural evidence of post-onset brain reduction in schizophrenia. *Archives of General Psychiatry, 64*(5), 521–529.

Salisbury, D. F., Shenton, M. E., Sherwood, A. R., Fischer, I. A., Yurgelun-Todd, D. A., Tohen, M., et al. (1998). First-episode schizophrenic psychosis differs from first-episode affective psychosis and controls in P300 amplitude over left temporal lobe. *Archives of General Psychiatry, 55*(2), 173–180.

Schulze, K. K., Hall, M. H., McDonald, C., Marshall, N., Walshe, M., Murray, R. M., et al. (2007). P50 auditory evoked potential suppression in bipolar disorder patients with psychotic features and their unaffected relatives. *Biological Psychiatry, 62*(2), 121–128.

Schulze, K. K., Hall, M. H., McDonald, C., Marshall, N., Walshe, M., Murray, R. M., et al. (2008). Auditory P300 in patients with bipolar disorder and their unaffected relatives. *Bipolar Disorders, 10*(3), 377–386.

Shin, K. S., Kim, J. S., Kang, D. H., Koh, Y., Choi, J. S., O'Donnell, B. F., et al. (2009). Pre-attentive auditory processing in ultra-high-risk for schizophrenia with magnetoencephalography. *Biological Psychiatry, 65*(12), 1071–1078.

Tiitinen, H., May, P., Reinikainen, K., & Näätänen, R. (1994). Attentive novelty detection in humans is governed by pre-attentive sensory memory. *Nature, 372*(6501), 90–92.

Uhlhaas, P. J., Haenschel, C., Nikolić, D., & Singer, W. (2008). The role of oscillations and synchrony in cortical networks and their putative relevance for the pathophysiology of schizophrenia. *Schizophrenia Bulletin, 34*(5), 927–943.

Umbricht, D., & Krljes, S. (2005). Mismatch negativity in schizophrenia: A meta-analysis. *Schizophrenia Research, 76*(1), 1–23.

van der Stelt, O., Lieberman, J. A., & Belger, A. (2005). Auditory P300 in high-risk, recent-onset and chronic schizophrenia. *Schizophrenia Research, 77*(2–3), 309–320.

Weisser, R., Weisbrod, M., Roehrig, M., Rupp, A., Schroeder, J., & Scherg, M. (2001). Is frontal lobe involved in the generation of auditory evoked P50? *Neuroreport, 12*(15), 3303–3307.

Yung, A. R., Yuen, H. P., Berger, G., Francey, S., Hung, T. C., Nelson, B., et al. (2007). Declining transition rate in ultra high risk (prodromal) services: Dilution or reduction of risk? *Schizophrenia Bulletin, 33*(3), 673–681.

Yung, A. R., Yuen, H. P., McGorry, P. D., Phillips, L. J., Kelly, D., Dell'Olio, M., et al. (2005). Mapping the onset of psychosis: The Comprehensive Assessment of At-Risk Mental States. *Australian and New Zealand Journal of Psychiatry, 39*(11–12), 964–971.

12 Stigma in early stages of psychotic illness: Connections with cognitive neuroscience

Lawrence H. Yang, Ahtoy J. Wonpat-Borja, Mark Opler, Michael T. Compton, Meredith Kelly, Valerie Purdie-Vaughns and Cheryl M. Corcoran

Introduction

Schizophrenia, a chronic and oftentimes severe mental illness characterized by the presence of hallucinations, delusions and potentially lifelong impairment, has been identified as the ninth leading cause of disability worldwide. Because the symptoms of psychotic disorders emerge during late adolescence and early adulthood (a crucial time of psychosocial development), such illnesses are particularly impairing in diverse educational, occupational and interpersonal domains. However, given that the onset of schizophrenia and related psychotic disorders is preceded in 80% of cases by subclinical psychotic symptoms and other prodromal features (Häfner et al., 1998), early detection promises to reduce the disease's public health burden. The psychosis risk syndrome has been classified as subthreshold psychotic symptoms that fulfil at least one of three criteria: attenuated positive symptoms; brief intermittent psychotic symptoms; and/or functional decline in the context of genetic risk (Miller et al., 2003). Use of this classification for identification as well as in initial randomized clinical trials of pharmacological and/or cognitive-behavioural methods of individuals who are "at risk" for psychosis (McGorry et al., 2002) has introduced the goal of reducing the prevalence of psychotic disorders by delaying onset or conversion to psychosis.

Despite the major potential benefits that early identification and treatment might confer, the question of the risk of stigma and its impact on individuals who are identified as being "at risk" for psychosis and their family members arises consistently (Corcoran, First, & Cornblatt, 2010; Corcoran, Malaspina, & Hercher, 2005; McGorry, Yung, & Phillips, 2001; Yang, Wonpat-Borja, Opler, & Corcoran, 2010). While a National Institute of Mental Health-funded study has demonstrated good reliability (κs > .80 at each site) and predictive validity of the psychosis risk syndrome (approximately 35% of individuals progress to psychosis within 2.5 years of identification; Cannon et al., 2008), over 50% of identified patients may not ultimately "convert" to psychosis. The risk of stigma is further amplified among the "false positives" who do not develop a future psychotic disorder (Corcoran et al., 2005, 2010). Because stigma comprises a potential risk for this "at-risk" designation, this chapter seeks to inform this issue by drawing upon the extensive theoretical and empirical literature on stigma to better identify how stigma might exert effects upon individuals identified as "at risk" for psychosis. First, we determine what dimensions within the multifaceted construct of stigma are most salient and categorize the possible mechanisms by which stigma might affect individuals identified as being "at risk" for psychosis. Second, because this designation will typically be made with teens and young adults whose identity is not yet stable and whose psychosocial development is rapidly evolving, we review the empirical literature describing how stigma related to mental illnesses occurs among adolescents to determine which of the stigma mechanisms identified above may manifest in the "at risk" for psychosis group. Next, we review the few studies that evaluate stigma in at-risk states and in individuals with an initial episode of psychosis, in both patients and families, with a brief review of ethnic differences. Finally, we discuss the existing cognitive neuroscience literature to identify likely brain regions involved in the experience of stigma. We conclude by recommending areas of future study for the "at-risk" designation that are suggested by this review of the conceptual and empirical literature.

Defining stigma

Rather than being restricted to a unitary definition, conceptions of stigma have ranged from formulations emphasizing internal psychological processes to more complex conceptualizations integrating evolutionary principles, institutional policies and sociopolitical forces (see Wraga, Helt, Jacobs, & Sullivan, 2007; Yang & Kleinman, 2008; Yang et al., 2007, for reviews). In this chapter, stigma is defined and mechanisms that most directly illuminate how an official psychosis risk label (i.e., a clinical diagnosis) might impact identified subjects are elaborated. In his classic conceptualization, Goffman (1963) defined stigma as "an attribute that is deeply discrediting" that diminishes the bearer "from a whole and usual person to a tainted, discounted one" (p. 3). Goffman viewed stigma as occurring when a discrepancy exists between "virtual social identity" (how a person is characterized by society) and "actual social identity" (the attributes truly possessed by a person; p. 2). Subsequent social psychological definitions described stigma as being comprised of a "mark" that—with its linked pejorative meanings—is viewed as "engulfing" how the person is perceived by society (Jones et al., 1984). A prominent group of social psychologists defined stigma as being socially constructed by defining whom is included in a stigmatized social group and whether an attribute confers a devalued social identity in a particular context (Crocker, Major, & Steele, 1998). These definitions emphasize the centrality of *stereotypes* and how such social processes lead to the devaluation of an individual's identity (Seibt & Förster, 2004).

The definition of stigma has more recently been expanded from narrower conceptions of stigma as an attribution or stereotype to encompass interrelated stigma components under a broad umbrella concept (Link & Phelan, 2001). *Labelling* occurs when people distinguish a human difference as significant (e.g., hearing voices and talking to oneself) and assign it a label (e.g., being "schizophrenic"). *Stereotyping* then takes place when a social group's beliefs link labelled persons (e.g., "schizophrenics") to negative characteristics (e.g., "dangerous and unpredictable"). Next, *cognitive separation* occurs when labelled individuals (e.g., "schizophrenics") are perceived as so different that complete distinction of "us" ("normals") from "them" ("deviants") is achieved. *Emotional reactions* (Link, Yang, Phelan, & Collins, 2004) include the affective responses to stigma felt by both stigmatizers (e.g., fear, disgust) and the stigmatized (e.g., shame, alienation). *Status loss and discrimination* occur when labelled individuals experience either devaluation (e.g., having their opinions disregarded) or unfair behavioural treatment from others. Discrimination may take place through person-to-person forms (i.e., individual-level discrimination such as being shunned or avoided) or when institutional practices place stigmatized groups at a systematic disadvantage (i.e., structural discrimination such as denying insurance due to a pre-existing psychiatric condition). Lastly, Link and Phelan proposed that the stigma process depends on the use of social, economic and political *power* that allows these stigma components to lead to discriminatory results. From these definitions, processes are identified involving awareness of societal stereotypes (and even more importantly, its application to the self via "*internalized stigma*", described below) as possible mechanisms to describe how this harmful social dynamic might affect individuals characterized as being in an "at-risk" mental state.

Models by which stigma impacts individuals

Building upon definitions of stigma, it is possible to begin identifying potential mechanisms through which stigma might affect individuals identified as being in an "at-risk" state for psychosis by briefly describing the most relevant models of how stigma exerts its negative effects on individuals (see Major, McCoy, Kaiser, & Quinton, 2003; Steele, Spencer, & Aronson, 2002, for extensive reviews). Social psychologists have conceptualized stigma as working through processes of cognitive categorization; i.e., stigma takes place when the mark links an individual via attributional processes to negative characteristics (Jones et al., 1984). Subsequent models have included the response of individuals to stigma; e.g., preserving self-esteem through cognitive coping strategies (Crocker et al., 1998) or through a combination of involuntary and voluntary coping responses (Major & O'Brien, 2005). A major contribution of these conceptualizations is that the stigmatized individual may *internalize* a negative stereotype, leading to harmful effects. An example of such internalization among stigmatized individuals is the concept called *stereotype threat*, whereby individuals are made aware of negative stereotypes about their own group (e.g., women) in relation to a specific situation (e.g., maths achievement) and the consequent threat to that individual's self-esteem then adversely impacts the person's performance (Steele et al., 2002). Specific brain areas (reviewed under "social perception, stereotype threat and cognitive neuroscience" below) have also been implicated with the experience of stereotype threat (Krendl, Richeson, Kelley, & Heatherton, 2008). With regard to people labelled with a psychiatric diagnosis, internalized stigma occurs once affected individuals become aware of societal stereotypes of mental illnesses and apply these stereotypes to themselves, which may lead to harmful psychological outcomes such as low self-esteem and depression (Ritsher & Phelan, 2004).

Of particular relevance to how stigma affects people with a mental illness is a sociological model known as *labelling theory*. Based on the concept of *symbolic interactionism* (Mead, 1934), this conceptualization proposes that social responses to deviant actions (e.g., behaving in a bizarre manner due to persecutory delusions) are constantly influenced by shared cultural languages and symbols (e.g., that "crazy" person is unpredictable and should be sent to a mental asylum). Self-conceptions then develop from perceptions of others' beliefs and responses, thus socializing an individual into *role identities* (e.g., being psychiatrically ill), which are linked with behavioural expectations (e.g., chronic disability). Link, Cullen, Struening, Shrout, and Dohrenwend (1989) proposed a *modified labelling theory* that all members of a society internalize ideas of what it means to be labelled with psychiatric illness as part of everyday socialization. These internalized conceptions are comprised of the extent to which all community members endorse that people with a mental illness will be devalued (i.e., lose status) and discriminated against (i.e., be denied life opportunities). Since official clinical/diagnostic labelling occurs via contact with the system of psychiatric care, expectations of community devaluation now become relevant to the individual. According to Link et al., labelled individuals may then respond to perceived anticipated rejection in two harmful ways: (1) *secrecy*, or concealing one's treatment history from others; and (2) *withdrawal*, or limiting contact to those accepting of one's condition (e.g., others who share a devalued status by virtue of having a mental illness). Previous empirical studies have demonstrated that labelling-induced stigma is linked with lower self-esteem (Fung et al., 2007; Link, Struening, Neese-Todd, Asmussen, & Phelan, 2001), demoralization (Link, Mirotznik, & Cullen, 1991), depressive symptoms (Link et al., 1991; Ritsher & Phelan, 2004), less adherence with treatment (Fung et al., 2007), constricted social networks (Link et al., 1989) and reduced social integration (Prince & Prince, 2002). Such effects also restrict opportunities to engage in life opportunities through increased unemployment (Link et al., 1991) and loss of housing (Page, 1977). These models highlight the process of what is termed *internalized stigma* (Corrigan, Watson, & Barr, 2006), whereby people with mental illnesses internalize negative societal stereotypes and experience negative emotional consequences as a result of applying these negative societal notions to the self (Link et al., 2004). Further, the deleterious behavioural coping strategies utilized by individuals with a mental illness to avoid potential harmful effects and to avert perceived anticipated rejection comprise another pivotal mechanism by which stigma operates (Link et al., 1989). These mechanisms (i.e., "internalized stigma" and behavioural coping responses to stigma) are highlighted as possible processes by which stigma might impact individuals designated as being "at risk" for psychosis.

Stigma and labelling among adolescents

Because the identification of individuals as at risk for psychosis typically occurs in adolescence, specific age-related aspects of this developmental period may influence the expression and impact of stigma for this group. Adolescence is a developmental stage during which identity formation is in flux; teens and young adults are faced with the challenge of reaching important developmental milestones, such as consolidating an autonomous self-concept, attaining educational and vocational achievement and forming social networks (Zarrett & Eccles, 2006). Adolescents' neurocognitive capacities also continue to develop during this stage and show differences from adults with regard to experiencing stigma-related social emotions (i.e., embarrassment). Becoming labelled (and all its effects) may impede one's transition into adulthood by interfering with the acquisition of personal assets or competencies, values and social capital (Zarrett & Eccles, 2006). For example, in a qualitative study of adolescents labelled as having mental-health problems, participants reported experiencing significant changes in their familial roles, their educational and career choices and their social standing, expressing specifically that their mental illness label got in the way of their becoming adults (Leavey, 2005). Because adolescence is a developmental period characterized by identity consolidation, the effects of labelling have the potential to be especially damaging as adolescents' self-concepts are less well formed and vulnerable to change. Receiving a label of a serious mental illness such as major depressive disorder, or plausibly the label of risk for serious mental illness such as schizophrenia, during this crucial stage might result in the lasting incorporation of negative conceptions into the foundation of one's social identity, thereby threatening a fundamental sense of normalcy (Wisdom & Green, 2004).

To shed some light on this process of diminishing self-concept, Lally (1989) proposed that after acquiring the label of an "ill person", such a role becomes central in defining an individual's identity. Interacting in this capacity over time diminishes other valued social roles, leaving only the "chronically ill" role behind. An *engulfment* into a stigmatized identity occurs when a person endorses beliefs of incompetence, defines him- or herself as "just being mentally ill", believes that others perceive him or her in terms of illness characteristics and perceives a future defined by disability. It is plausible that adolescents, whose identity formation is as yet in flux, may be particularly vulnerable to engulfment into a stigmatized identity. This is supported by in-depth interviews with adolescents with depression (Wisdom & Green, 2004), many of whom reported feeling that their diagnosis was an important part of their personal identity and that their condition might be permanent.

Stigmatized public attitudes toward mental illness are so pervasive that awareness of them is found even among young children (Wahl, 2002) and that children and adolescents can suffer their effects in terms of internalized stigma (Pescosolido, Perry, Martin, McLeod, & Jensen, 2007). According to community surveys (Penn et al., 2005; Pescosolido, Perry et al., 2007), both adults and youth think that adolescents with a mental illness are violent and likely to be rejected from social circles. Almost half of adults who participated in the nationally representative US General Social Survey endorsed the statement that "getting mental-health treatment would make a child an outsider at school" and that the stigmatization initiated during this time would persist into adulthood (Pescosolido, Perry et al., 2007). Similarly, adult respondents agreed that children with attention-deficit/hyperactivity disorder (ADHD) or depression were significantly more likely than other kids to harm themselves or others (Pescosolido, Fettes, Martin, Monahan, & McLeod, 2007). Furthermore, this perception of dangerousness was exacerbated (a fivefold increase) when "mentally ill" labels were independently offered (Pescosolido, Fettes et al., 2007). Youth respondents also shared a negative perspective, agreeing that peers with schizophrenia were more violent (72%), more suicidal (76%) and less likely to do well in school (70%; Penn et al., 2005). These attitudes extend beyond a diagnostic label, impacting treatment utilization, as evidenced by more than a third of adolescents reporting that there are moderate to high levels of stigma associated with seeking help for mental-health problems (Chandra & Minkovitz, 2006). Finally, while prior contact with people with a mental illness has been shown to decrease stigma in adults, it had the opposite effect among youth, increasing stigma through perceptions of personal blame and dangerousness (Corrigan et al., 2005). Taken together, these findings suggest that labelled adolescents' experience of stigma is at least equal to and perhaps more troublesome than that of adults.

Although the impact of the label of being in an "at-risk" mental state has yet to be systematically examined, two recent studies of approximately 60 teens (ages 12–18 years) have each documented changes in adolescent well-being and self-concept during diagnosis and treatment of disorders such as disruptive behaviour disorder, affective disorders and posttraumatic stress disorder (Moses, 2009a, 2009b). Despite reporting relatively low levels of perceived public stigma, diagnosed adolescents in Moses' study (2009b) endorsed expectations of societal devaluation toward youth receiving mental-health treatment, such as being teased, harassed, or looked down upon by peers. About half of respondents also reported experiencing peer rejection, such as being disrespected and others "hurting their feelings", which they attributed to use of mental-health services. These studies demonstrate that several key mechanisms proposed by *modified labelling theory* (Link et al., 1989) can be operative in adolescents. For example, adolescents who reported greater perception of societal devaluation were also more likely to report more self-stigma (such as feeling ashamed, different, or uncomfortable), which in turn was linked with increased secrecy about one's mental-health problems. Although the direction or causality cannot be established for certain, these stigma-related constructs were strongly associated with psychological well-being: endorsement of societal devaluation and self-stigma were linked with higher levels of depression and societal devaluation was significantly related to lowered self-esteem even after controlling for depression. While most adolescents were found to actively interpret (and in some cases resist) the label of a mental illness at the time of diagnosis, approximately 20% "self-labelled" by naming the mental illness as a key feature of their identity (e.g., describing "my" psychiatric disorder; Moses, 2009a). Of note, Moses (2009a) indicated that individuals whose onset of illness was later tended to be "non-labellers", as were boys when compared with girls, suggesting that individuals "at risk" for psychosis (who tend to develop symptoms and receive a risk label in later adolescence and who are primarily male; Woods et al., 2009) might be less prone to "self-labelling". Further, "self-labellers" had more self-stigma and depression than those who avoided self-labelling. Consistent with the proposal that teens may be particularly vulnerable, adolescents with an earlier age at initiating treatment reported more self-stigma, a higher likelihood of self-labelling and greater secrecy about their problems, regardless of the level of functional impairment (Moses, 2009a, 2009b).

These studies by Moses suggest that similar mechanisms could be at work in terms of the potential impact of stigma on young people identified as being "at risk" for psychosis. However, this is tempered by significant differences between Moses' cohorts and typical "at-risk" cohorts, including having an established diagnosis (vs. identification as "at risk"). Additionally, the Moses cohorts were characterized by much greater symptom severity and impairment (receiving services across multiple systems) and a higher prevalence of disruptive disorders. The impact of stigma in individuals identified as "at risk" for psychosis remains an empirical question that may be informed by preliminary studies.

Studies of stigma associated with psychosis and its risk states in patients and families

Despite the potential consequences of stigma for those identified as "at risk" for psychosis and for their families, research is scarce in this area. However, the few studies involving patients with a first episode of psychosis are illustrative and provide a useful potential point of reference in the examination of early stigma processes. A study by Tarrier and colleagues (Tarrier, Khan, Cater, & Picken, 2007) found that patients suffering from their first episode of psychosis reported experiencing stigma (53%), social exclusion (50%) and physical harassment (38%) as a result of their illness. Parents of patients receiving treatment for their first episode of schizophrenia also highly endorsed negative attitudes about mental illness (Czuchta & McCay, 2001). A qualitative study of family members of patients with recent-onset psychosis revealed themes of labelling, stereotyping, negative emotional reactions and coping strategies discussed earlier in this chapter (Gerson et al., 2009). Consistent with Link et al.'s (2004) definition of stigma, parents recognized that their children were labelled by their diagnoses, internalized the negative stereotypes that were attached to that label and responded with feelings of shame and attempts to conceal their child's condition. In this same cohort of families, anticipated stigma was reported, such as fearing that a son with a mental illness would be "treated like a rapist" and that a patient's siblings would be teased by others (Corcoran et al., 2007). This set of processes is exemplified by the statement (Gerson et al., 2009): "*People tend to stigmatize people who are mentally ill. I'm kind of ashamed, really, to tell somebody*". Anger and frustration accompanied a sense of hopelessness about the permanence of the label according to another parent of an individual with recent-onset schizophrenia: "Now we have to deal with this 's' word ... it's like, oh, this is a dirty word. I almost had a breakdown myself and I said, 'This is what I am dealing with and I'm going to be dealing with it for the rest of my life and I am angry'". Worst of all, these negative stereotypes were viewed as encompassing one's entire identity and predicting one's future experiences. As one mother shared, "I talked to a social worker who was nice, but she said I should look at it as that I have three kids, two are good and one is not good". Another parent remembered that her doctor "told my son to get used to it and he would be like this for the rest of his life" (Gerson et al., 2009).

Working backward from the initiation of treatment, researchers have attempted to assess stigma prior to this point of first treatment for psychotic symptoms. Much of this literature is focused on the role of stigma in help-seeking behaviour through retrospective interviews done at patients' first contact with the mental-health system. These studies are especially important in light of findings that significant delays occur in obtaining care upon first observing psychotic symptoms (Singh & Grange, 2006) and that reducing these delays may have a positive impact on mental-health outcomes (Norman & Malla, 2001). Franz and colleagues (2010) conducted qualitative interviews with 12 African-American family members about their experiences before their relative began treatment for psychosis. Using a grounded theory approach, they found that the themes generated from the interviews closely resembled the constructs of modified labelling theory (Link et al., 1989; Link & Phelan, 2001), beginning with caregivers' recognition of society's negative reactions toward someone labelled with a serious mental illness and continuing on to their consequent efforts to cope with stigma. Relatives cited both early signs of psychotic behaviour ("if they do something funny") and the official psychiatric diagnosis as sufficient labels that elicited stigmatizing attitudes and behaviours from the public, such as social distance ("They look at them strange. They don't seem like they want to be around them" and "They think, 'Don't fool with them because they are crazy'. They don't treat them nice.") and fear of unpredictability ("They automatically think, 'He's just gonna do something outrageous'."). Family members generally regarded their relative's condition with empathy and compassion and employed several strategies to avoid a label altogether, such as using alternative explanatory models involving external factors (Franz et al., 2010). Two small, retrospective, qualitative studies of patients' experiences confirmed many of these findings and stressed the critical importance of stigma-related coping strategies in prolonging treatment delays (Boydell, Gladstone, & Volpe, 2006; Judge, Estroff, Perkins, & Penn, 2008). Such strategies reflect both relatives' and patients' fear of the consequences of labelling and included secrecy ("You really don't want anyone to know because no one wants to be looked at in a different way, as abnormal"; Franz et al., 2010), withdrawal ("I tried to help myself. I stayed in solitary for six months ... in a motel room"; Franz et al., 2010) and avoiding help ("I wouldn't tell anyone about the voices. It never felt safe to do that. I pictured myself being locked up in a cell if I told the truth"; Judge et al., 2008).

Findings from these studies, which report experiences pertaining to stigma before entering treatment, suggests that internalization of negative attitudes and related behavioural coping responses may constitute processes by which stigma might affect individuals before they are labelled by the mental-health care system as having an established disorder. Further indirect evidence for possible stigma processes during the putative prodromal period comes from studies interviewing parents concerning observed changes during the course of illness among individuals at elevated risk for psychosis (Corcoran et al., 2003). Parents in some cases described their children during their evolution of symptoms as having undergone a profound alteration in identity, which suggests the potential initiation of internalized stigma processes; i.e., "he adopted a whole new identity" and "now my daughter is a case study". This same cohort of family members of putative prodromal patients, studied together with family members of patients with recent onset of psychotic disorder, were also evaluated in terms of stigma using the Opinions about Mental Illness scale (OMI; Cohen & Streuning, 1962) and the Family Experiences Interview Schedule (FEIS; Tessler & Gamach, 1995). This study, by Wong and colleagues (2009), suggested that stigma experienced by families of individuals in the early stages of a psychotic disorder may be less evident, particularly in those identified as "at risk" rather than those with a recent onset of psychotic disorder. Reflecting minimal endorsement of public stigma, the majority of families agreed with positive/supportive statements about people with mental illnesses concerning government assistance, voting rights, employment, trustworthiness and religious/spiritual coping, while few family members agreed with negative stereotypes and generalized stigmatizing statements, including the limited ability of people with mental illnesses to perform certain tasks, hold positions in law enforcement/public safety and be trustworthy around children (Wong et al., 2009). However, the items that were moderately or highly endorsed by families indicate areas where internalized stigma might potentially take root. For instance, the majority of both groups agreed that "dealing with a person with a mental illness can at times be like dealing with a young child" and that "although people with mental illnesses can look okay, it is important to remember that they are ill", and at least 44% of both groups agreed with statements that people with mental illnesses are irrational and that their condition is permanent (Wong et al., 2009). One third of family members of individuals in an "at-risk" state avoided going to social events due to their relative's emerging illness, although other stigma-related coping strategies were relatively low compared to families of first-episode patients who anticipated social rejection from their community (54%), felt ashamed and embarrassed about their relative's illness (64%) and felt the need to conceal it from others (64%). The authors discuss an important caveat to these findings in that the "at-risk" group only includes families who recognized putative prodromal symptoms in their relative, who then voluntarily sought treatment in a specialty research programme, as compared to the families of the recent-onset group, whose relatives often had an involuntary admission after developing a psychotic episode. By selection, this sample of families of individuals identified as being "at risk" might be less likely to be concerned about stigma associated with participation in this type of programme when compared with undetected community members with putatively prodromal symptoms (or perhaps with individuals who are identified as at risk for psychosis in the community, outside of an academic research setting). Nonetheless, these studies suggest that some precursors of stigma may develop early in the course of psychotic disorder—even during its risk state—and that they have the potential to take on greater influence, particularly if psychosis progresses and more intensive mental-health treatment is required.

The role of race and ethnicity in the effects of stigma

It is important to consider the role of race and ethnicity in perceptions of stigma and stigma's role in potentially complicating the help-seeking process during the pre-psychotic phase. Although one can only draw tentative conclusions from this small body of existing literature, studies in two cohorts have highlighted pervasive fear of labels of mental illnesses, prolonged treatment delays and police involvement in the hospitalization of African Americans with emerging psychosis (Franz et al., 2010; Gerson et al., 2009). Previous studies have found that African Americans have more concerns about the stigma of receiving treatment (Cooper-Patrick et al., 1997) and endorse more stigmatizing attitudes toward people with mental illnesses than Caucasians. Multiple studies, including those that document high rates of involuntary hospitalization among African Americans in the United States and African Caribbeans in the United Kingdom (Burnett et al., 1999; Commander, Cochrane, Sashidharan, Akilu, & Wildsmith, 1999; Morgan et al., 2005a, 2005b), as well as qualitative studies (Alvidrez & Havassy, 2005; Cooper-Patrick et al., 1997; Keating & Robertson, 2004), provide evidence that stigma is a deterrent to help-seeking in these ethnic groups. Thus, future studies of the relationship between stigma, course of illness, labelling and diagnosis and service utilization, might productively incorporate further examination of the complex dynamics introduced by ethnic, racial and sociocultural factors.

Social perception, stereotype threat and cognitive neuroscience

As described, mental-illness stigma may have myriad adverse psychological effects via internalization of pejorative stereotypes and harmful stigma-related coping strategies. Tools from social and cognitive affective neuroscience can help us to understand the mechanisms underlying these stigma processes—including the neural circuitry involved and how this may be modified by cognitive deficits and symptoms typical of the psychosis risk syndrome—and have effects on clinical course and functional outcome in young people identified as "at risk" for psychosis. Components of social stigma rely on social processing and understanding of self and other, mentalizing and one's own emotional experience, which may be compromised in psychotic disorders and their risk states. The processes of labelling and internalizing stigma require a sense of identity, as a distinct entity, that entails an ability to differentiate self and other. Attribution is also relevant, as in determining "agency" or the feeling of being involved in an action versus the action originating from a source other than the self; this is subsumed by the parietal cortex, especially the intraparietal lobule (IPL; Ruby & Decety, 2001, 2003, 2004; Seger, Stone, & Keenan, 2004). Mentalizing and perspective taking is also relevant to stigma processes and involves the medial prefrontal cortex (mPFC), posterior cingulate/precuneus, temporo-parietal junction (TPJ) and superior temporal sulcus (STS; Amodio & Frith, 2006; Gallagher et al., 2000; Ochsner et al., 2004; Ruby & Decety, 2004; Saxe, 2006; Vogley et al., 2001; Vollm et al., 2006). Caudal regions are considered to be key to mentalizing tasks (Benoit, Gilbert, Volle, & Burgess, 2010; Gilbert et al., 2007).

Developmental theories suggest that one way we define ourselves is through "reflected self-appraisals", a process by which we internalize our ideas of other people's beliefs about us (see Pfeifer et al., 2009). In the case of an at-risk patient experiencing stigma, his or her imagined idea of what others think about him or her is informed by his or her perception of social cues such as emotional reactions from others, which may also be affected by disease processes. The study of social perception requires recognition and response to a social-affective stimulus (Ochsner, 2008); brain regions implicated in this process include inferior occipital lobe and temporal lobe structures such as the superior temporal sulcus (STS), fusiform face area, temporal poles (Adolphs, 2001) and amygdala, which is believed to have a central role in processing the social relevance of information gleaned from faces by leading the viewer to orient toward the eyes.

The emotional experience of stigma may include emotions such as shame or embarrassment, emotions that require mentalization and are related to regions of the anterior rostromedial prefrontal cortex (rmPFC) and the temporal parietal junction/superior temporal sulcus (TPJ/STS; Takahashi, et al., 2004). Adolescents may be particularly vulnerable to shame as these underlying brain regions show increased activity in teens experiencing social emotions such as embarrassment or guilt when compared to adults engaged in the same social emotional task. Thus, the emotional experience of stigma may be particularly salient in this younger population of at-risk teens.

Beyond emotional consequences for the individual, there are behavioural consequences of stigma. At-risk patients may find themselves in situations where their actions and behaviours confirm negative stereotypes. The basic premise is that a person's "social identity"—defined as group membership in categories such as mentally ill, age group, gender, religion and ethnicity—has significance when rooted in concrete situations. For individuals labelled "at risk", any social situation that requires intellectual performance—a job interview, a test-taking situation, a diagnostic psychiatric test—can evoke concerns that they will be judged not on the basis of their ability, but rather on the basis of a negative stereotype about the intellectual ability of all individuals with a specific designation or label—a concern introduced above as "stereotype threat" (Purdie-Vaughns, Steele, Davies, Ditlmann, & Crosby, 2008; Steele, 1997; Steele & Aronson, 1995; Steele et al., 2002). Such a threat can prove sufficiently stressful to impede cognitive performance and may occur regardless of the accuracy of the label (Steele et al., 2002; see also Crocker & Major, 1989).

Laboratory research on "stereotype threat" identifies several cognitive and affective processes underlying the effect of this threat on behaviour, including not only intellectual performance but also physiological stress due to arousal (Ben Zeev, Fein, & Inzlicht, 2005; Blascovich, Spencer, Quinn, & Steele, 2001), negative thoughts that consume executive resources, such as working memory (Beilock, Rydell, & McConnell, 2007; Cadinu, Maass, Rosabianca, & Kiesner, 2005; Schmader & Johns, 2003) and self-regulatory changes in the aims of managing thoughts and emotions relevant to the stereotype (Johns, Inzlicht, & Schmader, 2008; Seibt & Förster, 2004). Although a dearth of studies focuses on the neurological implications of contending with stigma in concrete situations, neuroscience techniques have been germane to exploring the role of specific neural regions and systems implicated in stereotype threat. Using fMRI, concerns about being perceived through the lens of a negative stereotype have been shown to undermine cognitive performance in two ways. First, it disrupts normal recruitment of cognitive areas required for intellectual performance—specifically, failure to show increased recruitment of the inferior prefrontal cortex, left inferior parietal cortex and bilateral angular gyrus, all areas associated with learning performance (Krendl et al., 2008). Second, it *increases* the recruitment of areas that allow for the processing, regulation and control of emotions—specifically, increased activation in the ventral anterior cingulate cortex, an area that has been associated with emotional self-regulation and processing of affective information (Krendl et al., 2008).

These results were supported and further specified by Wraga and colleagues (2007) in an attempt to link brain activation associated with affective processing and reduced performance under stereotype threat. Functional MRI analysis revealed that individuals under stereotype threat showed increased activity in areas associated with emotional self-regulation (rostral-ventral anterior cingulated cortex) and social knowledge (right orbital gyrus; Wraga et al., 2007). The emerging picture suggests that merely contending with stigma in the context of intellectual performance leads to *both* reductions in cognitive efficiency *and* increases in affective processing and recruitment of brain areas associated with emotional regulation. Although our understanding of how stigma is linked with underlying brain structures is still in its infancy, the above links between social perception, stereotype threat and cognitive neuroscience provide a promising base from which to launch future investigations. Also, these consequences of stereotype threat may be particularly problematic for at-risk individuals, who already have relative impairments in motivation, working memory, learning and affect regulation.

Future directions

This review of definitions of stigma and mechanisms by which stigma occur reveals that internalization of negative societal stereotypes and subsequent stigma-related coping responses harmfully affect people diagnosed with a mental illness, in particular adolescents, and might also be operative in individuals labelled as being "at risk" for psychosis. The existing studies of stigma in patients with recent-onset psychosis and their families initially corroborate that internalized negative stereotypes about people with mental illnesses and related coping mechanisms to avoid labelling may be the most salient stigma-associated constructs for further study in this area. However, there are no studies yet of stigma in these patients themselves and different mechanisms may be more relevant for them; for instance, research on identity engulfment for the young individuals recently labelled. It appears plausible that stigmatization originates in the prevalent negative public stereotypes toward adolescents with mental illnesses and further develops through these two processes of internalization and potentially maladaptive coping, especially through secrecy. The emphasis of these themes among young people experiencing their first episode of psychosis also supports this assertion and initial lines of evidence make plausible the suggestion that these stigma-related processes may in some circumstances take root during the phase in which one is "at risk" for psychosis, prior to diagnosis and treatment initiation. However, in the single study of families of individuals "at risk" for psychosis in an academic clinical research programme, endorsement of stigma in these areas was still relatively low (Wong et al., 2009). Future studies examining the emergence of stigma during the "at-risk" phase must partial out whether these processes precede or coincide with the full manifestation of psychotic symptoms, the official diagnosis of a psychotic or other mental disorder and/or mental-health treatment. Furthermore, Wong and colleagues (2009) focused on families of individuals who were at elevated risk for psychosis and not the individuals themselves, a critical gap in the literature that will be addressed in future studies. Intriguing findings regarding race and stigma warrant an examination of the possible intersection between racial, ethnic and sociocultural issues and stigma-related processes during the "at-risk" phase of psychosis in future studies. Finally, initial studies concerning neurological and behavioural correlates of stigma might further inform our understanding of the neural structures that underlie any experience of stigma among "at-risk" patients, which may themselves be affected by disease processes. Future studies of stigma and cognitive neuroscience might further elucidate the neural processes underlying stigma in at-risk patients who, as a potentially stigmatized group, are at risk of perceiving chronic stress, threat and marginalization as part of their everyday experience.

References

Adolphs, R. (2001). The neurobiology of social cognition. *Current Opinion in Neurobiology*, *11*(2), 231–239.

Alvidrez, J., & Havassy, B. E. (2005). Racial distribution of dual-diagnosis clients in public sector mental health and drug treatment settings. *Journal of Health Care for the Poor and Underserved*, *16*(1), 53–62.

Amodio, D. M., & Frith, C. D. (2006). Meeting of minds: The medial frontal cortex and social cognition. *Nature Reviews Neuroscience*, *7*, 268–277.

Beilock, S. L., Rydell, R. J., & McConnell, A. R. (2007). Stereotype threat and working memory: Mechanisms, alleviation and spillover. *Journal of Experimental Psychology – General, 136*(2), 256–276.

Benoit, R. G., Gilbert, S. J., Volle, E., & Burgess, P. W. (2010). When I think about me and simulate you: Medial rostral prefrontal cortex and self-referential processes. *NeuroImage, 50*(3), 1340–1349.

Ben-Zeev, T., Fein, S., & Inzlicht, M. (2005). Arousal and stereotype threat. *Journal of Experimental Social Psychology, 41*, 174–181.

Blascovich, J., Spencer, S. J., Quinn, D., & Steele, C. (2001). African Americans and high blood pressure: The role of stereotype threat. *Psychological Science, 12*(3), 225–229.

Boydell, K. M., Gladstone, B. M., & Volpe, T. (2006). Understanding help seeking delay in the prodrome to first episode psychosis: A secondary analysis of the perspectives of young people. *Psychiatric Rehabilitation Journal, 30*(1), 54–60.

Burnett, R., Mallett, R., Bhugra, D., Hutchinson, G., Der, G., & Leff, J. (1999). The first contact of patients with schizophrenia with psychiatric services: Social factors and pathways to care in a multi-ethnic population. *Psychological Medicine, 29*(2), 475–483.

Cadinu, M., Maass, A., Rosabianca, A., & Kiesner, J. (2005). Why do women underperform under stereotype threat? *Psychological Science, 16*, 572–578.

Cannon, T. D., Cadenhead, K., Cornblatt, B., Woods, S. W., Addington, J., Walker, E., et al. (2008). Prediction of psychosis in youth at high clinical risk: A multisite longitudinal study in North America. *Archives of General Psychiatry, 65*(1), 28–37.

Chandra, A., & Minkovitz, C. S. (2006). Stigma starts early: Gender differences in teen willingness to use mental health services. *The Journal of Adolescent Health: Official Publication of the Society for Adolescent Medicine, 38*(6), 754.e1–8.

Cohen, J., & Streuning, E. L. (1962). Opinions about mental illness in the personnel of two large mental hospitals. *Journal of Abnormal Social Psychology, 64*, 349–360.

Commander, M. J., Cochrane, R., Sashidharan, S. P., Akilu, F., & Wildsmith, E. (1999). Mental health care for Asian, Black and White patients with non-affective psychoses: Pathways to the psychiatric hospital, in-patient and after-care. *Social Psychiatry and Psychiatric Epidemiology, 34*(9), 484–491.

Cooper-Patrick, L., Powe, N. R., Jenckes, M. W., Gonzales, J. J., Levine, D. M., & Ford, D. E. (1997). Identification of patient attitudes and preferences regarding treatment of depression. *Journal of General Internal Medicine, 12*(7), 431–438.

Corcoran, C., Davidson, L., Sills-Shahar, R., Nickou, C., Malaspina, D., Miller, T., et al. (2003). A qualitative research study of the evolution of symptoms in individuals identified as prodromal to psychosis. *Psychiatric Quarterly, 74*(4), 313–332.

Corcoran, C. M., First, M. B., Cornblatt, B. (2010). The psychosis risk syndrome and its proposed inclusion in the DSM-V: A risk-benefit analysis. *Schizophrenia Research, 120*, 16–22.

Corcoran, C., Gerson, R., Sills-Shahar, R., Nickou, C., McGlashan, T., Malaspina, D., et al. (2007). Trajectory to a first episode of psychosis: A qualitative research study with families. *Early Intervention Psychiatry, 1*(4), 308–315.

Corcoran, C., Malaspina, D., & Hercher, L. (2005). Prodromal interventions for schizophrenia vulnerability: The risks of being "at risk". *Schizophrenia Research, 73*(2–3), 173–184.

Corrigan, P. W., Lurie, B. D., Goldman, H. H., Slopen, N., Medasani, K., & Phelan, S. (2005). How adolescents perceive the stigma of mental illness and alcohol abuse. *Psychiatric Services (Washington, DC), 56*(5), 544–550.

Corrigan, P. W., Watson, A. C., & Barr, L. (2006). The self-stigma of mental illness: Implications for self-esteem and self-efficacy. *Journal of Social and Clinical Psychology*, *25*(8), 875–884.

Crocker, J., & Major, B. (1989). Social stigma and self-esteem: The self-protective properties of stigma. *Psychological Review*, *96*(4), 608–630.

Crocker, J., Major, B., & Steele, C. (1998). Social stigma. In D. Gilbert & S. Fiske (Eds.), *The handbook of social psychology* (4th ed., Vol. 2, pp. 504–508). Boston, MA: McGraw-Hill.

Czuchta, D. M., & McCay, E. (2001). Help-seeking for parents of individuals experiencing a first episode of schizophrenia. *Archives of Psychiatric Nursing*, *15*(4), 159–170.

Franz, L., Carter, T., Leiner, A. S., Bergner, E., Thompson, N. J., & Compton, M. T. (2010). Stigma and treatment delay in first-episode psychosis: A grounded theory study. *Early Intervention in Psychiatry*, *4*(1), 47–56.

Fung, K. M. T., Tsang, H. W. H., Corrigan, P. W., Lam, C. S., Cheung, W., & Cheng, W. (2007). Measuring self-stigma of mental illness in China and its implications for recovery. *The International Journal of Social Psychiatry*, *53*(5), 408–418.

Gallagher, H. L., Happé, F., Brunswick, N., Fletcher, P. C., Frith, U., & Frith, C. D. (2000). Reading the mind in cartoons and stories: An fMRI study of theory of mind in verbal and nonverbal tasks. *Neuropsychologia*, *38*, 11–21.

Gerson, R., Davidson, L., Booty, A., McGlashan, T., Malespina, D., Pincus, H. A., et al. (2009). Families' experience with seeking treatment for recent-onset psychosis. *Psychiatric Services (Washington, DC)*, *60*(6), 812–816.

Gilbert, S. J., Williamson, I. D., Dumontheil, I., Simons, J. S., Frith, C. D., & Burgess, P. W. (2007). Distinct regions of medial rostral prefrontal cortex supporting social and nonsocial functions. *Social Cognitive and Affective Neuroscience*, *2*(3), 217–226.

Goffman, E. (1963). *Stigma: Notes on the management of spoiled identity*. London, UK: Penguin.

Häfner, H., Maurer, K., Löffler, W., an der Heiden, W., Munk-Jørgensen, P., Hambrecht, M., et al. (1998). The ABC Schizophrenia Study: A preliminary overview of the results. *Social Psychiatry and Psychiatric Epidemiology*, *33*(8), 380–386.

Johns, M., Inzlicht, M., & Schmader, T. (2008). Stereotype threat and executive resource depletion: The influence of emotion regulation. *Journal of Experimental Psychology – General*, *137*, 691–705.

Jones, E. E., Farina, A., Hastorf, A., Markus, H., Miller, D., & Scott, R. (1984). *Social stigma: The psychology of marked relationships*. New York, NY: Freeman.

Judge, A. M., Estroff, S. E., Perkins, D. O., & Penn, D. L. (2008). Recognizing and responding to early psychosis: A qualitative analysis of individual narratives. *Psychiatric Services (Washington, DC)*, *59*(1), 96–99.

Keating, F., & Robertson, D. (2004). Fear, Black people and mental illness: A vicious circle? *Health & Social Care in the Community*, *12*(5), 439–447.

Krendl, A. C., Richeson, J. A., Kelley, W. M., & Heatherton, T. F. (2008). The negative consequences of threat: An fMRI investigation of the neural mechanisms underlying women's underperformance in math. *Psychological Science*, *19*(2), 168–175.

Lally, S. J. (1989). "Does being in here mean there is something wrong with me"? *Schizophrenia Bulletin*, *15*(2), 253–265.

Leavey, J. E. (2005). Youth experiences of living with mental health problems: Emergence, loss, adaptation and recovery (ELAR). *Canadian Journal of Community Mental Health [Revue Canadienne De Santé Mentale Communautaire]*, *24*(2), 109–126.

Link, B. G., Cullen, F. T., Struening, E., Shrout, P. E., & Dohrenwend, B. P. (1989). A modified labeling theory approach to mental disorders: An empirical assessment. *American Sociological Review, 54*(3), 400–423.

Link, B. G., Mirotznik, J., & Cullen, F. T. (1991). The effectiveness of stigma coping orientations: Can negative consequences of mental illness labeling be avoided? *Journal of Health and Social Behavior, 32*(3), 302–320.

Link, B. G., & Phelan, J. C. (2001). Conceptualizing stigma. *Annual Review of Sociology, 27*(1), 363–385.

Link, B. G., Struening, E., Neese-Todd, S., Asmussen, S., & Phelan, J. C. (2001). Stigma as a barrier to recovery: The consequences of stigma for the self-esteem of people with mental illnesses. *Psychiatric Services (Washington, DC), 52*(12), 1621–1626.

Link, B. G., Yang, L. H., Phelan, J. C., & Collins, P. Y. (2004). Measuring mental illness stigma. *Schizophrenia Bulletin, 30*(3), 511–541.

Major, B., McCoy, S. K., Kaiser, C. R., & Quinton, W. J. (2003). Prejudice and self-esteem: A transactional model. In W. Stroebe & M. Hewstone (Eds.), *European review of social psychology* (pp. 77–104). Hove, UK: Psychology Press.

Major, B., & O'Brien, L. T. (2005). The social psychology of stigma. *Annual Review of Psychology, 56*, 393–421.

McGorry, P. D., Yung, A., & Phillips, L. (2001). Ethics and early intervention in psychosis: Keeping up the pace and staying in step. *Schizophrenia Research, 51*(1), 17–29.

McGorry, P. D., Yung, A. R., Phillips, L. J., Yuen, H. P., Francey, S., Cosgrave, E. M., et al. (2002). Randomized controlled trial of interventions designed to reduce the risk of progression to first-episode psychosis in a clinical sample with subthreshold symptoms. *Archives of General Psychiatry, 59*(10), 921–928.

Mead, G. H. (1934). *Mind, self, and society.* Chicago, IL: University of Chicago Press.

Miller, T. J., McGlashan, T. H., Rosen, J. L., Cadenhead, K., Cannon, T., Ventura, J., et al. (2003). Prodromal assessment with the structured interview for prodromal syndromes and the scale of prodromal symptoms: Predictive validity, interrater reliability, and training to reliability. *Schizophrenia Bulletin, 29*(4), 703–715.

Morgan, C., Mallett, R., Hutchinson, G., Bagalkote, H., Morgan, K., Fearon, P., et al. (2005a). Pathways to care and ethnicity. 1: Sample characteristics and compulsory admission. Report from the AESOP study. *The British Journal of Psychiatry: The Journal of Mental Science, 186*, 281–289.

Morgan, C., Mallett, R., Hutchinson, G., Bagalkote, H., Morgan, K., Fearon, P., et al. (2005b). Pathways to care and ethnicity. 2: Source of referral and help-seeking. Report from the AESOP study. *The British Journal of Psychiatry: The Journal of Mental Science, 186*, 290–296.

Moses, T. (2009a). Self-labeling and its effects among adolescents diagnosed with mental disorders. *Social Science & Medicine, 68*(3), 570–578.

Moses, T. (2009b). Stigma and self-concept among adolescents receiving mental health treatment. *The American Journal of Orthopsychiatry, 79*(2), 261–274.

Norman, R. M., & Malla, A. K. (2001). Duration of untreated psychosis: A critical examination of the concept and its importance. *Psychological Medicine, 31*(3), 381–400.

Ochsner, K. N. (2008). The social-emotional processing stream: Five core constructs and their translational potential for schizophrenia and beyond. *Biological Psychiatry, 64*(1), 48–61.

Ochsner, K. N., Knierim, K., Ludlow, D. H., Hanelin, J., Ramachandran, T., Glover, G., et al. (2004). Reflecting upon feelings: An fMRI study of neural systems supporting the attribution of emotion to self and other. *Journal of Cognitive Neuroscience, 16*, 1746–1772.

Page, S. (1977). Effects of the mental illness label in attempts to obtain accommodation. *Canadian Journal of Behavioral Science, 9*(2), 85–90.

Penn, D. L., Judge, A., Jamieson, P., Garczynski, J., Hennessy, M., & Romer, D. (2005). Stigma. In D. L. Evans et al. (Eds.), *Treating and preventing adolescent mental health disorders* (pp. 531–544). New York, NY: Oxford University Press.

Pescosolido, B. A., Fettes, D. L., Martin, J. K., Monahan, J., & McLeod, J. D. (2007). Perceived dangerousness of children with mental health problems and support for coerced treatment. *Psychiatric Services (Washington, DC), 58*(5), 619–625.

Pescosolido, B. A., Perry, B. L., Martin, J. K., McLeod, J. D., & Jensen, P. S. (2007). Stigmatizing attitudes and beliefs about treatment and psychiatric medications for children with mental illness. *Psychiatric Services (Washington, DC), 58*(5), 613–618.

Pfeifer, J. H., Masten, C. L., Borofsky, L. A., Dapretto, M., Fuligni, A. J., & Lieberman, M. D. (2009). Neural correlates of direct and reflected self-appraisals in adolescents and adults: When social perspective-taking informs self-perception. *Child Development, 80*(4), 1016–1038.

Prince, P. N., & Prince, C. R. (2002). Perceived stigma and community integration among clients of assertive community treatment. *Psychiatric Rehabilitation Journal, 25*(4), 323–331.

Purdie-Vaughns, V., Steele, C. A., Davies, P. G., Ditlmann, R., & Crosby, J. R. (2008). Social identity contingencies: How diversity cues signal threat or safety for African Americans in mainstream institutions. *Journal of Personality and Social Psychology, 94*(4), 615–630.

Ritsher, J. B., & Phelan, J. C. (2004). Internalized stigma predicts erosion of morale among psychiatric outpatients. *Psychiatry Research, 129*(3), 257–265.

Ruby, P., & Decety, J. (2001). Effect of subjective perspective taking during simulation of action: A PET investigation of agency. *Nature Neuroscience, 4*, 546–550.

Ruby, P., & Decety, J. (2003). What you believe versus what you think they believe: A neuroimaging study of conceptual perspective-taking. *European Journal of Neuroscience, 12*(11), 2475–2480.

Ruby, P., & Decety, J. (2004). How would you feel versus how do you think she would feel? A neuroimaging study of perspective taking with social emotions. *Journal of Cognitive Neuroscience, 16*, 988–999.

Saxe, R. (2006). Uniquely human social cognition. *Current Opinion in Neurobiology, 16*, 235–239.

Schmader, T., & Johns, M. (2003). Converging evidence that stereotype threat reduces working memory capacity. *Journal of Personality and Social Psychology, 85*, 440–452.

Seger, C. A., Stone, M., & Keenan, J. P. (2004). Cortical activations during judgments about the self and another person. *Neuropsychologica, 42*(9), 1168–1177.

Seibt, B., & Förster, J. (2004). Stereotype threat and performance: How self-stereotypes influence processing by inducing regulatory foci. *Journal of Personality and Social Psychology, 87*, 38–56.

Singh, S. P., & Grange, T. (2006). Measuring pathways to care in first-episode psychosis: A systematic review. *Schizophrenia Research, 81*(1), 75–82.

Steele, C. M. (1997). A threat in the air: How stereotypes shape intellectual identity and performance. *American Psychologist, 52*(6), 613–629.

Steele, C. M., & Aronson, J. (1995). Stereotype threat and the intellectual test performance of African Americans. *Journal of Personality & Social Psychology, 69*(5), 797–811.

Steele, C. M., Spencer, S. J., & Aronson, J. (2002). Contending with group image: The psychology of stereotype and social identity threat. In M. P. Zanna (Ed.), *Advances in experimental social psychology* (Vol. 34, pp. 379–440). San Diego, CA: Academic Press.

Takahashi, H., Yahata, N., Koeda, M., Matsuda, T., Asai, K., & Okubo, Y. (2004). Brain activation association with evaluative processes of guilt and embarrassment: An fMRI study. *NeuroImage, 23*(3), 967–974.

Tarrier, N., Khan, S., Cater, J., & Picken, A. (2007). The subjective consequences of suffering a first episode psychosis: Trauma and suicide behaviour. *Social Psychiatry and Psychiatric Epidemiology, 42*(1), 29–35.

Tessler, R., & Gamach, G. (1995). *Toolkit for evaluating family experiences with severe mental illness*. Cambridge, MA: Human Services Research Institute.

Vogley, K., Bussfeld, P., Newen, A., Herrmann, S., Happé, F., Falkai, P., et al. (2001). Mind reading: Neural mechanisms of theory of mind and self-perspective. *NeuroImage, 14*, 170–181.

Vollm, B. A., Taylor, A. N., Richardson, P., Corcoran, R., Stirling, J., McKie, S., et al. (2006). Neuronal correlates of theory of mind and empathy: A functional magnetic resonance imaging study in a nonverbal task. *NeuroImage, 29*(1), 90–98.

Wahl, O. E. (2002). Children's views of mental illness: A review of the literature. *American Journal of Psychiatric Rehabilitation, 6*(2), 134–158.

Wisdom, J. P., & Green, C. A. (2004). "Being in a funk": Teens' efforts to understand their depressive experiences. *Qualitative Health Research, 14*(9), 1227–1238.

Wong, C., Davidson, L., Anglin, D., Link, B. G., Gerson, R., Malaspina, D., et al. (2009). Stigma in families of individuals in early stages of psychotic illness: Family stigma and early psychosis. *Early Intervention in Psychiatry, 3*, 108–115.

Woods, S. W., Addington, J., Cadenhead, K. S., Cannon, T. D., Cornblatt, B. A., Heinssen, R., (2009). Validity of the prodromal risk syndrome for first psychosis: Findings from the North American Prodrome Longitudinal Study. *Schizophrenia Bulletin, 35*(5), 894–908.

Wraga, M., Helt, M., Jacobs, E., & Sullivan, K. (2007). Neural basis of stereotype-induced shifts in women's mental rotation performance. *Social Cognitive and Affective Neuroscience, 2*, 12–19.

Yang, L. H., & Kleinman, A. (2008). "Face" and the embodiment of stigma in China: The cases of schizophrenia and AIDS. *Social Science & Medicine, 67*(3), 398–408.

Yang, L. H., Kleinman, A., Link, B. G., Phelan, J. C., Lee, S., & Good, B. (2007). Culture and stigma: Adding moral experience to stigma theory. *Social Science & Medicine, 64*(7), 1524–1535.

Yang, L. H., Wonpat-Borja, A. J., Opler, M., & Corcoran, C. (2010). Potential stigma associated with inclusion of the psychosis risk syndrome in the DSM-V: An empirical question. *Schizophrenia Research, 120*, 42–48.

Zarrett, N., & Eccles, J. (2006). The passage to adulthood: Challenges of late adolescence. *New Directions for Youth Development, 111*, 13–28.

13 Conclusions

Philip McGuire

Until relatively recently, there was almost no research on the period prior to the first episode of psychosis. The chapters in this monograph illustrate how much this has changed, with a great deal of work having been conducted across a diversity of topics. These range from psychopathology, diagnostic classification, cognitive function, psychosocial stressors, and ethics, to genetics, and the structure, function, chemistry and connectivity of the brain.

It is clear from reading these chapters that, to date, research within each domain has often been conducted separately from work in other areas. While this is unsurprising, psychosis is likely to result from the interaction of multiple genes and multiple environmental factors, and probably involves changes in several aspects of brain function. A key aim for future studies will thus be the integration of findings across different research modalities (Chapter 3). This entails assessing the same ultra-high risk (UHR) subjects with a variety of different research modalities, but there are logistical limits to what is feasible, both in terms of the cost of investigations and research staff, and in how much investigation a given subject can tolerate. Nevertheless, relatively demanding studies are better tolerated by UHR subjects than patients with a psychotic disorder, and a number of such studies have recently been completed. For example, the combination of different neuroimaging techniques in the same UHR subjects has provided new data on the relationships between reductions in grey matter volume (Chapter 7) and glutamate levels (Chapter 9), striatal dopamine function and prefrontal activation (Chapter 10), and between hippocampal glutamate levels and striatal dopamine function (Chapters 9 and 10). Other research has demonstrated how psychosocial stressors may impact on the risk of psychosis through effects on the hypothalamo-pituitary-adrenal axis (Chapter 5).

While the UHR population has only been the subject of concerted study relatively recently, there is a well-established history of research in other high-risk groups, such as those at increased risk through a family history of psychosis. Thus, there is an extensive literature on studies in twins discordant for psychotic disorders, and in the relatives of patients with psychotic disorders. While the latter are often described as being "genetic" high-risk groups, and the UHR as "clinical" high risk, the mechanisms underlying their respective vulnerabilities may be more similar than these terms suggest. Although there have been few direct comparisons, qualitative comparison of data from neuropsychological and neuroimaging studies in familial high-risk and UHR samples suggest that the findings in the two groups are similar. Moreover, careful psychopathological assessment in familial high-risk subjects reveals that, while they may not meet UHR criteria, a substantial proportion experience attenuated psychotic symptoms. Similarly, although only a minority of UHR subjects have a family history of psychosis, the few genetic studies that have been performed in this group report an increased prevalence of risk genes for psychosis. It is thus possible that much of the vulnerability of the UHR group to psychosis is conferred by genetic factors, but that this is only occasionally manifest in the form of frank psychosis in the subject's relatives. The contribution of genetic factors (Chapter 4) to the UHR state is still unclear, as the samples studied to date have been small. This may be clarified in future through studies in substantially larger samples, recruited from multiple centres. For example, the recently commenced EU-GEI study (www.eu-gei.eu) includes an investigation of genetic factors in UHR subjects collected from multiple sites across Europe and Australia.

The data presented in this monograph clearly illustrate that UHR subjects differ from healthy controls in many respects: psychopathology, cognitive function, psychosocial risk factors and neuroimaging measures. A key issue for translating these findings into clinical practice is whether some of these differences are specific to the later onset of psychosis, as opposed to simply being correlates of increased vulnerability. The data reviewed in the monograph indicate that certain symptoms, neuropsychological deficits and neuroimaging abnormalities that are evident at clinical presentation are associated with the later onset of illness. Moreover, evidence from longitudinal studies in UHR subjects suggests that some baseline abnormalities also progress in the subgroup of subjects who make the transition to psychosis. However, it is difficult to recruit large numbers of UHR subjects, and the samples studied to date have been relatively small. This is a particular issue when examining predictors of transition, as only a minority of the original UHR sample will later become psychotic. Collecting samples that are large enough to definitively identify predictors is likely to entail multi-centre studies, which can recruit samples that are an order of magnitude larger than collectable at a single site. Accordingly, ongoing research in the UHR field has seen the formation of multi-site consortia, such as NAPLS in the USA (http://napls.psych.ucla.edu), and EARN, the European At Risk Network, and these are beginning to yield results. Large samples also provide an opportunity to investigate prodromal features that vary with the type of psychotic disorder. In particular, studies to date have been too small to permit subdivision of groups comprising UHR subjects who later made a transition to psychosis according to whether the psychosis was schizophreniform or affective. Research of this kind could provide new data that would inform the longstanding debate about the classification of psychotic disorders (Chapter 2).

Research in people at UHR of psychosis has significant translational potential. A key problem in the clinical management of subjects at UHR of psychosis is that it is difficult to predict, on the basis of the presenting clinical features, which individuals will or will not go on to develop psychosis. However, as there appear to be differences between these subgroups in terms of cognitive performance (Chapter 6), neurophysiological alterations (Chapter 11) and neuroimaging findings (Chapter 8), this raises the possibility that these measures could be used to facilitate the prediction of clinical outcome in UHR subjects. However, most differences between those who will and will not become psychotic have been identified at a group level: the challenge is to use this information to allow clinicians to make decisions about management at the level of an individual subject. One of the most promising approaches that can be employed to address this issue is the application of machine learning software to data from UHR subjects. This permits an estimate of how closely, for example, MRI data from a given subject, match the mean MRI data from either a group of UHR subjects who later developed psychosis, or a group who did not. The closer the match to the group that developed psychosis, the greater the likelihood that the subject will fall into that diagnostic category. This approach has recently been employed in data from one centre, and application of this approach to larger multi-centre datasets is ongoing.

Research in the UHR phase is a potentially powerful means of investigating the mechanisms underlying the onset of psychosis. The findings reviewed in this monograph have advanced our understanding of the neurobiological, psychological and social factors (Chapter 12) that contribute to the development of psychosis, and have provided new information about the stage at which these factors may operate. These data provide a basis for the rational development of novel interventions in the UHR phase. To date, intervention in UHR subjects has largely involved the application of treatments that are well established in psychotic disorders, such as cognitive-behaviour therapy (CBT) and antipsychotic medication. However, research in the UHR may reveal other potential targets for intervention. For example, evidence that there are marked changes in central glutamate levels in the UHR subjects (Chapter 9) suggests that interventions that act on this neurochemical system may be useful, while evidence of altered phospholipid levels in UHR subjects provides a rational for the use of fish oil in this population. The next generation of clinical trials in UHR subjects may involve more novel interventions, and are likely to involve multiple clinical centres, in order to recruit samples large enough to provide sufficient statistical power. The recently initiated NEURAPRO study (http://rc.oyh.org.au/ResearchAreas/atrisk/neurapro), a trial of fish oil involving several sites in Europe, Australia and Asia, is an example of such a study.

This monograph can be seen as marking the end of an initial phase of research in the UHR population. This phase has been remarkably productive, providing new information about the mechanisms underlying the onset of psychosis, and contributing to the development of clinical early-intervention services. The next phase of research in this area is likely to involve larger scale studies, involving multiple rather than single centres, and the integration of data from a range of different research modalities. These may permit further advances that build on the findings from the first wave of studies that we have sought to review here.

Index